Learning to Teach
Psychology in Teacher Training

Learning to Teach
Psychology in Teacher Training

Edited by
Hazel Francis
University of London
Institute of Education

The Falmer Press
(A member of the Taylor & Francis Group)
London and Philadelphia

UK   The Falmer Press, Falmer House, Barcombe, Lewes, East Sussex, BN8 5DL

USA   The Falmer Press, Taylor & Francis Inc., 242 Cherry Street, Philadelphia, PA 19106-1906

First published 1985

Library of Congress Cataloging in Publication Data

Learning to Teach.

   Bibliography: P.
   Includes index.
   1. Teachers, Traning of—Great Britain—Addresses, Essays, Lectures. 2. Educational Psychology—Teacher Training—Great Britain—Addresses, Essays, Lectures. 3. Teaching—Psychological Aspects—Addresses, Essays, Lectures. I. Francis, Hazel.
LB1715.L42   1985   370′.7′1   85-12893
ISBN 1-85000-041-7
ISBN 1-85000-042-5 (soft)

Jacket design by Leonard Williams

Typeset in 11/13 Caledonian
Imago Publishing Ltd, Thame, Oxon.

Printed in Great Britain by Taylor & Francis (Printers) Ltd, Basingstoke

Contents

Contents

Good for Spring Term.

Preface

This book is intended to be a serious contribution to curriculum development in teacher training. In its own way it speaks to both tutors and students.

It was initially a brainchild of the Education Section of the British Psychological Society, which has given very welcome encouragement and support to the editor and the writing team. However, the book is in no way a consensus view, as readers will readily discern, nor can it be taken to represent an Education Section position.

The editor and authors hope that it will not be taken as a prescription for the psychology to be taught to student teachers, but rather as a basis for considering why and how psychology might be used. Much of what is currently taught is not referred to; not because it has been found wanting, but because decisions about what to teach, and how to teach it, must rest on the kind of prior considerations the authors have tried to pursue.

All are actively involved in teacher education. They speak from different institutions and different psychological interests, but are united in a common concern about the nature and quality of professional training.

Hazel Francis
University of London Institute
of Education
February 1985

Introduction

How shall I teach? This question taxes the tutor in teacher training as much as it does the student teacher, and there are no simple answers for either. Nor are there for others with responsibility for education.

The Secretary of State for Education and Science, having expressed a major interest in the quality of teaching, is now pressing his statutory right of approval of training courses. The new Council for the Accreditation of Teacher Education will be much concerned with the interpretation of course curricula in the light of the agreed criteria. This should be a matter for serious debate and wise judgment, especially since such curricula must vary with the philosophies and resources of training institutions and with the type of teacher to be trained. There is clearly no hard and fast line to be taken with the role of psychology, but an examination of issues and criteria in whose light it might be evaluated could usefully inform the debate.

Everyone has their own non-expert ideas of what teaching should be like, notions culled from experiences of education and from learning in everyday contexts. These ideas are open to inspection and to change in the course of becoming more expert. The experiences of student teachers on their courses and in schools, together with discussions with experienced teachers and course tutors, are likely to strengthen some beliefs and practices and to alter others, beginning that development of educational expertise which will continue through a teaching career. Tutors similarly gain in their own expertise through working with their students.

Some of the opinions held by students might be regarded as practical principles of teaching. If they influence practice and are open to change then their modification is central to training. Paul Hirst (1983) has recently questioned whether such principles can be drawn directly from academic disciplines such as philosophy, sociology and psychology, and has argued that the role of these disciplines is more properly to provide a critique of practice. He is doubtful whether the student teacher is ready to encounter such disciplines, seeing them as much more appropriate and important for their tutors and for more experienced teachers.

It may be, however, that he has overlooked the value of confidence from having some justification for the way one acts. Whatever the beginner's thoughts and actions in teaching, self-doubt and practical dilemmas abound. If conflicting principles are advocated the face validity of the practising teacher's position has considerable power, but what if experienced teachers disagree? Hirst may be correct in doubting the utility of normative theory as a direct source of guidance, but a tutor cannot be absolved from the responsibility of helping the student off the horns of a dilemma with the best information available. It is argued in some of the contributions to this book that there are principles of psychological practice available to tutors which can be used both to ease the student's predicament and to yield examples of how they are derived and evaluated, thus giving some yardstick for gauging practical principles of teaching. To suggest withholding relevant critical disciplines because the trainee is in some sense not experienced enough is to raise the old, old question of readiness. Of course whole disciplines cannot be understood at once, but some things can be encountered usefully even by a beginner. The problem is to identify which and for what purposes.

In this book psychologists face this problem in various ways. Issues are raised which cannot be perceived from standard psychology texts, for these largely comprise information from theory and research but rarely say anything to the problem of contextualizing it, even in psychological let alone educational practice. Moreover there may well be a failure to seriously link research with the values and attitudes behind it, yet psychologists no more see human behaviour in a single way than do non-psychologists. Equally they entertain different views of teaching, and if asked what they deem to be good will almost certainly not seek identical criteria of quality. Some such differences peep through, or are made explicit, in the following chapters.

Although it must be a central feature of initial training, the development of skill and principles for action in the classroom is but one aspect. The problem of how to teach leads to others of what to teach, to whom and where. All these imply training for work with professional colleagues in different kinds of classroom and school within an educational system. Some of the contributions to this volume address this wider professionalization of the teacher from psychological standpoints.

The structure of the book is simple. The first part sketches the way psychology's involvement in teacher training has developed and changed during this century, and how it looked in the recent Leicester survey of postgraduate courses. (The omission of a survey of BEd provision is a deliberate restriction, not an oversight. What follows in the book largely applies equally to both kinds of course.) It also sets out in the third chapter some discussion of what is involved in becoming a teacher in our schools. The second part deals primarily with the student's learning during training. It has implications for the conduct as well as the content of courses. The third part points to aspects of education in schools which suggest further thoughts about the role of psychology in the training curriculum. The final chapter discusses how consideration of psychology in curriculum development bears on teaching and on the development of training courses.

A brief postscript draws the book together, emphasizing the importance the authors give to psychological practice as distinct from theory, and to consideration of the human and educational values behind it.

Reference

HIRST, P. (1983) 'Educational theory' in HIRST, P. (Ed.) *Educational Theory and its Foundation Disciplines*, London, Routledge and Kegan Paul.

1
The Training and Development of Teachers

Introduction

To understand some of the present concerns about the role of psychology in teacher education it is helpful to read Margaret Sutherland's historical sketch and Gerry Bernbaum's survey of the part it plays now. Clearly there is a spirit of doubt abroad, although this is matched by a strong conviction that psychology ought, almost by definition, to be involved. This conviction is enhanced by Brahm Norwich's chapter on the ways teachers become absorbed into the profession, and by Geoffrey Brown's description of a course which deliberately involved the teaching profession more than is usually the case in teacher training. The problems uncovered in both chapters demand a psychological approach which starts with the nature of the trainee, the training, and the profession, rather than with a bland selection of useful psychology for teachers.

Psychology and the Education of Teachers

Margaret B. Sutherland,
University of Leeds.

In looking at the relationship between psychology and the education of teachers one has the impression of studying the history of a marriage that went wrong. For psychology, in the early days of teacher education, was regarded as an essential partner of education: it continued to be a close associate during many decades: then younger, aggressive rivals took its place or at least vied with it for that place: and now there is, in some teacher education at least, what could be regarded as a move to divorce the two, education and psychology. The question is, should divorce be made absolute or should we counsel a reconciliation, a re-establishment, possibly on slightly different terms, of the old alliance?

Let us consider the early days when the two seemed made for each other. In the nineteenth century, when the education of teachers became a matter of urgent concern and training colleges were being set up, claims were also being made for the establishment of education as an academic discipline worthy of a place in universities: and psychology was perceived as an essential auxiliary to education. For in the claim to academic respectability stress was laid — then as now — on being scientific. The philosopher Alexander Bain (1879) entitled an important contribution to the debate *Education as a Science*. The first holder of the Bell Chair of Education in the University of Edinburgh, Professor Laurie, set out a syllabus for the training of teachers which referred to education both as an art and a science: and psychology was the major component of the science of education (Ross, 1883). The relevant topics here were to be '(1) the intelligence; and conclusions from the intellectual nature of man with reference to his education: (2) the unfolding of intelligence or periods of growth: (3) the ethical nature of man: (4) auxiliaries of the processes and growth of mind: conclusions from mental growth with reference to education.' The art of education, on the other hand, dealt with discussion of various philosophical problems. But psychology possibly appeared also in 'methodick with a view to instruction and assimilation' and in methodology, which included references to intellectual rules and 'the intellectual habit'. Whatever the wisdom of looking to psychology to give proof of scientific respectability — according to Ralph Hetherington's presidential address to the British Psychological Society, it was not until 1982 that psychology finally received the accolade as a genuine science — teacher training, in this country, continued to include psychology as an essential component until fairly recent times: and still does so include it in a great many European countries.

What exactly was the science of psychology expected to offer the young teacher? Definitions can be found in James Sully's *Handbook of Psychology for the Teacher* which was first published in 1886 and went rapidly into a number of editions. (And see comment on Sully and the teaching of educational psychology in Tibble, 1966.) Sully was concerned firstly to point out the difference between scientific knowledge and empirical knowledge. The latter is based simply on observation of individual cases, that is, it is what the teacher may very well acquire in practice: the former offers laws or general principles, derived from the 'processes of revision and extension of everyday empirical knowledge which make up the work of science'. Such scientific study includes 'a wide survey of facts and accurate processes of observation and experiment'. Hence 'the conclusions properly drawn from scientific principles are perfectly trustworthy'. But empirical knowledge is not being decried: it is simply to be made more accurate and supplemented by scientific knowledge. The educator will always need to continue to study the individuals with whom education is concerned. At the same time Sully made it perfectly clear that psychology is auxiliary, not the dominant partner: for the aims of education are something which the teacher will have studied otherwise — even if they are hard to define: psychology is to help in translating those aims into practice.

It is also worth noticing that Sully, like others of the time, saw *two* sciences as contributing the framework, or foundations, for the process of education. The other science was physiology, including hygiene. This is a proposal which was implemented for a considerable time in teacher education in this country. It is worth asking ourselves why knowledge of the physical constitution and development of children — and of their diseases and physical afflictions (including *pediculosis capitis*) — seems to have been dropped from the catalogue of things teachers should learn. Physiology is knowledge not totally irrelevant to psychology itself as well as being one of the sciences which Spencer (1855) thought essential to complete living.

Psychology then was to provide teachers with a knowledge of the laws of human development and behaviour. Sense-perception, memory, association, reasoning and deduction were all to receive attention. But the contribution of psychology was not to be purely on the cognitive — or intellectual — side. There was to be attention to all three aspects, the intellect, the emotions and the will. Encouraging the inventive faculty, training the imagination, were topics to be studied. The development of feelings, children's fears, education of moral sentiment — they were all there. (One must admit that there is singularly little reference to what we should consider as research reports in this handbook: but psychology was still itself in the process of evolution. There are certainly plenty of references for further reading, including a goodly number in German.)

Psychology's contribution is thus widely defined at the beginning of the partnership. Even if education is seen as 'the communication of so much useful knowledge, it may be said that the teacher still needs to study other faculties than the acquisitive; for psychology teaches us that no power of the mind works in perfect isolation'. The teacher should learn all that the science of psychology can tell about human development and human behaviour. At the same time, the need for the teacher's own observation of individual children is stressed: 'the educator will always need to supplement his general study of mind by a careful observation of the individual minds which he is called upon to deal with, so as to properly vary and adapt his methods of teaching and disciplining'.

Sully's point of view was one shared by another eminent educator-psychologist of the times, John Adams who, after a distinguished contribution to teacher education in Scotland, became in 1902 the first Professor of Education in the University of London and Principal of the London Day Training College. Adams (1897) also wrote to provide teachers with psychological knowledge: his book, *Herbartian Psychology Applied to Education* was one of the most influential of its time, even if Herbart's views were closely intertwined with those of Adams himself. And Adams' now threadbare dictum that to teach John Latin, we have to know both Latin and John, set forth vividly in its time the importance of the study of the learner, the need to focus not only on what is to be communicated but on what is at the receiving end. The teacher, it was emphasized, must know the 'raw materials' — the learners — with whom the teacher is working.

In view of these nineteenth century definitions of the role of psychology in the education of teachers, it is interesting to see what is claimed today for this study. A very widely used psychology textbook (Child, 1977) offers this statement: 'Psychology teaches us about people — how they think, respond and feel, why they behave as they do and what initiates and sustains their actions. Such fundamental processes are so essential to our understanding of children's learning that they cannot help but form a substantial part of a course in teacher training. We cannot rely on our independent observation alone.' There is an admirable agreement of opinions in the past and in the present as to the advantages of the association.

Given this early recognition, psychology did indeed provide, during succeeding decades, a remarkable richness of information and illumination for the teacher. The introduction of new theories in psychology did not necessarily affect immediately the teachers' studies of the subject: some time lag, varying according to the social respectability and obscurity of the new topic, inevitably affected the definition of psychology in different courses, as did the personal interests and qualifications of those teaching the subject. But we may note some of the themes which played a large part in teachers' studies of psychology. For many years, there was the dominating influence of William McDougall's theory of instincts (McDougall, 1908 and 1932) a theory which lent itself well to school teaching and which did in fact, in its treatment of the self-regarding sentiment, foreshadow usefully present-day preoccupations with the development of the self-concept: by 1941 the *British Journal of Educational Psychology* was running a symposium (Burt *et al*, 1941–3) to answer the question 'Is the doctrine of instincts dead?', but the verdict was 'not proven', Burt concluding that some of McDougall's principles remained valid and only Vernon giving a positive affirmative answer to the question. Thorndike's Laws of Learning made a strong contribution on the cognitive side and behaviourism attracted enthusiastic support, at different points in time; in its earlier phase perhaps mainly with regard to learning but in its more recent return to popularity, in the form of behaviour modification. Gestalt theory also enriched some courses and there were all the intriguing developments in thinking about intelligence — Spearman's two-factor theory, American multi-factor interpretations, factorial analysis, intelligences A, B and C, multi-dimensional theory. There was intensive and devoted discussion of the nature-nurture controversy, with intriguing references to the Jukes and the Kallikaks and canal-boat children. There was study of the gifted and of the mentally handicapped. Then too there were the psycho-analytic interpretations. Freud's views were considered with some hesitations and misinterpretations but perhaps they

9

also entered teacher education indirectly through the work of two of his admirers, Homer Lane and A.S. Neill. Adler's theories on dominance, compensation, inferiority complexes, had admirers and exponents, though Jung didn't seem quite to make it into teacher education. More recently, personality development has been viewed via Erikson, Rogers, Cattell and Eysenck. And of course an important component has been the theory of stages of human development as perceived by Piaget.

Thus psychology can be said to have contributed richly to the marriage with education over these many years. What one cannot tell with precision is how much psychology, or what psychology, has entered into the formal education of teachers in different centres of training. (There is of course also the informal learning of psychology by teachers who continue to read during the years when they are hard at work in school — there are such teachers — and who manage in this way to acquire an extended knowledge of current theories and results in the discipline. There is also the contribution of psychology to in-service and higher degree courses for teachers, a contribution which is by no means negligible.) Courses of teacher education in this part of the world do not have — as they do in other countries — a centralized curriculum from which one can fairly reliably discover what is taught to the students. The flexibility of the British systems means that the content of the courses can vary greatly according to the tutors' interests and capacities and also according to the other demands made upon the students.

Further, there is a distinct difference between teacher education in England and Scotland (and Wales and Northern Ireland). England has made provision through a wide variety of colleges of education, some rather small, and through teacher education in university departments of education for those graduates who chose to train for teaching: it is only in the 1970s that training became compulsory for graduates — and until 1984 maths and science graduates could still escape this compulsion. Hence England has had a large proportion of teachers who are untrained and hence, presumably, uncontaminated by such study of psychology as training courses offer. In Scotland, since 1906, all teachers have had to undergo a course of professional training. Moreover, in Scotland that training has been provided, for most of the century, in the four large provincial centres for the training of teachers (and in the two Roman Catholic colleges). There has therefore been a much greater degree of uniformity in the courses offered to students in training and there has been a tradition of strength in the teaching of psychology in the training centres. Not only has there been, at some times in Edinburgh and St. Andrews, the combination of university chair and principalship of the college (Godfrey Thomson was a most notable holder of such a joint appointment) but some eminent psycho-logists — P.E. Vernon, for example — have spent part of their careers teaching in college departments of psychology (see Cruickshank, 1970). In Scotland too the creation of the BEd/EdB (now MEd) degree in the years after the first world war developed the association between college work and university and meant that many teachers went on to increase their knowledge of psychology in this way — the degree was in fact recognized generally for many years as an honours degree in psychology, qualifying for membership of the British Psychological Society. Those who completed the degree frequently became them-selves lecturers in psychology or educational psychologists: Scotland indeed developed a fair export trade in such specialists. The foundation of a child guidance clinic in association with the Glasgow University Department of Education in 1926 and the foundation of the Scottish Council for Research in Education in 1928 were further instances of the association of education and psychology in Scotland (Ibid, 1970). (Though in fairness one must note that, even there, departments of education and departments of psychology have not always been of one mind concerning the most appropriate fare for future teachers).

Hence it is probably easier to judge of the impact of psychology in the education of teachers in Scotland than in England. But, so far as can be judged, there has been a fair similarity in the topics thought appropriate for psychology's contribution even if the amount of atten-tion to psychology may have varied.

Perhaps at this point should be mentioned the extent to which psychology has been interpreted in teacher education as 'psy-chometrics'. The term has been generally used as one of abuse in recent discussions of the curriculum: strictly speaking it could apply to any attempt to measure objectively psychological traits or abilities; but the main onus of complaints seems to be that the study of psychology has involved excessive attention to intelligence testing and produced a belief that the results of intelligence tests are as gospel.

Now if one looks at textbooks of psychology, such an interpretation is not likely to be justified. Normally they make all the due reservations about the unreliability of testing in various circumstances, the limita-tions of tests, the differences between group and individual tests. Any acceptance of scores as absolute and invariable would seem to show inadequate learning on the part of the teachers. It is also evident from various sources that the teaching of psychology to intending teachers has not been exclusively devoted to this topic, even though public interest and controversies about eleven-plus selection procedures may have given it prominence. The traditional and customary teaching of psychology has included the affective as well as the cognitive side — and we may recall that for the originator of the testing movement, Binet, the personality differences shown in the responses by two young girls of his family to his test questions were a major source of interest (Binet 1903). We shall come back later to the attitude of teachers towards what psychologists have offered them: at this point, apropos of intelligence testing, it can be remarked that those teachers who are said to have accepted test results so trustingly that they saw little point in working hard to teach children designated as having low IQs must be balanced against those legions of teachers who devotedly set themselves to coaching their pupils to achieve better scores in intelligence tests, an activity which indicates all kinds of interesting evaluations of the tests and the psychologists who constructed them (though mainly it demonstrates the universal reaction of teachers that if there is an examination system, they can beat it). (Comment on such coaching appears in Vernon, [Ed.] [1957].)

At any rate, we find that for many decades the marriage of psychology and education proceeded harmoniously, even if the contribution of one partner changed from time to time — and even if, occasionally, psychology adopted the alias of experimental education.

The alienation of affections seems to have developed from the 1950s onwards. The study of education itself went through a period of turmoil, for various reasons. There was the vigorous attack on what was described as the 'undifferentiated mush' of some college courses in 'education'. There was a demand for a clearer analysis of educational concepts and theories. There was growing interest in the sociological factors which were being shown to relate to children's progress through the educational system. And other fields of educational studies were being explored. Perhaps the evolution which has taken place during the last thirty years can be illuminated by consideration of the change in content of the *British Journal of Educational Studies*. Founded in 1952 under the auspices of the Standing Conference on Studies in Education, an organization then uniting professors of education, the Journal initially set out to bring to its readers the results of educational research and new developments in education. At the time of its foundation, those responsible recognized (see *British Journal of Educational Studies*, 1952) the interest of educators in developments in psychology and statistics: but this need, they said, was already well catered for by the journals of the British Psychological Society. Thus the new Journal would be concerned with the other side of the partnership, with education: and within education, the studies noted were philosophy, history and comparative education — a manageable cluster. The evolution of educational studies during the following thirty years meant that in its thirtieth anniversary issue the *British Journal of Educational Studies* (1982) included articles on philosophy of education, sociology of education, educational administration, history of education, economics of education, comparative education — and educational psychology: and even so it was accused of serious omissions, notably of politics of education and the curious hybrid, curriculum development. The articles themselves showed how rich and varied was the evolution of these studies during the three decades, how specialized they had become, how diverse their literature and their professional organizations.

Thus educational studies proliferated and the simple duo of education and psychology no longer matched the times.

Another factor contributing to the break-up of the partnership may be found in the evolution of BEd degrees from the mid-1960s onwards. Such degrees gave a new emphasis and, eventually, more time to educational studies. They were also concerned to achieve academic respectability, so the specialist qualifications of those teaching for them became a matter of importance both for colleges and for university departments validating college-taught BEd degrees. In such a climate it becomes important for the teacher of philosophy of education to be recognized as a 'real' philosopher, for the educational sociologist to achieve recognition as a pure sociologist, and so on. (It has been asserted in comment on American university schools of education that their members have a problem of achieving respectability in the eyes of specialists in other university departments: thus, for example, it had been noted that the educational psychologist in such schools may make rather frequent 'casual' references to his membership of the American Psychological Association [Jarrett, 1983 reviewing *American Graduate Schools of Education* by H. Judge]). With such specialization there comes the demand for space in the curriculum for the teaching of that particular aspect of educational studies. Courses themselves diversify into modules. Hence, instead of a simple allocation of time to education and psychology, there is provision for the teaching of a number of educational studies, of which psychology is only one, and for various combinations of modules. Within psychology, while some BEd structures may maintain a basic course followed by options, some may allow of the study, even in the first student year, of special fields of interest — development of cognitive thinking, adolescence, counselling and so on. Interdisciplinary courses may further diminish the teaching of a coherent course of psychology. The offered range of options within programmes means that some students may concentrate on other educational studies: sociology in particular has attracted great interest and enthusiasm. Thus, while Stanley Nisbet (1967) could note that in three of the four Scottish universities validating BEd courses, educational psychology (in some designation or other) appeared still as a compulsory component, the trend of development in colleges, has been to break up the education-psychology marriage. Future teachers may receive, or opt for, little or no teaching in psychology.

These developments have similarly affected the courses provided for the one-year PGCE teachers-in-training. Given the already excessive amounts of work and variety of interests to be coped with in this much too short course, the impossibility of a serious study of each of what have come to be regarded as the four major disciplines — philosophy of education, history of education, educational sociology and educational psychology — has seemed to many teacher-educators self-evident. Thus in many universities, PGCE students are offered a choice and some can avoid psychology completely. Or they may be presented only with such aspects of psychology as seem relevant to their special teaching subject (relevance being narrowly interpreted). Or there may be an attempt to offer the students an 'integrated' course in which representatives of the various disciplines make a contribution related to a chosen theme, normally one which is classroom-centred and practically oriented (that is, related to the daily teaching work of the school).

This development of options brings to our attention the important fact that since the nineteenth century it is not only attitudes to marriage — of people or subjects — which have changed. In higher education too we have become more permissive. Teacher-educators seem to have moved from the view that certain subjects are essential for the teacher therefore all intending teachers must study them. A more child-centred (or learner-centred) philosophy seems to have been adopted, that the learner should have freedom to choose what to study and the learner will study better those subjects he or she has chosen to study. (McLeish, [1970] reviews studies of various researchers who have found that colleges and departments of education tend to produce a child-centred approach in their students: possibly teacher-educators have the rare distinction of acting — in one respect at least — on the principles they preach.) But, as in discussions of child-centred theory in general, the question arises, how do learners discover the delights and usefulness of certain subjects if the learners can opt not to study them at all? And does a brief, superficial acquaintance with a subject give sufficient foundations for deciding on its value or lack of value? If psychology does have something essential for student-teachers how can we, in an optional-modules system, make sure they receive it?

A similar change in social outlook may be noted with regard to attendance at courses. In the old days the student-teacher, like the school-child, was expected to be punctual and regular in attendance. Again, the new ethos in higher education is that, in most cases, students may attend as they see fit. Certainly the University of Leicester (1982) survey of PGCE courses in English university departments of education found that there were noticeable variations in proportions of classes attended and that method classes were more likely to have a high attendance rate than 'theoretical' classes. (Teaching practice, indeed, would seem to be the one part of training courses where attendance is expected to be 100 per cent and where failure to turn up is severely sanctioned.) From the point of view of psychology (and other educational studies) the answer to the question of attendance is perhaps easier than the answer to the 'options' question, at least theoretically. If students find a subject well taught, interesting, useful, there should be no problem about attendance.

But the new attitudes do produce difficulties if we do want to give teachers a common background of knowledge and interests. And this we may wish to do for more than one reason. If teaching is to be regarded as a profession then it can be argued that all teachers, as professionals, should share, not simply practical experiences, but knowledge of disciplines relevant to their work. This common professional background was provided for by the old concept of the marriage of education and psychology in teacher education. We have to think now whether a common professional foundation can still be achieved or whether we must have schools and staffrooms where some teachers have been educated by the study of psychology and others have not. But if we are tempted to reintroduce a common element of psychology as part of the knowledge forming a common professional background as well as an essential part of teacher preparation we must be very sure that what we offer is in fact valuable to the teacher.

So we come to the question of how teachers have in fact responded till now to what has been offered them by the parent disciplines of education and psychology. In particular, have they found the contribution of psychology as valuable as the nineteenth century and later enthusiasts predicted it would be? Again, it is difficult to generalize. If one reverts to the empirical or anecdotal form of knowledge, it can be said that many teachers have remained unimpressed by what they know of psychological ideas and of psychologists. A not unknown reaction of the experienced, down-to-earth teacher is that 'Psychologists are all daft!' (a view for which one might even find some research evidence, if one takes neuroticism as related to daftness). There have been instances of antagonism between teachers and educational psychologists, the former complaining that the latter take a period of some weeks in testing before coming to the conclusion that a certain child is suffering from the problem for which the teacher sought expert help in the first place. Or teachers have found that psychologists' suggestions for action fail to take into account the circumstances of classroom teaching and the factors deriving from the presence of a large number of other children. Nor have teachers — as indicated earlier — been universally willing to accept the psychologist's view of the abilities of a particular child, especially as indicated by an intelligence test score. If the score is not compatible with the teacher's own observation of the child and with impressions gained during repeated attempts to teach the child, then the teacher's conclusion will often be that the score is nonsensical. This is one reason for finding interpretations of the work of Rosenthal and Jacobson (1968) so hard to accept: or at least for finding that that particular slant on the self-fulfilling prophecy was erroneous. For in so many cases the experienced teacher, given a discrepant set of IQs by a psychologist, would simply dismiss them and go right on teaching that particular group of children as the teacher saw fit. (And it will be recalled that in the 'Pygmalion' investigation, such gains as were shown by some of the experimental group were not in fact gains in school achievement — with assessment dependent on the teachers — but in some idiosyncratic psychological test scores.)

So far as the student teachers are concerned, what they mainly look for, especially during the one-year course, is information on how to survive in the classroom. What is wanted is a recipe for effective class management and for effective communication of the subject(s). Hence the teaching of psychology shares with other theoretical aspects the disadvantage of being concerned with wider issues and with knowledge which, while even more important, does not necessarily provide those 'practical tips for teachers' which the student anxiously desires to have.

If in fact one looks at what is offered to teachers-in-training, can one claim that psychology is living up to the fine promises of the initial contract? Psychology is to explain the principles on which human learning takes place. So the student in the introductory course is presented with three or four or more theories of learning — behaviourist, Gagné, Ausubel and others; together with a sophisticated critique of their respective merits and weaknesses. Memory and forgetting are areas highly relevant to the teacher's work. So students learn about long-term and short-term memories and filtering and retrieval: they draw more or less elegant diagrams to illustrate these: and deduce the 'practical applications' that meaningful material is more likely to be remembered and that repeated rehearsal makes the efficient retrieval of what has been learned more probable. (Conclusions which might, one feels, have burst in upon them through empirical observation after a couple of weeks in the practical situation.) Psychology is concerned with the whole personality of the child who is to be educated: so students again find a rich selection of theories to choose from and they become adept in responding to requests to 'compare and contrast the personality theories of Cattell and Eysenck'. We offer them a similarly entrancing array of theories about human intelligence and a wide selection of evidence both for and against the heritability of that trait, if such a trait exists. The stages of development of children are described and analysed; stages of cognitive development are related to work in school subjects. Teachers are warned against attempting to teach beyond the maturity level of the child; except that, on further consideration, it may be that teaching accelerates the child's progress from one stage or level to the next.

We have come a long way from the 'perfectly trustworthy' conclusions to be drawn from scientific principles.

So at the present time we find that the position of psychology in the education of teachers is threatened by external and internal forces: it is ill-defined and variously interpreted. The Leicester survey of PGCE work (Op. Cit., 1982) shows clearly the diversity of what is offered in the shape of courses on educational theory (including psychology). We find that 'many departments' offered courses in psychology: but some others offered rather such things as courses on 'learning', 'language — use and acquisition', 'counselling', which would seem fragments of the basic study. A 'few departments' also offered courses on 'behavioural techniques', 'small group dynamics', 'slow-learning children' as well as courses which would seem to have some relationship with psychology — 'juvenile delinquency' and 'aesthetic education'. But other students in other departments attended 'integrated courses' and could not therefore say whether they had studied psychology or not. Among students who had recognizably studied psychology, there was in fact a fairly favourable reaction to the subject. Yet one should consider carefully the opinions of those students who were in a position to judge of the amount of insight they had gained into various topics: while the majority thought they had gained insight 'to a great extent' or 'to some extent' on topics such as child development and the psychology of learning, 20.9 per cent and 26.9 per cent thought that in these topics they had gained insight 'hardly/not at all'. And again, while some 60 per cent claimed to have gained some, or great, insight into intelligence testing, 38.1 per cent responded 'hardly/not at all'. ('Teacher-pupil interaction' is perhaps a 'mixed' area: but here also we find again 21.1 per cent in the 'hardly/not at all' estimates of gains in insight).

In these circumstances, what is the best advice we can give as to this long-established marriage between psychology and education? Should we leave both sides to drift apart? Should we recognize that the claims of rivals such as sociology are to be respected and so a permanent union cannot be maintained? Or should we propose a re-affirmation of the old contract and a new, stronger partnership, with both sides having abandoned the romantic illusions of youth but ready to contribute to an understanding and effective relationship?

We do not receive any very clear answers to this question if we look at the advice of the central authorities in England as to the future training of teachers. Some move there certainly seems to be towards greater uniformity in what is provided in teacher education. But the exact contribution of psychology is not precisely defined.

Circular No. 3/84, *Initial Teacher Training: Approval of Courses* (DES, 1984) includes these statements of criteria for approval:

> Students should be prepared . . . to teach the full range of pupils whom they are likely to encounter in an ordinary school, with their diversity of ability, behaviour, social background and ethnic and cultural origins. They will need to learn how to respond flexibly to such diversity and to guard against preconceptions based on the race or sex of pupils. They should be helped to understand the different ways in which pupils develop and learn, and the factors which can affect that process, such as the quality of the exchange of language between teacher and pupil and the contribution of parents to their child's development. Students should learn to recognize children who are very able or gifted and appreciate how their potential can be developed; they will also need to acquire an understanding of the more common learning difficulties. This will require experience of the purpose and practice of the assessment of pupil performance and a knowledge of the appropriate levels of performance to be expected from children of differing ages, abilities and aptitudes. Students should be introduced to ways of identifying children with special educational needs . . . Courses should also pay attention to . . . staff collaboration in a collective professional approach to the curriculum and the pastoral and administrative responsibilities of teachers . . . Students should be made aware of the wide range of relationships — with parents and others — which teachers can expect to develop in a diverse society . . .

They will also need to have a basic understanding of the type of society in which their pupils are growing up ... in particular, ways in which pupils can be helped to acquire an understanding of the values of a free society and its economic and other foundations.

(The authorities don't want much, do they? No wonder there are proposals for the lengthening of the one-year course of training.)

Psychology is most obviously in there somewhere, lots of it, intertwined with sociological and other studies. But to teach psychology adequately in such conditions is probably an impossible task: there is simply too much to be done. The marriage of psychology and education must be maintained: but in different circumstances: not as something to be got over or treated superficially in the brief period of pre-service training of teachers but as indeed a life-long union. That is to say, we must recognize that psychology, like the theory of education, is not something to be learned and understood at a given point in time, once and for all. It cannot be crammed into a brief pre-service course (especially a one-year course): nor is it adequately presented in bits and scraps here and there. Individual teachers take many years before they can develop their own individual theory of education — a theory which must include some acceptance of psychological explanations of the nature of human beings to whom and by whom education is given. Theory is better understood, criticized and appreciated when it is brought into relationship with real experience. So in the study of psychology, the young teachers should certainly receive an introduction to some part of what it can offer during the period of initial training. But the real study of psychology is to be pursued later — by in-service courses (a provision which should be compulsory, and frequently available to all teachers) as well as by individual study. In teaching, empirical observation must lead the teacher to questioning how far the behaviour of individuals does correspond to general principles. So teachers can enjoy discovering psychological findings which throw light on the behaviours and situations they have observed (in staffrooms and elsewhere, as well as in classrooms): and they may join in research to establish further principles of this kind. Such developments may also help them to discriminate among weird and wonderful 'psychological' theories with which teachers and the public are bombarded. Above all, teachers are working with people. Let us make a value judgment: they should therefore be interested in people, how their minds work, how they feel. Psychology may not yet have arrived at agreed explanations of human behaviour but it has undoubtedly many insights to contribute. It is a growing discipline, with new and stimulating theories and findings to offer in future: though it must be selective and sensible in its offerings to teachers. Above all, psychological studies can encourage in teachers the habit of regarding children and young people and adults — and colleagues — not simply as representatives of social class III (manual) or social classes I and II, or as members of such-and-such an ethnic or cultural group, but as individuals whose individual reactions can be understood in the light of general principles and whose behaviour stimulates and contributes to the greatest of all human interests, the interest in human thinking and feeling itself.

References

ADAMS, J. (1897) *Herbartian Psychology Applied to Education*, London, D.C. Heath and Co.

BAIN, A. (1879) *Education as a Science*, London, Kegan Paul.

BINET, A. (1903) *L'Etude Expérimentale de l'Intelligence*, Paris, Schleicher Frères.

BRITISH JOURNAL OF EDUCATIONAL STUDIES (1952) 1, 1.

BRITISH JOURNAL OF EDUCATIONAL STUDIES (1982) 30, 1.

BURT, C., VERNON, P.E., THORNDIKE, E.L., DREVER, J., PEAR, T.H., MYERS, C.H. (1941–3) 'Is the doctrine of instincts dead?' in *British Journal of Educational Psychology*, 11, 3; 12, 1, 2, 3; 13, 1.

CHILD, D. (1977) *Psychology and the Teacher* (2nd edn.) London, Holt, Rinehart and Winston, p. 3.

CRUICKSHANK, M. (1970) *A History of the Training of Teachers in Scotland*, University of London Press, pp. 165, 181.

DEPARTMENT OF EDUCATION AND SCIENCE (1984) *Initial Teacher Training: Approval of Courses*, London, DES, Circular No. 3/84, and Welsh Office, Cardiff, Circular No. 21/84, Annex, pp. 8–9, paras 11–12.

JARRETT, J.L. (1983) reviewing JUDGE, H., *American Graduate Schools of Education* in *British Journal of Educational Studies*, 31, 3, p. 268.

McDOUGALL, W. (1908) *Introduction to Social Psychology*, Boston, Luce.

McDOUGALL, W. (1932) *The Energies of Men*, London, Methuen and Co.

McLEISH, J. (1970) *Students' Attitudes and College Environments*, Cambridge Institute of Education, Chapter 8.

NISBET, S. (1967) 'The study of education in Scotland', in *Scottish Educational Studies*, 1, 1, pp. 8–17.

ROSENTHAL, R., JACOBSON, L. (1968) *Pygmalion in the Classroom*, New York, Holt, Rinehart and Winston.

ROSS, D. (1883) *Education as a University Subject*, Glasgow, J. Maclehose and Sons, Appendix B.

SPENCER, H. (1855) and (1929) 'What knowledge is of most worth?', in

Education, Intellectual, Moral and Physical, London, Watts and Co., pp. 13–16.

SULLY, J. (1886) *Handbook of Psychology for the Teacher*, London, Longmans, Green and Co., pp. 2, 12, 14.

TIBBLE, J. (1966) *The Study of Education*, London, Routledge and Kegan Paul, p. 8.

UNIVERSITY OF LEICESTER, SCHOOL OF EDUCATION (1982) *The Structure and Process of Initial Teacher Education within Universities in England and Wales*, p. 115 and chapter 6.

VERNON, P.E., (Ed.), (1957) *Secondary School Selection, A British Psychological Society Enquiry*, Methuen and Co.

Psychology in Initial Teacher Education[1]

Professor Gerry Bernbaum[2]
University of Leicester

Enthusiasts for the high pressure sales techniques of the American Express Company will have recently been invited to give consideration to their Christmas presents, and, most particularly, to the advantages supposedly found in fruit cake. The advertisement for the Collins Street bakery in Corsicana, Texas, informs us that 'What Dom Perignon is to champagne and Romanoff is to caviar, the Collins Street Bakery is to fruit cake', and, indeed, one might add, psychology is to teacher education! For there is no doubt that, historically, psychology has been seen as the most relevant academic discipline to the training of teachers and that, moreover, the development of the discipline of psychology can to a large degree be explained in terms of its close association with teaching and learning and above all with the mental testing of young persons. It is equally the case that the research that we have undertaken at Leicester,[3] a description of which will fill a large part of this lecture, shows clearly that in the contemporary Postgraduate Certificate in Education in universities, psychology occupies a good deal of the students' time and is the discipline which has the greatest impact upon them.

Despite the central position that psychology has occupied, and continues to occupy, there is an ambivalence about its role in teacher education, as there is about the role of the other academic disciplines such as sociology and philosophy which might bear upon practical matters. To a very large degree this ambivalence can be explained by the traditions and origins of teacher education and the ideologies which surround it. The origins of teacher education in the nineteenth century were such that the earliest colleges were predominantly places which taught students the subjects which they might be required to teach and provided some practical induction into the teaching of those subjects.

The staff were ex-school teachers and were mainly concerned with very practical affairs as the title 'Master of Method' which was bestowed upon them indicated. By the early part of this century the standard of student entrant to the training college had improved and it therefore became possible for the courses in the colleges to take a somewhat broader and more liberal view of the nature of teacher education. At the same time standards in schools had improved and training colleges could move away from their 'model' schools and utilize for teaching practice a range of neighbouring institutions. It was this development which gave rise to the more modern notion of teaching practice. The improvement of the quality of students on the one hand and the development of a more broadly based teaching practice on the other did, however, produce a schism in the older concept of the work of training college staff. As this century progressed there was always a tension between those who were the experts in the subjects such as geography, history, English, which students were to teach in schools and who had responsibility for teaching those subjects to the students, and those on the other hand who had responsibility for the students in the schools and who were concerned with the administration and operation of teaching practice. This last group found it very difficult to establish any firmly based claim to academic expertise. They were essentially practising school teachers employed as college staff concerned with the induction of young teachers. It was this staff that formed the basis of the education departments within teacher training and who, in the first instance, most particularly in the inter-war years, seized upon the developing discipline of psychology as the vehicle by which their work could be given academic vigour. Thirty years later, in the 1960s and 1970s, the same enthusiasm was to be shown for sociology on precisely the same grounds.

It follows from what has gone before that there is within teacher education an emphasis upon the practical business of teaching in schools, and this emphasis is very powerful at the point when staff are recruited. Historically, the great majority of the staff in teacher education are recruited from schools. The nature of school teaching as an occupation and the career line which successful teachers might be encouraged to follow hardly allow for the nascent educationalist to develop an expertise in educational research, its methods and its problems. Education staff, when appointed to their new posts, have in effect to begin a new career. It is not always possible for all of them to make the transition successfully. These difficulties are further exaggerated at an institutional level in respect of those subjects that do not figure extensively on the school curriculum. Subjects like psychology, which is hardly taught in schools at all, therefore, find it very difficult to recruit practitioners well-versed in theory, method and empirical data, and who at the same time meet the conventional criteria of successful classroom experience. What has tended to happen, therefore, is that those without formal training in psychology but with practical classroom experience have, within the confines of the education department, taken on responsibility for the teaching of psychology, most particularly, as has already been argued, where this might seem to give academic legitimacy to their practical activities. Little wonder that the McNair Committee of 1944 noted that 'The small size of many colleges means that one lecturer must play many roles' (p. 71).

If there is any value in this analysis, the consequences of appointing staff on the basis of their presumed excellence in school teaching is that such staff have what might be termed an action orientation. The nature of the task places the lecturer and the students close together. The students are inevitably emotionally concerned with their own impact upon children and it is easy, therefore, for the staff to become totally absorbed in the practical activities of day-to-day teaching and almost impossible for them to appear less enthusiastic about teaching than they are inviting their own students to be. Such a heavy practical engagement inevitably takes time away from the more detached and scholarly pursuits whose results, if any, are likely to be at some distance in the future. It is particularly the case that work in psychology and sociology, which by its very nature is likely to be hedged with qualifications and constrained by methodological considerations, will appear problematic. The limitations of the work are likely to be such that no clear or immediate policy recommendations emerge, no dramatic cues to action are enunciated, and even where such action and such policies might be implicit, there is likely to be a lapse of time before implementation, and an untidiness brought about by unintended consequences after implementation. Those in teacher education, therefore, who adopt the mantle of psychology are likely to do so only in limited and partial fashion. The benefits of academic respectability and of the insights offered by the discipline are likely to be contained within a selective view of the subject and emphasis upon those parts of it which are practical in their concerns, and which apparently shed light upon immediate issues. Nor should it be forgotten that such an approach is likely to devalue complex issues relating to, say, research methodology, in favour of a more generalist and eclectic view of the study of education, most particularly when such a view can be justified on ideological grounds linked to the supposed benefits of inter-disciplinary inquiry and breaking down subject barriers.

These structural features of the historical development of teacher education are barely separable from the normative climate which has characterized the training of teachers over the last 150 years. The origins of teacher education in the middle of the nineteenth century were closely linked both to the churches and to the need to provide teachers for the children of the new inhabitants of the growing cities. Thus, the Newcastle Commission could argue that 'a set of good schools civilizes a whole neighbourhood'. This civilizing process, however, was not conceived of in intellectual terms. As the future Bishop of Manchester argued in 1858, it was possible to teach a working-class child 'soundly and thoroughly, in a way that he shall not forget it, all that it is necessary for him to possess in the shape of intellectual attainment by the time that he is ten years old' (Glass, 1961). Such opinions did not encourage the view that the teachers would require great intellectual qualities, though of course they might require much moral fortitude. Thus it was that Kay-Shuttleworth (1843) could describe as the main object of his initial teacher training scheme 'The formation of the character of the schoolmaster'. It is 'essential', he said, 'for the teachers of the poor to accept for themselves a way of life little different from that of their charges' (p. 65). Under these conditions, therefore, the commitment of teachers was essential. The moral, virtuous, but essentially unspecific nature of the teaching task seemed to demand above average commitment. 'Are you aware,' students seeking admission to the College of St. Mark and St. John were asked, 'that your path of duty on leaving the college will be principally, if not entirely, among the poor?' (Taylor, 1969, p. 255).

It was, however, not just religion which enabled teachers, in Jean Floud's graphic phrase, 'to carry light into dark places' (Floud, 1962). It was also the influence of those thinkers who were concerned about the impact of urbanization and industrialization upon the life, values and attitudes of nineteenth century citizens.

Many such authors were anti-industrial and associated their hostility to industrialism with romantic notions of the past. Secular ideas propounded in the eighteenth century by Rousseau began to be enthusiastically adopted by liberal and anti-industrial critics. These ideas were frequently incorporated into the dominant religious imagery when applied to education and to the training of teachers. Edmond Holmes, for example, in *What Is And What Might Be* insisted that 'the business of the teacher is to foster the growth of the child's soul', and emphasized the value of self-realization by which the 'idea of education begins to merge itself into the larger idea of salvation' (Holmes, 1911, pp. 60–61).

Those who held such beliefs came to emphasize the commitment and training of the teacher no less than did the religious bodies which had such a powerful hold on teacher education — to breathe new life into the mass of urban poor and to recreate the lost sense of community whilst, at the same time, encouraging social justice, was to be no easy matter. Clearly, it would require teachers of the most special kind — with compassion, hope, virtue and an inspirational commitment. Thus, until the most modern times the study of education remained firmly in the hands of the religious bodies or of those whose secular ideologies took on the characteristics of religious faith.

It is possible to argue that a subject such as psychology, which, in one of its dominant traditions at least, adopts the scientific mode, stands in an uncomfortable relationship with what Martin Bressler (1963) has called 'the conventional wisdom of education'. As has been argued, that conventional wisdom is characterized more by dogma and faith than by free scientific enquiry. In Bressler's own words, 'In the conventional wisdom of education, truth and wish are one'. The scientific study of social phenomena, as undertaken by much psychology, can too readily be seen as a challenge to faith and dogma, whilst the caution of intellectual reservation and qualification might be seen as heresy rather than doubt. As a result it has frequently been the case that what counts as evidence in the eyes of educationists is frequently an insubstantial and vague selection of information designed to support a stated point of view. Again, therefore, theory, method and research are placed in a secondary and ambiguous position.

This analysis of the structure of teacher education and of the normative climate in which it has been practised provides a helpful framework within which to analyse the development of psychology in teacher education. In 1959 the British Psychological Society, along with the Association of Teachers in Colleges and Departments of Education, published the results of an inquiry into the place of psychology in the training colleges of that time. The report of the joint working party points out how the early teaching of psychology was undertaken by the Master of Method or by the junior or infant method lecturer. Almost from the beginning, therefore, psychology was immersed in general education courses and undertaken by staff who, in the main, lacked specialist qualifications in the subject.

As recently as 1959 the joint report showed how difficult the colleges found it to estimate the amount of time spent on psychology because, in as many as seventy-six out of the ninety-eight colleges who replied, the psychological aspects of education were not separated from the study of aims, values, history and philosophy. The inquiry also looked at examination questions in psychology, which may be taken as a possible guide to what the staff consider significant and as an indication of the areas to which the students' attention must be drawn. Again, the ideological elements in the courses were immediately apparent and the concerns with the problems of practical experience were especially noted. As the authors of the report conclude, 'There were — relatively few questions on educational attainment of normal children, but many on educational failure and remedial treatment — over three-quarters of the questions on adjustment were on the causes, diagnosis and treatment of maladjusted children — on the whole, the approach appeared to be empirical rather than theoretical. The questions on learning, for example, seemed to be based on a knowledge of established classroom practice together with some of the more important experimental findings. Very few asked for general underlying theoretical principles about learning — Again, the questions on intelligence were almost wholly on the practical appreciation of tests in schools.' The report also noted the wide variation in the psychological qualifications of those staff concerned with the teaching of psychology and showed that 39 per cent of those with responsibility for teaching psychology had no formal qualifications whatsoever in the subject. What appears to have happened in effect is not that psychology or psychologists emerged as serious challenges either to the personnel of teacher education or to the dominant ideological strands in the rhetoric of teacher education, but that at both a personal and an intellectual level they were incorporated within the staff and into the established intellectual framework.

We are now in a position to examine more closely the material on the teaching of psychology in university PGCE courses which has been yielded by our study, the Structure and Process of Initial Teacher Education (SPITE) within Universities in England and Wales. This study, conducted in 1979–80, gathered a great deal of data from students on PGCE courses in universities in that year, and from the staff who taught them. The number of students involved in the inquiry was initially 4350, but by the end of the academic year usable responses were obtained from a reduced number, 3350. Nevertheless, both of these figures represent high response rates of 88 per cent and 68 per cent respectively. The staff in university departments of education provided us with 762 usable replies, a response rate of 60.7 per cent. It should be noted, however, that non-response rates amongst the staff were highest from that group of staff who did not have extensive PGCE responsibilities but whose work was mainly concentrated in in-service and advanced work. This group of non-respondents included a number of individuals whose main responsibility was the teaching of psychology.

Nevertheless, we are confident that, though the original formulation of the SPITE research was not designed specifically with either this lecture in mind or with a view to obtaining information on psychology teaching as a special topic, we do have a great deal of significant and relevant information about the teaching of psychology in initial one year courses of teacher training in universities.

The SPITE project embraced all university departments in England and Wales that taught the PGCE. Information was gathered from students in all departments by means of survey questionnaires, and seven of the thirty departments were selected for special study. Samples of students from those seven departments, as well as being given additional questionnaires, were interviewed and were invited to keep diaries whilst on their course. Data from all staff were gathered by survey questionnaire, and a small sample of staff in the seven sub-sample departments participated in semi-structured interviews.

As far as the PGCE is concerned, there is clear evidence that the situation in the universities in 1980 with respect to the teaching of psychology was not entirely dissimilar to the description given by the joint BPS/ATCDE working party on psychology in the colleges of education twenty years previously. There is a great deal of psychology taught. Not all of it, however, is taught in what might be termed regular psychology courses. Some psychology, quite properly, appears within integrated topic or issue-centred courses along with, say, sociology. But it is clear from our study that much psychology appears in a group of diverse topics such as teaching children with learning difficulties, special educational needs, women's studies, language, learning, class-room control and discipline, assessment, and also within method work. As a result, therefore, it is not surprising that the staff involved in the teaching of psychology have diverse qualifications. What might be termed the 'elite' corps are the thirty-seven respondents to our questionnaire who can be identified as teaching specialist named courses in psychology within the PGCE framework. Of these thirty-seven, however, nine appeared to possess no qualifications in psychology at all, and a further fourteen did not have a first degree in psychology but had acquired their psychology training at a postgraduate level only. The range of first degrees possessed by those who did not have a first degree in psychology covered the school curriculum and included such subjects as geography, mathematics and English.

As already noted, in addition to the thirty-seven tutors responsible for specialist courses in psychology there were a further seventy staff who claimed to be teaching topics in the field of psychology. The qualifications of these staff were even more diverse. Only eleven possessed any degree in psychology. The remaining fifty-nine had no specialist degrees, first or otherwise, in psychology, and it is interesting to note that out of the total of seventy more than a fifth had previously been teachers of English in secondary schools. In all of this, however, we need to remember that there is another side to the uncertainty about the relationship between qualifications and teaching responsibilities. Some of the staff upon whom we have commented have master's degrees in education or first degrees in social science which might contain elements of psychology not readily apparent in the title. We also gathered a great deal of other information about the staff responsible for psychology courses in some form or other, and will return to these data shortly. It is clear from what we have said already, however, that those teaching psychology on PGCE courses possess a diverse range of qualifications reflecting the policy of the departments in recruiting mostly staff who have had practical experience of teaching in schools, and the need for lecturers in education to perform many diverse roles. Thus, there is both diversity of staff and diversity of courses.

In addition, our study of the various psychology curricula, reading lists, essay titles and the like, shows clearly the ways in which the action-oriented, problem-centred approach so dominant in the educationalist context is reflected in the psychological components of the PGCE.

In describing the course it is important to keep in mind the distinction between those departments in which psychology is offered as a specialist subject and those where psychology appears as part of a adolescence and intelligence. Where courses are integrated the domitopics covered show a strong emphasis upon language, learning, adolescene and intelligence. Where courses are integrated the dominance of language and learning is maintained, but problem-oriented areas such as special educational needs, educational disadvantage and counselling are frequently mentioned by the students. It should be remembered that in all types of departments psychology is also taught within other popular options on the PGCE, such as particular courses on pastoral care, languages, learning, evaluation and assessment. It is not surprising, therefore, that by the end of the year it is the psychological aspects of their PGCE course which the students name as having dominated their non-method work experience. Not surprisingly, also, in view of the extent of their exposure to psychological topics, the students claim to have found psychology the most intellectually stimulating part of their non-method PGCE course, and also the most academically interesting. With the exception of their courses on discipline (which undoubtedly included some psychology) the students also found their psychology courses the most useful part of educational theory when they were in schools.

In the light of the exposure to psychology and the apparent enthusiasm shown for it by the students, at least in comparison with other parts of their course, it is no surprise that psychology heads the list of topics upon which students claimed to have written essays during their PGCE year. It is also the case that psychology-related fields such as discipline, language and learning, careers and counselling, grouping (including mixed ability teaching), examinations and assessment and special educational needs are topics upon which a high proportion of students claimed to have put pen to paper.

The students in our sub-sample were invited to tell us which books that they had read on their PGCE course they had found stimulating. Psychology books received the second highest number of mentions, but, more significantly the students expressed far and away the greatest enthusiasm for books dealing with special educational needs, maladjustment and remedial education. When we came to examine in detail the titles of books that the students had found so rewarding, it emerged that the most popular were books which might be seen to be on the margin of psychology — John Holt's books, for example, *How Children Fail*, *How Children Learn*, and Michael Marland's *The Craft of the Classroom* were without doubt the most popular. Other books popular with the students, which give some indication of the problem- and action-oriented perspectives which they adopted, were Clegg's *Children in Distress*, Hannam *et al's Young Teachers and Reluctant Learners*, Barnes' *Language Across the Curriculum*, Francis' *Beyond Control?* Of the conventional psychology books, Dennis Child's *Psychology and the Teacher* was far and away the most frequently mentioned. As Child himself notes, however, his book has limited and practical objectives, its 'central aim' he writes, 'is to introduce teachers to elementary ideas in psychology which have some relevance for their work with young people'. The books nominated by the students, therefore, only serve to emphasize the practical nature of much of the psychology teaching within the PGCE course, and the whole picture of work done is illustrative of the arguments developed in the first half of this lecture.

In examining the place of psychology in initial teacher education it is also interesting to consider in some detail the characteristics of the teaching staff, most particularly when the groups teaching psychology can be compared with the total number of education staff who replied to our enquiries.

In making such comparisons, however, it is important to remember that consideration must be given to two groups who teach psychology — those who are clearly responsible for specialist courses in the field, and those, on the other hand, who teach on other kinds of courses which contain a psychological component. Overall, as will be clear, what might be termed the generalist psychology staff differ little from the large group of education lecturers, but the specialist psychology tutors, though small in number, stand apart from both. Of the thirty-seven who were responsible for specialist courses, fifteen had joined their departments since 1975. This figure of almost 43 per cent compares with 26 per cent for the seventy who were teaching psychology outside of a specialist framework, and 24 per cent for the total of our 762 respondents. Quite simply, the specialist teachers of psychology were more likely to have been recently appointed. Not unexpectedly, therefore, they were also younger. The total sample had just 24 per cent of the respondents under the age of forty, but almost 50 per cent of the specialist psychologists were favoured with such youth. The generalists in psychology were closer to the total educationalists in that 26 per cent only were under forty. The same point can be made another way. Of the total sample, 33 per cent were aged fifty or over, and, of the generalists in psychology, as many as 30 per cent were aged fifty or over. The specialist psychologists, however, were younger, with only 23 per cent having reaching fifty.

There were interesting sex differences between the three groups also. Of the total of 762 respondents, only 17 per cent were women, of the generalist psychologists only 11 per cent were women, yet, of those responsible for specialist psychology courses, 35 per cent were female. As might be expected, the larger proportion of females amongst the specialist psychologists had as a corollary the fact that a slightly higher proportion of this group originated in the middle class as compared with the other two groups.

The arguments about the traditions and structure of teacher education from which I began also make the question of the school teaching experience of the staff extremely significant. Of the total sample of staff 93 per cent had taught in schools or in FE at some stage in their careers, and this proportion was almost exactly the same for the non-specialist psychologist. For the specialist psychologists, however, the proportion dropped dramatically to 73 per cent.

There were also differences in the types of schools in which our respondents taught. Of the total sample, 15 per cent had experience of only primary or middle school work and this proportion fell to 10 per cent in respect of the generalists. For the specialist psychologists, however, the proportion rose to 43 per cent. The subjects taught by our respondents when they had been school teachers covered the full range of the school curriculum. Thus, amongst the specialist psychologists there were ex-teachers of German, English, history, geography, classics, biology, physics, mathematics and music. Interestingly enough, as noted earlier, 22 per cent of the generalists had at some time or other been teachers of English. The professional experiences of the different groups in respect of promotion was also notably distinctive. Of the total sample, 19 per cent had never obtained a promoted post in a school. For the generalist psychologists this figure fell to 12 per cent yet 43 per cent of the specialist psychologists had never obtained a promoted post in a school, and despite the relatively high incidence of primary school teaching experience amongst the specialists, none of them had achieved the post of head or deputy head. Not suprisingly, amongst the psychology staff there was a high proportion who had previously worked either as educational psychologists or in educational research. The picture that emerges from this review of the careers of staff is one which yet again emphasizes that the specialists stand a little way apart from the educationalist context.

Overall they are younger and are less likely to have had extended school teaching careers. Even the careers they had had are not typical of those most commonly experienced by the educationalists. It is also clear that the teachers of non-specialist psychology are much closer in terms of their previous experiences to the total sample of education lecturers than they are to the specialist teachers of psychology. A greater proportion of the psychology staff than of the total number of respondents possesses a higher degree. This provides further evidence of a difference in career, and interestingly, one that bears a relationship to the duties of the specialist teacher of psychology when compared to all other staff. Our study shows clearly that a higher proportion of psychology staff than of others are likely to be teaching on advanced diploma courses, teaching on master's courses and supervising research degrees. Indeed, 50 per cent of the psychologists claimed that the course on which they spent the most time was at master's level, compared with just 22 per cent of the total sample. Our data show also that smaller proportions of psychology staff than of all staff are likely to be involved in the administration of national committees relating to their work, in the administration of university committees and in the administration of the PGCE course and of in-service courses.

The specialist teachers of psychology are in turn more likely to be engaged in research, particularly research funded by external bodies.

Not surprisingly, therefore, they are more likely to have published research reports than are education lecturers as a whole, and more likely to have published university textbooks and made contributions to academic books. The education staff, on the other hand, are more likely to have published school textbooks. Just over half of each category had published complete academic books. The specialist psychologists, however, were more likely than their colleagues to claim that they were currently engaged in work which they expected would lead to publication.

Not surprisingly, therefore, we find that whereas 53 per cent of all respondents see the balance of their university work predominantly in terms of teaching, only 38 per cent of the specialist psychologists take the same view. In general, the psychologists give greater weight to research than do the educationalists.

In concluding this discussion of the staff, it is worth noting that the differences in career, qualifications and structural position have their counterpart in differences in educational attitudes and values held by the two major groups under consideration, the psychologists and the educationalists. Compared with the education lecturers, for example, the psychologists are more likely to agree with the view that PGCE students are over-taught. They are more likely to agree with the view that university tutors do not have sufficient time to visit students on teaching practice, and to see this as a major problem. Psychologists are also more likely to agree with the view that supervising teaching practice takes up tutors' time which could be better spent on other things. The group of psychology staff are also less confident than are the educationalists about the part that practising school teachers might play in teacher education. They are less likely to agree with the view, for example, that the main responsibility for supervising students on teaching practice should be with school teachers, notwithstanding the fact that they see teaching practice supervision as absorbing a great deal of time. The psychologists are also much more likely than education lecturers generally to express strong agreement with the statement that 'It should not be so easy to pass the PGCE'. Not unexpectedly, the psychology staff see as more desirable than do the education staff the possession on the part of teachers of knowledge of educational research.

The illustrations offered to demonstrate the differing values and attitudes held by the different groups of staff further emphasize the ambivalence and ambiguity which characterize those who are responsible for basic academic disciplines taught within an educational context. Perforce they came to adopt Janus-like attitudes, looking on the one hand towards the body of theory, methodology and empirical data which is central to their scholarly concerns, and, on the other, to the more immediate world of action, optimism and bright pragmatism.

Thus, I would argue that there is a uniformity of pattern to the picture that I have presented. The origins of teacher education, and the ideologies which pertained to it, albeit outside of universities, have been powerful influences in determining the work of education departments in universities for over 100 years. The structural divisions within teacher education have emphasized the divisions between those whose concerns are close to the schools and to the everyday practicalities of the classroom, and those whose work in education departments is directed more heavily towards the world of learning and the scholarly departments within the university. Both sets of personnel and both kinds of professional cultures are necessary within teacher education, but there is ample evidence that they do not always sit comfortably together. This evening I have drawn particular attention to the differences between those responsible in the main for specialist courses in psychology within the PGCE and the general group of education lecturers, the majority of whom are responsible for method work in the subject areas of the school curriculum. There is no doubt in my mind that, had there been a higher response to our questionnaire from those who had few if any responsibilities on the PGCE, the differences which I have described would have been even more marked.

The differences that have been spoken of this evening are not likely to disappear. We are a long way from the time when what might be termed a scientific perspective on educational debate will end ideological disputes by some kind of empirical judgment. Indeed, it is unlikely that the model of scientific perspective implicit in that statement will ever be capable of yielding such decision-making power. Nevertheless, it is possible that all who work in education, most particularly in an educationalist context, might be required to think more rigorously about what might constitute evidence, and to confront that evidence when we have it. Philip Vernon, whose name we honour this evening, understood the need to tread a careful path between the practitioners on the one hand and the scholarly psychologists on the other. He also knew that the path was likely to be a very long one. As long ago as 1950, in his inaugural lecture (Vernon, 1980, p. 117) he wisely observed: 'The psychologist, when asked for the answer to any educational problem — should realize that his own judgment is often no better or even poorer than that of the parent, the teacher or the administrator who may have consulted him. In the absence of good scientific evidence, his reply should be: here are the most relevant previous researches, these are the tools of my trade: your problem can best be investigated in such a manner; but until this is done, I must confess ignorance'.

Notes

1 This lecture was delivered as the second Vernon-Wall lecture to the British Psychological Society Education Section Annual Conference, 1982.
2 In preparing this lecture I have been helped greatly by Mrs. Helen Patrick, Research Associate on the SPITE Project.
3 The Structure and Process of Initial Teacher Education, DES funded Research Project, 1979–1983.

Bibliography

BARNES, D. (1977) *Language Across the Curriculum*, Heinemann, London.

BRESSLER, M. (1963) 'The conventional wisdom of education and sociology', in PAGE C.H. (Ed.) *Sociology and Contemporary Education*, Random House, New York.

CHILD, D. (1977) *Psychology and the Teacher* (2e) Holt, Rinehart and Winston, London.

CLEGG, A. (1973) *Children in Distress*, Penguin, Harmondsworth.

FLOUD, J. (1962) 'Teaching in the affluent society', *British Journal of Sociology*, 13, 299–308.

FRANCIS, P. (1975) *Beyond Control? A Study of Discipline in the Comprehensive School*, Allen and Unwin, London.

GLASS, D. (1961) 'Education and social change in modern society', in HALSEY, A.H., FLOUD, J. and ANDERSON, C.A. (Eds.) *Education Economy and Society*, Free Press of Glencoe.

HANNAM, C. (1977) *Young Teachers and Reluctant Learners*, Penguin, Harmondsworth.

HOLMES, E. (1911) As quoted in MATHIESON, M. *The Preachers of Culture*, George Allen and Unwin, London.

HOLT, J. (1969) *How Children Fail*, Penguin, Harmondsworth.

HOLT, J. (1970) *How Children Learn*, Penguin, Harmondsworth.

KAY-SHUTTLEWORTH, J. (1843) *Report on Battersea*, as quoted in RICH, R.W. *The Training of Teachers in England and Wales During the Nineteenth Century*, Cambridge University Press, Cambridge.

MARLAND, M. (1975) *The Craft of the Classroom*, Heinemann, London.

McNAIR, A. SIR (1944) *Committee to Consider the Supply, Recruitment and Training of Teachers and Youth Leaders*, HMSO, London.

PEEL, E.A. (1962) *Joint Working Party on the Teaching of Educational Psychology in Teacher Training*, British Psychological Society and Association of Teachers in Colleges and Departments of Education, London.

TAYLOR, W. (1969) *Society and the Education of Teachers*, Faber and Faber, London.

VERNON, P.E. (1980) 'Modern educational psychology as a science', in GORDON, P. (Ed.) *The Study of Education*, Vol. 1, Woburn Press, London.

Aspects of the Professional Socialization of Teachers

Brahm Norwich
University of London Institute of Education

Introduction

Any discussion of the contribution of psychology to teacher training and education would be incomplete without some consideration of what is involved in becoming a teacher. This process, sometimes referred to as professional socialization, is important in that it emphasizes not only the acquisition of skills but the acquisition of values and attitudes. Professional socialization is usually taken to refer to the process of becoming a member of a professional group (Lacey, 1977). The aim of this paper is to raise several issues about the professional socialization of teachers with a view to discussing some possible implications for teacher training and the position of psychology in it. There is an extensive literature in this field particularly from a sociological perspective. Only certain areas have been selected in an attempt to focus the discussion on the structure of teacher preparation.

This chapter covers three broad areas; teaching as a profession; the occupational culture of teachers and the sources of teachers' outlooks and practices; and the position of psychology as a foundation discipline in teacher preparation. It is inevitable that in covering such a wide range some significant issues may be overlooked. The aim in selecting particular sources for the chapter has been to focus attention on the organizational context in which teachers are trained and work.

Teaching as a Profession

One of the most striking features of teaching as an occupation is its divided nature (Lacey, 1977; Judge, 1980; Hanson and Herrington,

1976). The divisions can be described in terms of the training and social origin of teachers, the status and function of the schools in which they work and the expertise and understanding teachers bring to the classroom and schools. In the United Kingdom, teachers can be classified in terms of their graduate or non-graduate status. However, neither graduate or non-graduate categories are homogeneous (*Teaching Quality*, HMSO, 1983). In England and Wales, about 13 per cent of graduate teachers had no initial training and of the remainder, 27 per cent were holders of the BEd degree. The majority of non-graduates were trained on courses leading to a Certificate in Education. This course was extended from two to three years in 1960 and admitted its last students in 1979, following the move to an all graduate entry to teaching. As Judge (1980) points out, the divisions within the teaching profession reflect those within the school system and society more generally. The divisions of the school system into maintained and independent sectors, and within the maintained sector into grammar and secondary modern until quite recently, are too familiar to dwell on. These divisions led to the range of different systems of training; universities for the grammar and public schools, training colleges for other schools. In view of these divisions teaching can be seen as a number of different careers (Lacey, 1977). In this respect it differs significantly from other professions.

There is a considerable body of sociological literature about teaching as a profession. School teaching has been seen as a relatively new profession compared to law and medicine, showing certain characteristics with other so-called semi-professions (Etzioni, 1969). What has interested certain sociologists has been the nature of these semi-professions; shorter training, less public status, less specialized bodies of knowledge and less autonomy from supervision and controls by society compared to the traditional professions. Etzioni considers that sub-groups within professions like school teaching (in the USA) have aspired to fully-fledged professional status despite an awareness that this is not deserved. These aspirations are seen as generating social tensions as there are, from this viewpoint, limitations within society on the extent to which occupational groups can become professionalized (Goode, 1969). The key to full professional status in this analysis is professional autonomy, that is, having occupational behaviour judged by colleagues and peers and not by outsiders. Professional autonomy is seen to be based on the mastery of a field of specialized knowledge and on a commitment to the ideal of serving the client. It is seen as resulting from an exchange between the occupational group, which agrees to control its members, and society which concedes autonomy because effective service depends on individual judgment and application of specialized knowledge and techniques. The granting of professional autonomy therefore sets up professional principles based on the authority of knowledge. This is seen to be incompatible with organizational principles of authority based on administrative hierarchies where controls are exerted from higher positions in the organization outside the occupational group. As Goode (*op. cit.*) argues, tensions between the principles of professional autonomy, the commitment to the serving client, and the knowledge base, can come about in several ways, all undermining the occupation's claim to autonomy. One possibility is that the occupational group can be supervised by a bureaucratic organization as the substance of its work requires little autonomy. School teaching is seen as an instance of this.

It is important to balance against the above theoretical perspective another framework which sees teaching not simply as a technical occupation but as having a particular social function in the system of economic relations in society (Harris, 1982). Teachers are considered to be in an invidious occupational position. On one hand, they are charged with the noble ideal of educating and facilitating some degree of social and personal development. On the other hand, they work in institutions which are assigned the social purpose of moulding new generations to a social order which is held to deny education to the majority of people because of the overriding influence that the system of economic relations has on social institutions such as the education system. Such a framework makes it possible to look at the relationships between the social institutions, the economic base of society, and the occupational position of different groups. The professional position of teachers can be seen within the broader social and economic system, and the possibilities of change in the occupational group can be related to wider constraints.

The uncertain position of teachers in relation to other occupational groups is highlighted in the differing conceptions that teachers themselves have about their occupational position (Ginsberg *et al*, 1980). This diversity of teacher views is reflected in the divisions between teacher organizations, and has made occupational unity a distant prospect. Teacher organizations can be seen as expressions of the snobbery and class consciousness of English society (Perkin, 1983). The National Union of Teachers has made several failed attempts to unify the occupation from the 1920s to the present period. These failures have been attributed by some commentators to the fears of the better paid minorities that they would be absorbed into the lowest common denominator (Perkin, *op. cit.*). This disunity is reflected in the failure of teachers to establish a Teachers' Council in England and Wales which would have a major influence on teacher selection, training and qualifications. The proposal for such a Council in 1960 was thwarted by the Government which was reluctant to relinquish control of the entry requirements for teachers. The Weaver Report proposals for a Teaching Council in 1970 were also rejected by the NUT because the DES reserved the right to accept or reject Council recommendations about entry qualifications (National Union of Teachers, 1971). The Scottish Teaching Council has advisory powers in this area and is therefore not seen as a model for England and Wales by the NUT. Proposals have been made more recently for a general teachers council covering the range of teachers from school to further education and higher education institutions. Such a council would influence the content of training and confer qualified teacher status, a function currently performed by the Secretary of State (Ross, 1984).

This section has emphasized so far the way in which teaching as an occupation has reflected divisions within the school system and teacher training. From the perspective of certain sociological analyses teaching cannot be considered a profession in the sense of having the professional autonomy some teachers aspire to. According to these analyses, in view of the nature of teachers' tasks they are unlikely to work within an organizational system which could grant such autonomy. Despite these limitations, some commentators have identified occupational developments which might lead to improved teacher status (Hoyle, 1983). The implications of these for teacher education will be discussed in a later section.

Occupational Culture and Socialization of Teachers

Another perspective on teachers is the investigation of how teachers see themselves as an occupational group and how they think about their practice. Such an ethnographic approach has tended to be neglected (Hargreaves, 1980; Jackson, 1977), resulting in the underestimation of the significance of the occupational culture in influencing educational practices and innovations, including training. Jackson (*op. cit.*) observed (on the basis of a study of US elementary teachers) that these teachers preferred to talk about children's education in theoretically unsophisticated child-centred as opposed to teacher-centred terms. Many elementary teachers had romantic beliefs about the innocence, goodness and uniqueness of childhood. These beliefs were associated with an impatience for generalizations about children which ignored idiographic approaches. Jackson doubted whether this distrust of analysis and rationality could be accounted for in terms of the predominance of female teachers. He considered that there was a fit between these teacher characteristics and the demands of their classroom tasks and roles. The dependence on intuition is reinforced, according to this analysis, by the complexity, number, pace and uncertainty of classroom events and actions.

A US author (Lortie, 1969) has commented on the culture of elementary school teaching as not encouraging teachers to record their experiences in a way that it can become the property of the occupational group. Lortie has also observed an absence of a refined technical culture in the talk of elementary teachers. This has led him to portray teaching in the following way:

> The general status of teaching, the teacher's role and the
> condition and transmission arrangements of its subculture point
> to a truncated rather than a fully realized professionalization.
> (Lortie, *op. cit.*)

In this country Hargreaves (1978, 1980) has emphasized the significance of the occupational culture particularly in relation to secondary teachers. The hazards of secondary teaching are identified as emotional exhaustion, professional isolation and alienation. These can lead, according to Hargreaves, to defensive strategies of withdrawal in which teachers stick to what can be done, avoid what is new and feel threatened by educational discussions. Hargreaves repeats a comment first made by Waller (1932) that teachers who teach according to a transmission model of teaching tend to have reduced abilities to learn themselves. They become 'bad learners' with the consequence this has for initiating and adapting to change.

Differences within the teaching profession make it difficult not only to generalize about teacher characteristics but also to conjecture about the different influences on teachers and trainees. This point needs to be emphasized when considering empirical studies and theoretical accounts about teacher socialization.

Nevertheless, there have been a series of studies in this country which illustrate the changing pattern of attitudes to education as student-teachers become class-teachers (Butcher, 1965; Finlayson and Cohen, 1967; Hanson and Herrington, 1976; Whiteside, Bernbaum and Noble, 1969; Lacey, 1977). Despite differences in theoretical orientations and research method, these studies indicate that students moved to more progressive, child-centred views about education during training and then reverted to more traditional views as they entered class-teaching. Such changes have been explained in terms of a two-phased process in which student-teachers pass initially under the influence of training tutors who put forward an ideal concept of the teacher's role (Musgrave, 1979). Professional training promotes a conception of teaching which goes beyond the everyday aspects of the teacher's job. The purpose of the occupation is put forward in diffuse and grand idealistic terms (Jackson, 1977) which contrasts with the realities of school and classroom life. In this second phase, teachers succumb to custodial values (Willower *et al*, 1967), seeing themselves as practising teachers who take advice now from their colleagues. The colleague group becomes the context in which teachers find comfort and sympathy for the difficult task of class-teaching. As Waller (1932) put it:

> The landmark of one's assimilation to the profession is the moment when he decides that only teachers are important.

Lacey's (*op. cit.*) study of the impact of a school-based method of teacher training at Sussex University is of particular interest. A model of socialization was adopted in which the individual teacher is seen as using social strategies and negotiating with the existing school culture. This reverses the usual functionalist approach in which socialization involves fitting the individual teacher to the school structure. School is seen rather as the arena in which newly trained teachers strive to be accepted into the existing structure and strive to make the school resemble the kind of place where they would like to teach. English and primary trainees were found to score consistently highest and physics and chemistry lowest on scales designed to assess naturalist, radical and tender-minded attitudes. This was taken as indicative of a subject subculture and that becoming a teacher was to some extent a multi-stranded process.

Lacey suggested that student involvement with the subject started five to six years before the PGCE and was likely to have given rise to specialized preoccupations. Based on a case-study of three years of student-teachers, four phases of the training period were identified. At first, there was a honeymoon period in which students were optimistic about overcoming difficulties. This was followed by a phase of searching for materials and ways of teaching in which attempts were made to compensate for lack of class control and teaching ability by elaborate preparation. Students then faced a crisis stage when they felt they were not in control and not getting through to the children. These problems were coped with by blaming either the system or the children, what is called a radical or establishment displacement. The final phase of the training period involved learning to get by or possibly failing. In this phase strategies were adopted for sharing problems with the others or for keeping problems to oneself and not talking about them. The average student was observed to use different strategies in the university compared to in school. The typical university strategy was a collectivist one, the typical school strategy was a private strategy. The questionnaire responses indicated that students were actively engaged and interpreted their experience rather than merely internalizing behaviour and judgment. Lacey also found that the Sussex scheme failed to involve teachers and school-based tutors in collective teaching. Teaching strategies devised within the collectivised atmosphere of the university simply disappeared when faced with school realities.

Lacey investigated student-teachers' reasons for going into teaching both before and immediately after training in five universities including Sussex. Initially, there was a clear attachment to idealistic reasons, such as interest in children's progress, doing something creative and using one's talents. After the training year, factors such as job security, holidays and income, became more important and factors concerned with the challenge of the task and being creative became less important. The components of the courses which retained their importance for the students were those concerned with the practical and subject aspects. The theoretical aspects involving psychology, sociology and philosophy all failed to achieve their initial promise. Examination of commitment to teaching suggested that there was a decline in all universities, though least in those with traditional courses. The most committed student-teachers were those who chose to teach at an early stage and saw subjects as important for teaching. Two streams of motivation to teach were identified, a commitment to teach *per se* with a career in the classroom and school — a professional commitment and, secondly, a view of teaching as a means to a broader educational end, so that if class teaching proved ineffectual some other broadly education occupation could be chosen — a radical commitment. Results of the attitude measures showed significant and widespread though small decreases in tender-mindedness, radicalism and naturalism after one year of teaching. Open-ended questioning revealed agreement that teaching problems were posed largely by socially-disadvantaged and less able children. Yet, the remedies offered varied according to the teachers' earlier commitment to teaching. The teachers with a more radical commitment saw the problems emerging from the staff and school organization whereas those with a less radical commitment favoured excluding children who presented difficulties. As Lacey comments, it appears that streams of socialization identified in student-culture flowed into the schools.

Mardle and Walker (1980), by contrast to Lacey, put forward a less active and interpretive model of teacher socialization, placing less emphasis on the active use of strategies of negotiation and redefinition as ways of coping with the school arena. They see students as newly trained teachers adjusting to and redefining situations, but in a less dramatic way, since the origins of teachers' commonsense knowledge are considered to derive not only from constraints within the classroom but from their total experience of the education system. Experience of teacher training and schooling is considered as a coherent and developmental process in which teachers do not become re-socialized in training, nor in the classroom reality, as they have never actually lost the influence of classroom reality. Mardle and Walker's focus is on the hidden curriculum of teacher training, what is acceptable behaviour, and what are rewards and sanctions, emphasizing the development process from school to college to school again. This perspective highlights the socialization process as restrictive, pervasive and showing continuity. Those students who go into teacher training are seen as different from both those who go into other professions and those who go into manual occupations in their experience of schooling and their intellectual achievements and character traits. Teacher training is seen as restrictive in not allowing scope for trying out different methods. What is taught as education theory is not seen by these authors as radically oriented as it conveys a style of 'liberal individualism' in which educational failure is construed mainly as individual inadequacy. These conclusions were based on interviews with a group of trainee teachers who had studied sociology. It was also found that students rarely used or criticized the new concepts they were taught. The socialization process, according to Mardle and Walker, involved students in assimilating the notion that differentiation between them on the course was a necessity for the requirements of the university and the job market. Accepting the need for differentiation in the schools was seen as a simple extension of this notion. From this perspective, the influence of teacher training and education is not the provision of practical techniques but the hidden curriculum which is thought to impart a cognitive style which penetrates all aspects of professional practice (Dale, 1977). This cognitive style is considered to involve assumptions which predispose theories in particular directions, that is, towards the view that problems are seen mainly as deriving from individuals and that solutions be directed at individuals. This cognitive style — 'liberal individualism' — is also thought to be linked to the classroom conditions in which teachers work. It is observed that although teachers are given much autonomy within classrooms they adopt similar methods and ideas.

These similarities are attributed to the physical constraints of class-rooms, the experiences teachers had themselves as pupils and the influence that pupils have on them.

Another theorist who attributes styles of teaching to the formal structure of school organization (Denscombe, 1980) distinguishes between the official and competent membership of an organization. Official membership refers to the system of DES teacher registration based on initial training and probation. Competent membership is accomplished not through official but through routine activities and the modes of understanding which relate to these activities. Such under-standing is distinct from and owes little to pedagogical principles and training. Gaining competent membership in this framework is learned mainly on site and results from being included in the teacher culture. According to this framework, competent membership derives from the way teachers cope with practical work problems and the way these problems derive from the formal organization, three of which are identified. Class teaching involves relatively few material resources, is technically unsophisticated and depends on personal interactions. Class management is therefore concerned with the allocation of personal resources. Time as a resource is officially allocated leaving individual class teachers with little power to control schedules. Similarly, staff-pupil ratios reflect organizational policy. The second broad area con-cerns the clientele teachers work with. Children's characteristics in terms of their abilities and motivation are a strong influence on teachers' understanding of appropriate activity. The third broad area, account-ability, is concerned with the degree of supervision experienced by competent members. That teachers are encouraged to operate indi-vidually is seen to be related to the need for classroom flexibility and discretion and not their professional autonomy.

Denscombe (1982) relates this distinction between official and competent membership of an organization to a distinction between formal and hidden pedagogy. Competent membership depends on beliefs and methods about teaching which are considered to contrast with the formal educational theory taught during initial training. The hidden pedagogy, an implicit set of aims and methods of teaching, is characterized by its pragmatic nature. It is tacitly understood by teachers and has its roots in school experience and classroom practice. These pragmatic beliefs and practices are common to many teachers despite the variety of their training, subjects and schools in which they work because they share one overriding influence on their attitudes and approaches to the job — classroom experience. Denscombe also agrees with other authors (Hanson and Herrington, 1976; Mardle and Walker,

1980) about the continuity in the preparation of teachers. The discontinuity in attitudes between training courses and actual teacher activity is seen as context specific and of minor importance compared to the influence of classroom experience which operates before training, when trainees were pupils in classrooms, and after training when newly trained teachers respond to the practical demands of the classroom.

The pragmatic and largely implicit ideas about teaching which make up the hidden pedagogy involve beliefs about the need to establish classroom control and to maintain the privacy of the situation as prerequisites for successful teaching. These beliefs can continue from generation to generation of teacher without much change and despite alterations in formal theory because the structural features of classrooms discussed above remain largely unchanged. However, there may be difficulties with the notion of a hidden pedagogy, whether it is the most accurate and useful way of referring to classroom-generated beliefs about teaching, what it refers to in detail and what its relationship is to formal theories. Nevertheless, there is some consensus among various theorists that the social organization of schools is a major influence on teaching and that training programmes have a short-term influence on much subsequent classroom teaching. A concept like hidden pedagogy is valuable in drawing attention to the routine activity and practical thinking used by teachers. It draws attention to factors that training programmes need to acknowledge in order to influence the classroom behaviour of new and experienced teachers. The implications of some of the above analyses for the organization and content of training programmes will now be discussed, with the emphasis being on *professional* training.

Educational Theory, Psychology and Teacher Training and Education

Not only has the effect of much teacher training been seen as transitory and marginal to subsequent classroom teaching, there have also been accounts of student disaffection with the courses (Taylor and Dale, 1971). As mentioned above, the system of training has traditionally reflected the divisions within the school system. Nevertheless, there have been changes in teacher training towards greater professionalization (Hoyle, 1983), a process in which teaching as an occupation meets more of the criteria attributed to the established professions. The length of training has increased, the idea that all teachers should be trained has been extended, the academic content of courses has increased (BEd) and educational studies are more grounded in foundation disciplines and underpinned by a growing body of research and scholarship. Despite these changes and the Government's white paper on initial training courses (*Teaching Quality*, 1983) and *Circular 3/84*, it is uncertain to what extent these changes will improve professional status or improve professional development.

A major obstacle to establishing effective training and education is a lack of clarity about the very nature of education and what is involved in the preparation of teachers (Wilson, 1975). This relates to the issue of the nature of the knowledge base which might characterize the profession. Teacher preparation has tended to seek professional status by increasing the academic content of courses. The development of the BEd, as Judge (1980) has pointed out, is interesting in showing up the doubts about the content of initial training courses. With no confident tradition in higher education or within the teaching profession to define the proper content, other disciplines (psychology, sociology, philosophy) were brought in to contribute to education theory. Yet, without a clear way of co-ordinating these contributions, the result was a set of theoretical contributions lacking in unity and not necessarily relevant to educational theory (Wilson, *op. cit.*). Chambers and Chambers (1984) have characterized most BEd degrees as stressing academic/theoretical concerns rather than professional/practical concerns. Despite guidelines which encourage professional skills, most BEd submissions to the CNAA were found to cover only a limited range of professional skills. This was attributed by these authors to the academic demands of main subject and education course components involving foundation subjects such as psychology and sociology. Chambers and Chambers consider this emphasis as an obstacle to offering coherent professional preparation.

Other approaches to educational theory may be based on considerations of the nature of professional practice. The Government's recent plans to improve initial teacher training (*Teaching Quality White Paper*, 1983, *Circular 3/84*) involve setting up a Council for the Accreditation of Teacher Education to advise the Secretary of State on the approval of initial training courses in England and Wales. Various criteria are stipulated for approving initial courses with the aim of increasing the match between teacher training and future work. Some of the requirements relate to the recognition of the need for subject expertise; adequate attention to teaching method in the chosen main subjects; the professional elements to provide trainees with adequate mastery of basic professional skills; and closer links with practical experience in schools, involving the participation of experienced teachers. Although these proposals are welcome for bringing teacher education into a more open role in the education system and for the emphasis placed on pedagogical skills and school partnership, there are some important gaps. What is left out is some consideration of education theory and its relationship to practice. These plans and recommendations are based on the assumptions that teacher quality can be improved without the guidance of theoretical considerations and that there are few doubts about the kinds of experience trainees need to be exposed to. These proposals, despite aiming to match training to the tasks of teaching, also take little account of the socialization factors discussed above. Involving practising teachers in training is a commendable development, but it does not involve changes in the structure of and resources for training which are based on an acknowledgement of the influences of classroom and school realities.

Proposals for innovation which take account of classroom and school factors have been derived from some of the analyses discussed above. It is suggested that teacher training would benefit from a more developed system of internship (Denscombe, *op. cit.*). New teachers would be relieved of many of the responsibilities and anxieties normally associated with moving into the classroom and would be helped directly by a collaborating senior teacher. This suggestion relates to the position of Dreeben (1970) that the elements of teaching need to be identified so that new teachers can master each component of the job, task by task. By providing new teachers with opportunities to identify parts of their work and to analyse the tasks it may be possible to counter the tendency noted by Jackson (1977) for teachers to approach educational affairs intuitively rather than rationally. Secondly, Denscombe proposes that team-teaching practices could be valuable in encouraging teachers to observe colleagues, observe themselves and learn from experience. The tendency to privacy could be reduced and responsibility for control shared by the team. Considerations of the influence of the hidden pedagogy on teachers, according to Denscombe, lend support to the value of in-service training courses. Experienced teachers are less likely to be as anxious about control and will be more likely to try new ideas and methods. Dreeben (*op. cit.*) bases his proposals not only on an analysis of traditional classroom organization but draws lessons from the preparation of other professions. The most pressing question according to this view is a rethinking of the relationship between school systems, and training institutions. Though his views derive from the system in the USA, they are relevant to the British system. Teacher training is considered to be far too short and superficial to exert the kind of influence on trainee teachers necessary to develop a strong occupational identity. The proposed model of teacher preparation would involve greater integration between training and school institutions as in the case of medical schools linked to teaching hospitals. Such proposals could take a variety of forms but the common element involves some form of apprenticeship. The trainee teacher could, for example, learn the job task by task under the supervision of experienced specialists. This might involve multi-teacher classrooms with trainees at various stages of apprenticeship. Responsibility for training could be taken by supervisors who would have joint school and training institution appointments. This kind of training model would require that schools be willing to adopt new norms about who does teaching and there would be a need for a clearer dialogue between staff members within schools and between schools and training institutions.

There has been a growing recognition in the UK that for teacher training to have some impact on professional practice the realities of classroom life need to be more connected to the training process. This is shown in the IT-INSET programme started in 1978 involving twenty training institutions (Ashton, 1983). In this scheme of teacher training supervisors work in schools with serving teachers and trainees. In another project in Liverpool, college lecturers and class teachers devised a programme to encourage trainees to learn craft skills from practising teachers and to engage in professionally focused discussion about classroom skills (McNamara and Desforges, 1979). Such linking between training and service institutions, it has been argued, could also facilitate the integration of theory and practice. Although the use of teaching experience as a way of approaching educational theory has been advocated in this country (Peters, 1977), there has been considerable doubt about the nature of educational theory, the integration of its foundation disciplines or their relationship to practice (Wilson, *op. cit.*).

From this perspective it is not so surprising that educational theory during training courses does not fulfil its promise. The problem of translating theory into practice is not only related to the organization of classrooms and training but to the nature of what passes as educational theory. As McNamara (1976) commented, on returning to the chalk face from lecturing in a training institution:

> Once working again as a teacher I lost all desire to keep up to date with literature. This was not because my mind went soggy or because I became too involved with the minutiae of day to day problems. It was simply that the world of academic journals seemed completely irrelevant to classroom life.

McNamara considers that much theory and social science research criticises teachers implicitly, and at times professes to instruct the teacher about how much to teach. This makes him wonder whether there is any other occupational group which supports an establishment of experts who do not practice the activities they talk about. The problem is connected, according to this view, with the nature of much current psychology and sociology. As social sciences they attempt to provide generalized explanations in a mode of discourse and with aims which avoid direct commitment to action. It is understandable that many teachers would distrust such generalizations for not relating directly to practical theorizing and for not taking account of individual cases (Jackson, 1977).

McNamara derives several proposals aimed at relating theory to practice from his analysis. There is a need for an informed and critical teaching force which can come together with educationalists and researchers to think in realistic terms about the relationship between theory and practice. In another piece he considers that the time is opportune to abandon the disciplines of education in the training of teachers (McNamara and Desforges, 1978). These could be replaced by a body of professionally relevant knowledge which is academically rigorous and practically useful. It is recognized that such a body of knowledge is lacking at present, as indicated by the unwritten and largely unexamined views of the teaching profession. Teacher trainers are urged to work with trainees and school teachers to build such a systematic body of knowledge.

The difficulty with the McNamara and Desforges approach is that it is presented as a choice between academic social science research and theory and research and theory based on professional practice. By contrast, Dreeben (*op. cit.*) advocates two related kinds of research and theory. In addition to the substratum of theoretical foundation knowledge he sees no reason why teachers could not undertake 'clinical' research given particular organizational conditions similar to the tradition of clinical medical research. However, in order to conduct such indigenous research, some teachers would need to learn relevant skills as a part of their training and have their job descriptions altered to include such activities. The benefits of establishing such a tradition could be that useful material might be gathered and distributed among teachers facing similar problems, a medium of communication might be set up within the occupational group whose members typically work in isolation, and the content of this research could feed directly into the theoretical and empirical problems studied by academic social scientists. Dreeben considers this last point to be most important as it has direct relevance to those working in institutions of higher education. A natural link between school and university conducted research could be established:

> ... the generalized scientific knowledge of the academic can inform the subsequent work of the teacher doing 'clinical' research in the schools, and of course the flow of knowledge also travels the other ways.... It is difficult to imagine the development of teaching technology without direct contact between the two institutions and their members and contact is not likely to be made without a universe of common discourse and actual pieces of research relevant to each. (p. 212)

The development of theory directly relevant to educational practice and derived out of such practice calls into question conventional ideas about the nature of educational theory and the relationship of foundation disciplines in the social sciences and philosophy to educational theory and practice. Hirst (1983) has been concerned to correct the view that the disciplines provide a justification for practical principles and practices. In his current formulation, the rationale for educational theory is seen as the justification and development of practice and the enlightenment of practitioners. It is to be distinguished from theories in the social science disciplines which are explanatory rather than prescriptive in form. This gap between the discourse of practice and that of the foundation disciplines is critical to the position of a discipline such as psychology in justifying practice and therefore in the preparation of teachers. At the centre of Hirst's current views is a rejection of a particular type of rational model of action which over-emphasizes premeditated planning and action based on validated theoretical principles. By accepting that some actions are immediate and therefore not derived from premeditated action and theoretical principles, Hirst argues that successful educational practice can be a basis for valid practical principles.

In this scheme the disciplines of psychology, sociology and philosophy are no longer at the centre of educational theory. This is to be derived from educational practice and to be in the form of general practical principles. The theoretical principles associated with the foundation disciplines can be of help, according to Hirst, in the process of rationalizing the amalgam of practical principles. The disciplines can feed in more basic beliefs and principles, inspire new practice through this process and offer a sustained critique. As such they provide a background of theory and a perspective from which education theory as practical theory is criticized and validated.

Hirst's current formulation has important implications for how education theory is organized and how educational research and training institutions function. With education theory seen in terms of practical theories and principles the people who would work directly with such principles are practising teachers, advisers, educational administrators and methods tutors. These methodologists at various positions in the wider education system would need to take into account the implications of the foundation disciplines. As Hirst would argue, educational methodology would be deficient unless it was informed by these disciplines. The social scientists and philosophers in education would not in this formulation be directly responsible for practical theory and methodology. They would be aware of the concerns of methodologists and involved in various kinds of dialogues with methodologists. The theories and beliefs of methodologists would be the field of contact between the methodologists and social scientists and philosophers who work in the educational field. Initial teacher training in this formulation would give priority amongst other factors to helping trainees learn educational theory which consisted of justifiable practical principles. Trainees would need to engage in discourse about practice and need to grasp the justification of such practical principles. Only if there was time on courses would there be a place for studying aspects of the social sciences and philosophy. At an in-service training stage teachers would be in a better position to examine the justification for practical principles and the relationships between practical theories and the theories of social scientists and philosophers.

One of the dangers of Hirst's reformulation of the relationship between foundation disciplines and educational theory is that in moving practical theories to the centre of the stage it can understate the complex relationships between practical theories, explanatory theories and ethical issues. Within the social sciences there are various schools of thought based on different theoretical assumptions and rationales. To suggest that a discipline such as psychology provides a context and framework in which practical educational theory can be assessed could be too simplistic. Depending on the theoretical assumptions adopted in, say, psychology, so the links between psychological assumptions and theories and practical theories will be different. Not only is there the complexity introduced by different theoretical frameworks within psychology and sociology, but there are special difficulties in the relationship between philosophical approaches and educational theory as practical theory (White and White, 1984). Hirst's reformulation is based on the assumption that successful practice is the ground on which practical theories are constructed. This may seem acceptable but actually the notion of successful practice in education is problematic as it depends on what are considered to be the aims of education. Where there are differences over these aims, conceptions of successful practice will differ. White and White argue from a philosophical perspective that practical theory depends not only on successful prior practice but on ethical considerations. This implies that broad issues concerned with educational aims are central to the development and assessment of educational theory. Similarly, theoretical frameworks and principles in the social sciences do not only provide a context for assessing practical theories but are likely to influence the development of these theories.

Hirst's reformulation of the relationship between educational theory and the foundation disciplines can be interpreted less as representing a major change in the current relationship and more as recognizing the importance of practice and practical theory in the relationship. This could be seen by some psychologists in education as a threat to their traditional position in training, research and service fields. Psychologists could be seen as playing a reduced part in the broad education service. However, this view could only be supported if the contribution psychologists are willing to make is limited to the traditional offerings. The Hirst reformulation could by contrast be construed as providing an improved opportunity for psychologists to work with methodologists at all levels of the education system. In the LEAs, professional psychologists could collaborate with educational administrators and advisers, and, in schools, with teachers at all levels on matters covering not only children with special needs but on general teaching and learning issues. In the field of curriculum development and research, psychologists could collaborate with methodologists in a variety of ways. In initial teacher training, psychologists could be involved in collaborating with methods tutors and school-based tutors in designing and developing the system of training, in particular, the system of supervising training (Stones, 1979, 1984). Psychologists working in different parts of the education system are nevertheless in an unusual and difficult position. On one hand, they need to be up to date with current ideas and theories in psychology, possibly participating in theory led research, but also aware of the conceptual foundations of the discipline and the competing theoretical frameworks. On the other hand, they need to have some experience and be up to date with a wide range of current issues and practices in education. Finding ways of linking theoretical schemes and investigative methods used in psychology to the educational concerns of school teachers, parents, advisers and methods tutors is a complex task. But perhaps even more demanding is the challenge presented by various accounts of the professional socialization of teachers of which initial training is but a part.

References

ASHTON, P. (1983) *Teacher Education in the Classroom*, Croom Helm.

BUTCHER, H.J. (1965) 'Attitudes of student teachers to education: a comparison with attitudes of experienced teachers and a study of changes during training courses', *British Journal of Social and Clinical Psychology*, 4, pp. 17–24.

CHAMBERS, J. and CHAMBERS, P. (1984) 'Teacher educators and teachers' in ALEXANDER, R.J., CRAFT, M. and LYNCH, J. (Eds.) *Change in Teacher Education*, London, Holt, Rinehart and Winston.

DALE, I.R. (1977) *The Structural Context of Teaching*, Open University.

DENSCOMBE, M. (1980) 'The work of teaching: an analytic framework for the study of teachers in classrooms', *British Journal of Sociology of Education*, 1, 3, pp. 279–291.

DENSCOMBE, M. (1982) 'The hidden pedagogy and its implications for teacher training', *British Journal of Sociology of Education*, 3, 3, pp. 249–263.

DREEBEN, R. (1970) *The Nature of Teaching, Schools and the Work of Teachers*, Scott Foresman and Co.

ETZIONI, A. (Ed.) (1969) *The Semi-Professions and Their Organization*, Free Press.

FINLAYSON, D.S. and COHEN, L. (1967) 'The teachers' role: a comparative study of conceptions of college of education students and headteachers', *British Journal of Educational Psychology*, 37, 1, pp. 22–6.

GOODE, W.J. (1969) 'The theoretical limitations of professionalization' in ETZIONI, A. (Ed.) *The Semi-Professions and Their Organization*, Free Press.

GINSBURG, M.B., MEYENN, R.J. and MILLER, H.D.R. (1980) 'Teachers' conceptions of professionalism and trades unionionism: an ideological analysis' in WOODS, P. (Ed.) *Teacher Strategies*, Croom Helm.

GORDON, P., PERKIN, H., SOCKETT, A.H. and HOYLE, E. (1983) *Is Teaching a Profession?* Bedford Way Papers No 15, University of London Institute of Education.

HMSO (1983) *Teaching Quality*, Cmnd 8836.

HANSON, D. and HERRINGTON, M. (1976) *From College to Classroom: The Probationer Year*, Routledge and Kegan Paul.

HARGREAVES, D.H. (1978) 'What teaching does to teachers', *New Society 9*, pp. 540–2.

HARGREAVES, D.H. (1980) 'Occupational culture of teachers' in WOODS, P. (Ed.) *Teacher Strategies*, Croom Helm.

HARRIS, K. (1982) *Teachers and Classes: A Marxist Analysis*, Routledge and Kegan Paul.

HIRST, P. (1983) *Educational Theory and its Foundation Disciplines*, London,

Routledge and Kegan Paul.

HOYLE, E. (1983) 'The professionalization of teachers: a paradox' in GORDON, P. *et al, Is Teaching a Profession?* Bedford Way Papers, No 15, University of London Institute of Education.

JACKSON, P.W. (1977) 'The way teachers think' in GLIDEWELL, J.G. (Ed.) *The Social Context of Teaching*, Gardner Press.

JUDGE, H. (1980) 'Teaching and professionalization: an essay in ambiguity', in HOYLE, E. and MEGARRY, J. (Eds.) *World Yearbook of Education 1980, Professional Development of Teachers*, Kogan Page.

LACEY, C. (1977) *The Socialization of Teachers*, Methuen.

LORTIE, D.C. (1969) 'The balance and control in elementary school teaching' in ETZIONI, A. (Ed.) *The Semi-Professions and Their Organization*, Free Press.

MCNAMARA, D. (1976) 'On returning to the chalk face: theory not into practice', *British Journal of Teacher Education*, 2, 2, p. 155.

MCNAMARA, D. and DESFORGES, C. (1978) 'The social sciences, teacher education and the objectification of craft knowledge', *British Journal of Teacher Education*, 4, 2, pp. 18–31.

MARDLE, G. and WALKER, M. (1980) 'Strategies and structure: some critical notes on teacher socialization' in WOODS, P. (Ed.) *Teacher Strategies*, Croom Helm.

MUSGRAVE, P.W. (1979) *The Sociology of Education*, London, Methuen.

NATIONAL UNION OF TEACHERS (1971) *Teaching Council*.

PETERS, R.S. (1977) 'Education as a specific preparation for teaching', in PETERS, R.S. *Education and the Education of Teachers*.

ROSS, A. (1984) 'An education for tomorrow's teachers' in ALEXANDER, R.J., CRAFT, M. and LYNCH, J. (Eds.) *Change in Teacher Education*, London, Holt, Rinehart and Winston.

STONES, E. (1979) *Psychopedagogy: Psychology Theory and the Practice of Teaching*, London, Methuen.

STONES, E. (1984) *Supervision in Teacher Education: A Counselling and Pedagogical Approach*, London, Methuen.

TAYLOR, J.K. and DALE, J.R. (1971) *A Survey of Teachers in Their First Year of Service*, Bristol University Press.

WALLER, W. (1932) *The Sociology of Teaching*, London, Wiley.

WHITE, P. and WHITE, J. (1984) 'Practical reasoning and educational theory', an unpublished paper, University of London Institute of Education.

WHITESIDE, M.T., BERNBAUM, G. and NOBLE, G. (1969) 'Aspirations, reality shock and entry into teaching', *Sociological Review*, 17, 3, pp. 399–414.

WILLOWER, D.J., HOY, W.K. and EIDELL, T.L. (1967): *The School and Pupil Control Ideology*, University Park Press, Monograph No 24.

WILSON, J. (1975) *Educational Theory and the Preparation of Teachers*, National Foundation for Educational Research.

The Roles of Schools and Teachers in Teacher Education

Geoffrey Brown
University of East Anglia

Introduction

Close examination of many professional and industrial training procedures is likely to uncover either pockets of highly disgruntled educators,
trainers and practitioners, or, at very least, certain issues on which
uneasy compromises are tolerated with varying levels of good grace by
the different factions. Medical training, and the education of engineers
and teachers have all shivered under the cold light of close scrutiny at
some time or another. The fact that the pseudonymous Saber-Toothed
Curriculum (Peddiwell, 1939) insinuated itself onto so many reading
lists for teachers in training is testimony enough to the steely realism
beneath that particularly jocular spoof. One must certainly take seriously the possibility that educational or training systems, whilst ostensibly
mounted to equip students for forthcoming roles in society, develop
their own self-justification and logic which are insensitive to changes in
those roles, or, even worse, lose sight of these roles altogether. It is
perhaps to the credit of teacher-educators that their misgivings are not
always swept under the carpet, and that innumerable experiments, both
small and large, have been, and are being conducted into methods for
the education and training of teachers. What follows is an attempt to
make some general observations from a small-scale study at the
University of East Anglia. The purpose of writing it is to invite
colleagues to test the generalizations against their own experiences, for
unless training establishments and schools are prepared to explore these
issues, and to use their combined expertise to delineate the issues in
systematic fashion, they may find themselves impelled headlong into
change instigated by nothing more substantial than political dogma.

Rationale

In the academic year 1981–2 discussions took place within the School of Education of the University of East Anglia which attempted to identify sources of unease in the views of students, tutors, and teachers in the local schools. (For the sake of clarity the terms student, tutor and teacher will be used, although the similarity of the roles of tutor and teacher should not be overlooked). A number of inter-related issues were made explicit.

The hierarchical ordering of aspects of their courses by students was, in tutors' views, implicit in the priorities afforded by allocation of time and effort. School practice was the most important; 'subject studies', particularly those with extensive content of what to teach and how to teach it, were of secondary importance; and 'education' and its contributory disciplines were of least relevance, although some students charitably conceded that they were interesting. It was difficult to escape the implication that that view would have been more fully expressed as 'they would be interesting if we were not engaged in more important matters'.

The views expressed above would have been serious enough if they had been unanimously declared to be misguided by the tutors, but this was not the case. Indeed the order of precedence perceived by the students was highly correlated with the extent of concern on the part of some tutors, although issues were seen as more complex by the latter. A considerable degree of sympathy for the students' perceptions was expressed. Tutors were not surprised that the prevailing preoccupation was with the novel and testing world of the classroom rather than the lecture theatre with which they were so familiar. Nevertheless tutors felt that it was important that students were introduced to the wider issues thrown up by 'education', though how to demonstrate their importance was not clear.

The Programme

The problem was articulated as a need to ensure that the students' activities in the three areas were indeed part of the same endeavour, and to make this explicit to all parties. To this end the Board of the School of Education sanctioned a pilot project for a new type of PGCE programme for the twenty-four students who entered to study English in October 1982. The project was extended in 1983 with another intake of the same size. The two cohorts were made up of almost equal numbers of 'main' and 'subsidiary' English graduates, but in keeping with current policy the two were taught together. A programme was devised in which pairs of students were attached for two days per week throughout the year to a local school, and it was initiated by inviting teachers from the schools to discuss the intentions and to join tutors in devising a programme. The prime target was to produce a meaningful blend of work in the University and work in the classrooms by devising a sequence of classroom-based tasks which could be built upon in seminars and lectures. Tutors produced a week-by-week schedule of their activities, which was approved by the teachers during regular visits to the university. The tasks which were set were to be accomplished in addition to a gradual introduction to class teaching supervised by the teachers in consultation with the tutors. As the programme developed students would begin to introduce matters which they had encountered in schools and these were also incorporated into the programme. It was anticipated that long-term school attachment would reduce the 'assessment' orientation of the conventional 'block' practice. The assessment aspect would be left as late as possible and then accomplished in detailed consultation between teachers and tutors.

What follows is a record of the negotiations and transformations which took place after the scheme's inception. Four tutors were involved in the scheme, two were specialists in training teachers of English, the others were from the 'education' team — a psychologist and a sociologist. The tutors had been unable to agree upon whether attachment to a single school was ideal. It was favoured by those who stressed the continuity of the experience, the opportunities to see the various phases of a school year — Christmas festivities, internal and external examinations, PTA meetings, sports day etc., and the increased likelihood that the students would become sufficiently incorporated into the life of the schools that they could repay the early efforts of the staff by taking additional responsibilities towards the end of the year. Counter-arguments stressed the unique nature of a school's English scheme and argued that, at interview, students would be handicapped if they had had experience of only one school. The teachers appreciated the two viewpoints, but a sizeable majority favoured the latter. It was therefore decided that the normal pattern would be for students to change schools mid-way through the year, unless teachers and students requested otherwise; and in the event two schools and their attendant students did so.

Early Developments

At one of the earliest meetings after the programme had started teachers made strong protests on two other matters. The more fundamental of these was the inherent limitation of attachment for only two days per week. They argued that the secondary school timetable rarely allowed access to a reasonable cross-section of work, age-range, or ability levels on only two days. Furthermore, the students would not get the 'real experience' of being a class teacher unless they had several uninterrupted weeks of block practice. In recognition of these strongly held views the programme was altered so that two-day attachment led up to block attachments late in the autumn term and in the summer term. The second protest was that the assignments set by the tutors for students to accomplish in their schools were too time-consuming, and interfered with the induction into classroom teaching practices. In recognition of this some tasks were withdrawn. This problem was exacerbated by what were found to be irreconcilable principles — the one, to gear the school experience to current activities back at the university — the other, to leave the disposition of students within the school to the professional judgment of the supervising teacher. Within a few weeks it became clear that there was considerable asynchrony of student experiences which considerably reduced student participation in some aspects of the curriculum.

It is the view of this writer that these two first encounters with teacher colleagues revealed a rather fundamental difference of opinion as to what professional training demanded. Both issues suggested that the teachers saw the 'real' business of the year as a form of apprenticeship which involved total immersion in the classroom life of a teacher, a professional 'sitting next to Nellie'. Tutors, on the other hand, favoured a gradual introduction, more in the nature of a progressive integration of identified subskills. However, these differences were never articulated in such stark explicitness.

The two 'education' tutors also experienced a sense of what can only be described as professional vulnerability on this scheme. Whilst both had volunteered to be involved because of personal dissatisfaction with the 'disciplines' approach to education, the new curriculum emerged as so practically oriented that tutorials were in danger of becoming anecdotal and unchallenging. Whilst this could, with ingenuity, be avoided, it had to be accepted that much of the 'conventional disciplines' content would not be examined. In one sense this was the *raison d'être* for the scheme, but in another it removed the familiar authority-base from which the tutors had operated. As one observed 'I feel myself becoming an old-fashioned Master of Method rather than a Psychology Tutor'.

Tutors had also desired to make a much closer integration of 'English' and 'education' in the new programme, but this happened to only a limited extent. In spite of a relatively lavish tutor-student ratio demands on tutors' time were high, and much of the university-based content was developed independently by the two pairs of tutors, though the other pair was always fully advised.

Perhaps because of this pressure upon staff resources; and perhaps partly because of the negotiated re-introduction of some degree of block teaching practice tutors also found themselves working under the spectre of the old scheme, particularly when visiting students and teachers in the schools. The intention was to use the classroom as a workshop, as a working environment in which the student could learn by observation and experiment with tutor and teacher as guides and collaborators. In the event tutors found themselves inexorably drawn back into the role of assessor, visiting briefly, making comments and offering suggestions, estimating competence and departing. Whilst the ultimate requirement for a training establishment to assess was never denied, it had been the firm resolve that such an activity would be relegated to a late part of the year. The habits of many years of conventional teaching practice supervision proved harder to break than had been anticipated. Furthermore these old patterns of behaviour were reinforced by colleagues in the schools who recognized them as familiar.

Meetings were held between the four tutors at very frequent intervals — weekly in the early stages and every three or four weeks towards the end of the year. Schools were invited to send representatives to the preliminary meeting before the scheme began, and all schools were visited by the tutors. During the year meetings were held at the university twice each term in the late afternoon. These meetings were largely taken up with the day-to-day logistics of the scheme — problems of timetabling, availability of resources etc. The content of the university-based work was offered for negotiation, but in the event it was 'received' or 'approved' with little or no comment. Whether this was indicative of its perceived low priority in the minds of teachers, or of deference to the tutors who 'knew their own business best' was not clear. A simpler explanation was that, after a full day's work in schools, teachers were ill-prepared for tackling weighty curriculum issues.

Consultations with students also took place throughout the year. Informal comment was obtained almost daily, but in addition all students were interviewed by tutors at the end of the first term of the programme, and written comments were invited at the end of third term. Without exception the comments supported the general intentions of the scheme, and most felt that it was superior to the programmes being followed by their peers. The vast majority of the problems concerned individual difficulties within particular school establishments and were typical of the issues to which all school attachment programmes are hostage — non-availability of appropriate classes, pressure of time of teachers making consultation infrequent and brief, etc.

Later Developments

During the second year of the programme, with another intake of students, some interesting developments took place, and some new errors were substituted for old ones. The first of these mistakes was a move from an over-definition of demands upon students to an under-definition. Tutors had assumed that a relaxation of the restricting schedules would permit teachers to pace work for their charges more realistically in terms of the particular school organization. Sometimes this happened, but in other cases the result was a total stagnation, with students being made to revert to a passive observer role for long periods. There is here no criticism of the teachers intended, but simply a belated recognition that they had neither the time nor the experience to determine what was required.

The intention is now to attempt some intermediate phasing of university-based assignments, such that students and teachers will be asked to attempt to investigate and record certain aspects of schooling within a period of weeks, maybe a school half-term. This should allow the teachers the flexibility they need, but its sacrifice will be the concurrency of experience in the school and follow-up work at the university. The extent to which tutors will be able to operate such long-term assignment schedules remains to be seen.

The pessimism engendered by the apparently different views of what form school experience should take was ameliorated on the one hand by a recognition that block practices did, in the students' views, give a quite different vision of the 'real world' of the teacher, where priorities may need to be ordered differently than on a one or two day attachment; and on the other hand by a number of the teachers beginning to use their professional experience in analysing the needs of the students and suggesting forms of graded experience leading up to full-scale classroom teaching. In other words, there was a recognition of the potential value of a sub-skills integration approach.

es of the evening meetings for tackling the wider
ducation programme led to a suggestion from the
ly conference should be held, during school term
rking parties would discuss curriculum content,
spite of unintentional sabotage by union withdrawal
nference was held, albeit with reduced numbers.
Whilst little in the way of specific curriculum content resulted from this
a number of suggestions for the hierarchical ordering of school-based
tasks was forthcoming, and a detailed discussion of classroom performance assessment led to a small working party of teachers producing a
redrafted student assessment schedule, which is now being evaluated.

Discussion

The exhortation to involve teachers more intimately in the recruitment
and education of new teachers has such intuitive appeal that there is a
danger of it blinding the profession to the complexities of such a
procedure. In the implementation of this scheme some lessons are quite
clear. No amount of documentation, however good, is adequate substitute for personal visits from informed tutors. Once a programme is
established frequent meetings of tutors and teachers are essential for its
progress; and for joint consideration of complex issues, such as curriculum content and student evaluation, longer day-time conferences are
necessary. The implications in terms of resources for universities,
colleges and schools are obvious. If, in some quarters, there is a hope
that the increased involvement of teachers will ease the load on hard
pressed tutors, experience on this project suggests that that may be
misguided, or at least a very long-term objective.

If such a long-term objective is entertained it is, of course, one
which passes on some of the workload to teachers who are themselves
hard pressed. Tutors at the University of East Anglia have found an
almost universal willingness in teachers to be involved, and a strong
desire to be a part of the training process. Yet the demands made upon
them are already very high, and without some alleviation of these,
tutors constantly run the risk of being over-demanding. Bearing in mind
the pressure under which tutors found their volunteer colleagues in the
schools, the prospect of involving their more reluctant colleagues does
not augur well.

Understanding the nature of the teacher-education process is not
something which can be conveyed immediately to teachers any more
than it can be to students. It was paradoxical that some teachers, whose

job involved organizing learning programmes for so
recognize a similar requirement in the training of
profession. To some extent it must be experienced
about, and this takes time. Only in the second year
seem to be developing. Perhaps a more efficient
accelerate that development, but perhaps not.

Increasing the contact with schools and teacl ⌐⌐⌐gs other
pressures. Whilst it is relatively easy to declare that links will be forged
between lectures, seminars and school-based work, the quality of these
links may vary enormously; and in some cases they may be hard to
make. Important decisions need to be made about the wider aspects of
education and their salience as perceived by the student. Is it reasonable to send out a qualified teacher who knows nothing of the
philosophy of education, or who has never considered the place of the
school in the social structure of society? Yet whilst these are seen as
important issues by very many tutors and teachers it may be some years
before the student recognizes them.

To some extent any attempts to modify current patterns of teacher
education are hamstrung by the knowledge that for many students this
experience may be all they get throughout their professional years. If it
were possible to set our sights upon a pattern of teacher education
which would necessitate in-service courses at certain times throughout
the teacher's career, then perhaps the tutor responsible for initial
training would have less guilt at omitting some of the areas of study. It
would be comforting to think that we could start to organize our courses
around the question 'What does the novice teacher need to know?' and
to work out a scheme with our teacher colleagues which would embrace
initial training and professional probation. The more complex and
abstract issues could then be left until the teachers returned, bringing
several years of professional experience to enhance their studies.

A more radical appraisal might suggest that the duality of tutor and
teacher is a poor basis from which to develop teacher education. It is
perhaps inevitable that tutors, because of the experience and qualifications required for their appointments, quickly become outdated in a
rapidly developing school system. It is equally apparent that the role of
the teacher, as presently defined, leaves little room for the assumption
of new training activities. Perhaps a closer look at the medical model
where tutors are also practitioners, and training establishments fully
working hospitals, offers a better pattern. Is it not possible that integration may be easier and less contrived in a teaching school, wherein
teachers were also tutors and where classroom research went on
alongside classroom teaching? It would seem that the current moves in

63

er education, the increasing emphasis on classroom based re-
arch, and the popularity of the 'teacher as researcher' and 'research
based teacher education' notions, however these last two are defined,
would all be more effective within such a scenario.

Note

The views expressed are those of the author, and not necessarily those
endorsed by the School of Education at the University of East Anglia, nor of
other members of the project team.

Reference

PEDDIWELL, J.A. (1939) *The Saber-Tooth Curriculum* N. York, McGraw-Hill.

2

Becoming a Teacher

Introduction

Learning to teach makes heavy demands on the student. Noel Entwistle shows how learning can be achieved through guided reflection on, and analysis of, one's own learning experiences. Guy Claxton challenges trainers to face up to the personal development of the student in training, to their difficulties and trauma, their satisfactions and joys, whilst Peter Tomlinson considers a model of skill development as a guide to training. All three point to the wisdom of selecting salient concepts and practices for trainees.

Learning from the Experience of Studying

Noel Entwistle,
University of Edinburgh

Introduction

Most graduates come into teacher training with little or no knowledge of psychology, and within a year they are expected to emerge as teachers with professional skills and an understanding of some of the main psychological ideas which underpin the practice of teaching. In presenting psychological ideas to student teachers, we are faced with a problem about the nature of our discipline. Educational psychology is not just a body of knowledge to be presented to students; it also contains theories about learning which should be exemplified in the way the subject is taught. Yet psychologists seem to have taken surprisingly little interest in the implications of psychological research for their own work as university teachers. As Bannister (1982) complains:

> Conventional psychology teaching derives virtually nothing from psychology as a discipline. The teaching methods of the average psychology department ... are largely indistinguishable from those of the departments of history or geography or biology or what have you. This in spite of the fact that psychologists have discoursed grandly on the nature of learning, motivation, cognition, group interaction and many other topics which might be thought to be germane to any educational venture ... Our discipline should be reflexive ... Any assertion we make about human behaviour should logically apply to doing psychology. (p. 73)

Bannister goes on to stress the importance of making use of the student's own experience

> In line with the reflexivity argument, students should be
> encouraged to interrogate their personal experience and convic-
> tion, to become more aware of it, to question it in terms of
> psychological literature and to question psychological literature
> in terms of personal experience. In short, courses in psychology
> should start from where the student is. (p. 73).

In degree courses in psychology a student's general experience of
life may be utilized, but within the short time available in a teacher-
training course, it is necessary to focus attention on those aspects of a
student's experience which are likely to enhance sympathetic understanding of teaching and learning in schools. The student's own experience as a pupil is rather distant, but it is possible to draw on the
immediate past and current experiences of studying, and by linking
them to the systematized experiences of other students, to introduce
some more general psychological concepts and ideas.

Research on Student Learning

The impetus for a new wave of research into student learning came from
the research group in Gothenburg led by Ference Marton. His ideas,
and those of Gordon Pask, have since been extended by researchers in
Britain, Holland, and Australia to provide a substantial body of research
evidence. A wide, and potentially confusing, array of concepts and
terminology has been introduced in the process of this research (see
Marton *et al*, 1984). So, in presenting these ideas to student teachers, it
is necessary to limit the detail and the conceptual complexity while
retaining the essence of those ideas which have the greatest applicability
to schools.

The way in which this body of research might be built into a course
will be discussed later: first the main concepts must be described.

The starting point is to see academic learning as a purposeful
activity. To understand students' learning processes, we have to consider first why they are studying — either in general terms or, to
simplify matters, in relation to a particular piece of work set by a
teacher. The psychology of learning has proved rather ineffective in
guiding educational endeavours, largely because it has sought generality. Take problem-solving as an example. Gestalt psychologists and
information processing theorists have offered explanations of what it
takes to solve problems. But neither theory explains what happens
when teachers ask students to solve problems, because it is assumed

that the task is the central focus of the student's attention — that the intention, first and foremost, is to understand the problem and then solve it. In fact, it seems that students are so much aware of the general educational context, that their attention is more often focused on trying to meet the perceived demands of the teacher or the formal requirements of the course.

Diana Laurillard (1984) investigated how students tackled problems on the design of a control program for a microprocessor. She found that:

> the focus of their attention (was) not on the problem itself, but on the problem as set by a teacher in the context of a particular course. We might expect that the first stages in solving such a problem would be to consider what kind of microprocessor it is, what kinds of control would be needed, which instructions are relevant etc. But the students' attention is focused not on the program to be written, but rather on what they think the teacher requires . . . . Each step, and each strategic decision made, refers to the immediate context of the problem as it occurs in that course. The criterion is not 'Is that what this type of micro-computer needs?', but 'Is this what this teacher is looking for?' For these students, the problem situation is quite different from those featured in experimental studies. The problem is not an isolated event; it comes after a certain lecture, and is likely to relate to it. It will also be marked by a particular lecturer, and the solution should take that into account as well. (p. 131)

Of course, students do also concentrate on the meaning underlying academic tasks, and it was just this sharp contrast between students who actively search for personal understanding and those who seek only to fulfil task requirements in a reproductive manner, which led Ference Marton to introduce the concept of *approach to learning*. The crucial distinction between 'deep' and 'surface' approaches is intentionality; but 'approach' also describes important differences in the processes of learning and in the organizational principles involved in remembering (Entwistle and Marton, 1984). The deep approach is also holistic in its ways of organizing and restructuring information and ideas. The surface approach is atomistic: it focuses on the sequential processing of the elements of knowledge, generally by rote learning.

Marton derived his concepts from experiments in which students were asked to read academic articles and 'to be ready to answer questions afterwards'. The form of the questions was unspecified (as is often the case in education) and so students were left to make their own interpretations of what was required. Moreover the students had unlimited time — a luxury not enjoyed in normal studying.

When time is restricted in similar experiments (Entwistle and Ramsden, 1983) students are less likely to exhibit the fully deep approach. Instead, among those attempting to understand, some students focus mainly on evidence and detailed arguments, while others grasp the general meaning but not in relation to the details. Thus within the deep approach there seems to be a further distinction which parallels Gordon Pask's (1976) dichotomous learning styles — comprehension learning (holist) and operation learning (serialist). A holist style involves understanding through seeing relationships, through using analogies, and through reflecting on personal experience. A serialist style follows step-by-step learning, examining information cautiously, and looking at logical connections. Full understanding generally demands the *versatile* use of both styles of learning — but lack of time will prevent full alternation of these styles, leaving the students exhibiting the different types of partial understanding indicated above.

Table 1. Relationships between Intention, Process, and Outcome.

Intention	Process	Outcome
Deep	Versatile	Understanding of ideas in relation to details
	Holist	Understanding of main ideas
	Serialist	Understanding of evidence
Surface	Rote	Reproduction of main points or specific details

Table 1 presents a simplified outline of the connections between intention, process, and outcome.

Another important concept introduced by the Gothenburg group is that of *outcome space* (Dahlgren, 1984). Marton and his colleagues have been interested in qualitative differences in the outcomes of learning. When students, or pupils, are asked a fairly open question about what they have learned, the answers can generally be classified into different levels of understanding. In most of their analyses there tend to be three or four main categories which have similar characteristics to those described by Peel (1971). 'Mentioning', 'describing', and 'explaining', each represent a qualitatively different response to questions about a prose passage or problem.

A further extension of these attempts to identify different levels of understanding is the work of Biggs and Collis (1982) on their SOLO taxonomy (Structure of the Observed Learning Outcomes). Their approach was based on ideas on human information processing applied to an analysis of students' essays (Schroder *et al*, 1967). Their classification system has been built around four main categories relating to 'the way an individual receives, stores, processes and transmits information'. At the *unistructural* level there is little recognition of a problem: an immediate, over-simple and usually erroneous answer is provided after little or no reflection, almost as a reflex response to a stimulus. When two or more aspects are recognized (*multistructural*), these are presented without recognition or acknowledgement of possible links or contradictions between them and so lead to incomplete, conflicting, or inconsistent judgments. *Relational* responses point out and attempt to resolve conflicts, and show how similar ideas are related. They fall short, however, of the most sophisticated category of response, *extended abstract*, which provides explanations and develops into generalized statements drawing on a wide range of relevant information and theoretical ideas.

The mapping of the main categories produced in the answers creates an 'outcome space' for that question, which will, of course, depend not just on the question topic, but on its *form* (Pollitt, *et al*, 1984) — the narrower the question, the more restricted the outcome space produced.

Links with Other Psychological Concepts

An attempt was made previously to show how the research on student learning could provide a framework within which to introduce mainstream constructs in educational psychology (Entwistle, 1981). Since then new research findings would allow the connections to be made more fully, but they can only be indicated here.

Analysing outcome space can be a useful first step towards understanding the representation of knowledge in the memory. Differences in students' answers reflect both the way the information has been stored (cognitive structure and the memory) and how it has been processed. The level of outcome depends on the sophistication of thinking applied — which, through the SOLO taxonomy, can be linked to both cognitive and conceptual development.

The approach to learning adopted by a student will be affected by previous knowledge (particularly in science — Ramsden, 1982) and self-confidence in relation to intellectual skills. But it is also affected by the student's motivation — not just its level, but also its *type*. Intrinsic motivation (learning out of interest in the subject matter) is closely associated with a deep approach and meaningful learning (Biggs, 1978; Entwistle *et al*, 1979), while the surface approach and rote learning is linked either to fear of failure (or anxiety about the specific task, Fransson, 1977), or to extrinsic motivation (concern about qualifications).

Style of learning, in turn, seems to be related to more fundamental aspects of personality. A factor of 'deep holism', for example, has been found to have high loadings on such personality traits as thinking introversion, theoretical orientation, aestheticism, complexity, and impulse expression. (Entwistle and Ramsden, 1983).

Thus approaches to learning are associated with many key concepts in educational psychology and can be used to introduce those concepts in ways which root them in the students' own experiences, as well as in supporting evidence from research.

Links with the Practice of Teaching

The research into student learning can also be used to demonstrate the effects of teaching on learning outcomes — again not just on the quantity of information learned, but on its quality. The main influence on the approach to learning adopted by a student seems to be the assessment procedure and its form. Students are influenced not so much by the stated objectives of a course, but by what they perceive as the requirements which will earn them credit in the concrete form of marks — the 'hidden curriculum' (Snyder, 1971). Thus the use of examinations or tests which emphasize factual information (multiple choice or short answer questions) are likely to induce surface approaches to learning (Marton and Saljo, 1976; Ramsden, 1981) unless carefully balanced by other assessment techniques.

Even attempts to improve an examination procedure can have unintended consequences on student learning. For example, Newble and Jaeger (1983) have reported an interesting innovation in measuring clinical competence. The traditional examination involved 'oral' procedures in which the student was questioned by a series of examiners. The subjectivity of this examination was recognized, and it was replaced by a form of 'continuous assessment' in the wards. Within two years it was found that students' clinical competence had declined. They had discovered that the ward assessments almost never resulted in failure — and so students were spending their time on rote learning for the theory examinations where there was a substantial failure rate. Changes to a more objective form of clinical examination counteracted this effect once more, to provide a convincing illustration of how assessment procedures affect approaches to studying.

Another example of a similar kind has been provided by Gibbs (1981). He was approached by a psychology department which was concerned that the students were doing very little reading. It was thought that they might need workshops to improve their reading skills. Gibbs interviewed the first-year students involved and found that they were spending most of their time writing up their laboratory reports, because they had been led to believe that these played an important part in deciding who would proceed into the second year. In fact assessments of these reports had only a marginal effect on end-of-year results. In an attempt to persuade students to take the reports seriously, the unintended consequence was to deflect the students from the more important task of supplementing lecture material by their own reading. It is thus all too easy to blame students for their ineffective studying, when their approaches will be, in part at least, determined by the actions and comments of the teaching staff.

Students' approaches to studying are affected not just by assessment procedures, but also by the work-load, the extent of choice allowed to students, and above all by 'good teaching' (Ramsden and Entwistle, 1981). Students described good teaching in terms of pitching the material at the right level, thorough preparation, an awareness of sources of potential difficulty, and, above all, the communication of enthusiasm.

> If they have enthusiasm, then they really fire their own students with the subject, and the students really pick it up ... I'm really good at and enjoy (one subject) but that's only because a particular tutor I've had has been so enthusiastic that he's given me an enthusiasm for it and now I really love the subject (Entwistle and Ramsden, 1983, p. 169).

In fact lecturers seem to be able to shift students, at least temporarily, from viewing lectures as having only extrinsic relevance (for fulfilling course requirements) to having intrinsic relevance (through the subject matter) by their style of teaching (Hodgson, 1984). It also appears likely that the different styles of teaching identifiable in higher education will suit different types of student (Entwistle, 1981). For example, Pask (1976) reported the effects on the outcomes of learning of matching and mismatching students who preferred holist or serialist learning strategies with programmed learning materials based on holist or serialist principles. The matched groups, both holist and serialist, learned exceptionally well, with almost no overlap with the performance of the mismatched groups.

In general, it seems likely that student teachers will begin to teach as they prefer to learn, but if that style is extreme in either holist (informal) or serialist (structured) directions, some students will almost certainly find it unnecessarily difficult to learn.

Links with Classroom Learning

There is, of course, a danger of developing ideas about 'approaches to learning' so much in relation to the student's own experience of learning that it fails to capitalize on the need, also, for perceived professional relevance. 'This is all very interesting, but how is it going to help me to become an effective classroom teacher?'

The first question that needs to be answered is whether the distinction between deep and surface approaches to learning applies only in higher education. Selmes (1985) has carried out interviews with pupils entering the sixth form and has shown that not just the two main categories of deep and surface approaches are readily identifiable, but also the three main subdivisions in each are present in the interview protocols. Thus a deep approach involves 'personal integration of the material, the seeking of relationships, or of meaningfulness in the material'. In contrast, a surface approach depends on 'isolating aspects of the material or task, memorization of the material, or passivity to the task'. Selmes indicated that pupils seemed to find little opportunity to adopt deep approaches during their 'O' level year.

Attempts to measure approaches to studying by questionnaire among school pupils have also been successful (Entwistle and Kozeki, 1985). Three main study orientations — meaning, reproducing and strategic — have been identified by factor analysis separately in Britain and Hungary. The effects of the form of assessment may also be discerned in the responses to this questionnaire. In Hungary, where there are no external examinations in secondary school, a higher proportion of pupils endorse items indicating a deep holist approach (but without the supportive serialist strategies), while pupils in the fourteen to seventeen years age range in Britain have higher scores on 'surface approach', 'instrumental motivation', and 'serialist style'.

The importance of a deep approach to learning can also been seen even among very young children learning to read. Francis (1982) has described how pupils who learn to read easily seem already to have an intuitive idea about what reading involves. They thus approach books in a way which implies a recognition that they will be able to extract meaning from the words in due course. In contrast, difficulties in mastering the early stages of learning to read seem to stem from a failure to recognize the purpose of reading, or even the links between letters, words, sounds, and meaning. The strong effects of the hidden curriculum have also been demonstrated among young children. Desforges *et al* (1985) have provided a number of illustrations of how teachers may affect their pupils' learning endeavours.

> For example, a teacher was recently observed to talk to a class of six year old children for forty-five minutes about the countries of origin of the produce commonly found in fruit shops. This monologue was illustrated using a tiny map of the world and extensive reference was made to many foreign countries. She finished by asking the children to 'write me an exciting story about the fruit we eat'. The children had to decide what she meant by this! They were helped in part by the fact that they had heard the instruction before in respect of other contents. In fact the children wrote very little. They took great pains to copy the date from the board. (The teacher did not ask them to do this. It was presumably taken for granted as part of the task specification). They formed their letters with great care and used rubbers copiously to correct any slips of presentation. Whilst this went on the teacher moved about the class commending 'neat work' and 'tidy work' and chiding children for 'dirty fingers' and 'messy work'. No further mention was made of 'exciting' content or of 'stories'. It seemed that the children knew perfectly well what the teacher meant when she asked for an 'exciting story about fruit' even though in this case, the overt task definition (i.e. the teacher's instructions) stood in sharp contrast (although not necessarily in contradiction) to the reward structure (page 000).

The perception of these children, inevitably, would be that imagination was not required, but that accuracy and neatness led to compliments and, presumably, to better marks. Such examples can be used to illustrate the ways in which a teacher shapes the pupils' approaches to studying and the quality of their learning outcomes, in powerful, but often unrecognized, ways.

Thus ideas about approaches to learning, emerging from research on students, can be used first to root important psychological constructs in students' own recent experiences of learning, and then to show some of the ways in which teachers influence students' or pupils' learning by their methods of teaching and particularly by their assessment procedures. But how might these ideas be introduced into a graduate teacher-training course?

The Experience of Studying

The general intention in using research on student learning would be to start with the student firmly in the role of learner, and gradually encourage a shift in perspective, towards that of the teacher. The starting point, as in Marton's own experimental work, might thus be to give out a short article to be read preparatory to answering questions on it afterwards. (See Entwistle, 1981, page 61 for further details of this type of exercise). This is a familiar task and the subsequent questions provide the typically coercive element contained in many classroom situations. The article used for this purpose needs to be relevant to the course, easy to read, with detailed information together with a strongly developed argument within about 1500 words. After reading the article, the students might be asked first a series of, say, five detailed questions related to the informational content of the article, followed by an invitation to write a one-page summary of the article (without further reference to it), and to answer a question which requires a discussion of implications — in other words that takes the student beyond the information presented in the article.

The next step might involve using a common classroom ploy — passing the answers to a neighbouring student to mark. The factual answers could be marked on a 2-1-0 scale, while students could be asked to put marks (out of, say, ten for the summary and five for the implications) on to a separate sheet along with their comments and an explanation of the marks awarded. Adding the marks together provides a total out of twenty-five and multiplying by four produces a percentage mark. Answer and comment sheets could then be exchanged, followed by discussions between the student pairs about the marks awarded.

This simple introductory exercise has been described in detail because it can provide a source of subsequent discussion of many important concepts and ideas. The discussion of marks will probably start with arguments about whether the open-ended answers have been appropriately graded, but these can be guided towards a consideration of criteria. How do we decide the relative worth of different answers? The idea of qualitative differences in the outcome of learning can then be introduced, and this represents a first step into the research literature.

Peel (1971) was one of the first to try to apply Piaget's stages in cognitive development to pupils' responses to questions. His initial distinction between explaining and describing, and the subsequent elaborations of his students (for example, Sutherland, 1982), provide a way of introducing the concept of *outcome space* and the SOLO taxonomy. Biggs and Collis (1982) provide a striking illustration of the differences in Australian pupils' answers to a simple geographical question, and this can be used to point up the relevance to schools of this concept. They described the range of pupils' answers to the question:

Why is the side of a mountain that faces the coast usually wetter than the side facing the interior?

1 'Dunno'
2 'Because it rains more on the coastal side'
3 'Because when we go to our cabin that's right on the coast, it's always wetter there than on the road crossing the mountain that gets us there. Never fails, my Pop says. I reckon we ought to move; like get us a cabin for hunting which is better'n fishing anyway. Besides, I hate rain.'
4 'Because the sea breezes hit the coastal side of the mountain first.'
5 'Cos air from the sea gets kinda damp, like fog and that. It settles on the coast first and so it rains and all the wetness falls on the coast and there's none left for the other side of the mountain.'
6 'Because the prevailing winds are from the sea which is why you call them sea breezes. They pick up moisture from the sea and as they meet the mountain they're forced up and get colder because it's colder the higher you get from sea level. This makes the moisture condense which forms rain on the side going up. By the time the winds cross the mountain they are dry.'
7 'This is likely to be true only if the prevailing winds are from the sea. When this is so, they pick up the water vapour evaporated from the sea which is carried to the mountain slopes where the damp air mass rises and cools. Cooling causes the water vapour to condense, and being heavier than air, the water droplets deposit as rain. Not only is the wind now drier, it is possible that it is carried up the mountain further where it is compressed, which warms it like a bicycle pump gets warm. It is therefore less saturated than before for

two reasons. The effect is like the chinooks experienced on the eastern slopes of the Rockies in Canada in winter. If there was no mountain, there would likely be no difference between the coast and inland. It all depends on the land features and the prevailing wind and temperature conditions. If these differed, then the energy exchanges would be different, resulting in quite a different pattern.' (Biggs and Collis, 1982, pp. 4–5).

This example can be supplemented by others from Biggs and Collis or a similar one from Peel (1971, pp. 90–2) to provide students with a good feel of qualitative differences in the outcome of learning.

Returning to the exercise, the students might be asked to comment on the fact that they had been asked to produce a percentage mark to indicate how much they had learned. What is the connection between the percentage mark awarded and the underlying attribute — knowledge about the article? What does the percentage mark mean? How useful is it? These questions provide a peg on which to hang later discussions about assessment techniques in schools.

To maintain initial momentum, however, discussion should be switched towards 'strategy'. How did the students tackle the task they had been given? Why did they use that approach? This discussion should soon highlight the sequence in school learning of intention, process and outcome (see Entwistle and Marton, 1984). Again it is unwise to lean too heavily on the initial discussion of experiences. The purpose of the initial learning task is to ensure that theoretical constructs are rooted in the personal realities of previous experience. But to rely on the experiential approach too heavily would convey the impression that educational psychology is built out of anecdote and intuition. Thus, the initial discussion on strategy should lead on to a description of the research on student learning. These studies provide illustrations of the techniques of collecting data in educational research and of the difficulties in interpreting them. They show how the collective experiences of many individuals can be systematically condensed, and eventually represented by a model or a theory.

A discussion of the concept of approach among students can be seen as the pivotal point of this introduction to educational psychology. From that point, alternative avenues open up. The simplest path follows the effects of previous knowledge and different forms of motivation, on approaches to learning.

It is probably best to introduce the concept of style while the original learning exercise is still fresh in the students' minds. The most dramatic way to introduce 'style' is perhaps through the use of Pask's TEACHBACK protocols. Students who have learned in different ways are asked to explain what they have come to understand. In one of Pask's (1976) examples, the students have learned the characteristics of the sub-species of an imaginary Martian animal, the Gandlemuller. A serialist explains the taxonomy as follows:

> Zoologists have classified the Gandlemuller on the basis of physical characteristics. The three main types are Gandlers, Plongers, and Gandleplongers. Gandlers have no sprongs. Plongers have two sprongs, Gandleplongers have one sprong. There are four sub-species of Gandler: M1, M2, B1, and B2. The Ms have one body, the Bs have two bodies. The M1 and B1 have a single cranial mound. The M2 and B2 have a double cranial mound ... etc.

At the opposite extreme, a holist presents an entirely different form of explanation.

> I want to tell you about a funny Martian animal which has been recently discovered and classified by scientists conducting surveys. They are funny sluglike things with various protuberances. These animals are called Gandlemullers, because they churn about the swamps near the Equator and Gandle is the Martian for swampmud, hence the swampmudmiller (Muller is German for miller). These things churn through the mud eating it by some curious process which means they eat and excrete at the same time. (see Entwistle, 1981, p. 91)

Which of these explanations is best? Both, eventually, provided all the information correctly, but in very different ways. Why are they different? Clearly students have stored the information according to different organizational principles. What are those principles? Here a discussion of the representation of knowledge in the memory could be begun, linking back to the SOLO taxonomy. But the main springboard from both approaches and styles is into the effects of teaching and assessment procedures on pupils' learning. Some of the supporting research from schools was mentioned earlier, and it seems to be a fast-developing research area which will provide a rich variety of illustrations describing the classroom experiences of pupils in terms of their perceptions of the teacher's requirements.

As other psychological and educational research evidence is introduced, it will be important to help students to make the imaginative projection from their own experiences and the research on student learning, to pupils' experiences and the learning contexts of differing school classrooms. This can be achieved partly by a careful choice of research studies which emphasize the pupil's perspective on learning, and by the use of additional experiential methods, such as those described by Guy Claxton elsewhere in this book.

Alterable Variables and Potent Concepts

Bloom (1979) has argued that educational research should aim not at general description or explanation, but at identifying 'alterable variables' over which teachers have direct influence — like the allocation of time on task. A parallel argument would be that, given the severe time constraints in teacher training courses, a very limited number of psychological concepts should be introduced. We should therefore choose those concepts which are most likely to provide powerful tools for teachers in their thinking about their classroom experience. It should be clear by now which psychological concepts are seen as 'potent'. To provide an indicative summary, Figure 1 presents the main concepts derived from research on student learning and the ways in which these can provide links into other 'potent' concepts.

In taking a course on psychology within a teacher training course,

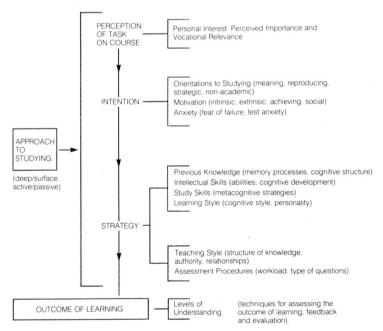

Figure 1.   *Psychological topics associated with concepts derived from research on student learning*

students do not have time to read widely around the subject. They cannot be expected to develop a sophisticated understanding or a detailed knowledge of psychological theories or methods of enquiry. Concentrating on a small number of 'potent' concepts, and case studies of research methods, provides a limited focus from which to encourage (through the assessment requirements) students to project their own experiences of learning into the classroom situation, guided by psychological ideas.

The ritual reproduction of detailed information should be played down, if we want to follow the implications of the research which guided this approach to educational psychology. If we teach psychology as a body of knowledge which we expect students to apply to their teaching, without appearing to believe it is worth applying to our own teaching, the outcome is inevitable. Students will see psychology as a largely irrelevant academic discipline to be coped with by surface learning ploys, to be memorized for the examinations, and then promptly forgotten. Whichever way of introducing educational psychology to student teachers we adopt, we should surely encourage them to be active in their learning, to seek relevance and linkages with personal experience, and to develop a style of teaching which encourages these same characteristics in their own pupils. Research on student learning provides one such approach. Don Bannister (1982) saw an alternative way of challenging the existing orthodoxies of teaching psychology through the use of Personal Construct Theory and biographies. However, his conclusion gels with our own.

It may be that our teaching style should aim to involve our students in the framing of interesting questions rather than to urge them to recite dull answers (p. 79).

References

BANNISTER, D. (1982) 'Personal construct theory and the teaching of psychology' *British Psychological Society Education Section Review*, 6, pp. 73–9.

BIGGS, J.B. (1978) 'Individual and group differences in study processes' *British Journal of Educational Psychology*, 48, pp. 266–279.

BIGGS, J.B. and COLLIS, K. (1982) *Evaluating the Quality of Learning, the SOLO Taxonomy*, New York, Academic Press.

BLOOM, B. (1979) *Alterable Variables: The New Direction in Educational Research*, Edinburgh, Scottish Council for Research in Education.

DAHLGREN, L-O. (1984) 'The Outcome of Learning' in MARTON *et al*, see below.

DESFORGES, C. (1985) 'Understanding the quality of pupils' learning experiences' in ENTWISTLE, N.J. (Ed.) *New Directions in Educational Psychol-*

ogy: *Learning and Teaching*, Lewes, Falmer Press.

ENTWISTLE, N.J. (1981) *Styles of Learnng and Teaching* London, Wiley.

ENTWISTLE, N.J., HANLEY, M. and HOUNSELL, D.J. (1979) 'Identifying distinctive approaches to studying' *Higher Education*, 8, pp. 365–380.

ENTWISTLE, N.J. and KOZEKI, B. (1985) 'Relationships between school motivation, approaches to studying, and attainment among British and Hungarian adolescents' *British Journal of Educational Psychology*, (forthcoming).

ENTWISTLE, N.J. and MARTON, F. (1984) 'Changing conceptions of learning and research', in MARTON *et al*, see below.

ENTWISTLE, N.J. and RAMSDEN, P. (1983) *Understanding Student Learning*, London, Croom Helm.

FRANCIS, H. (1982) *Learning to Read*, London, Allen and Unwin.

FRANSSON, A. (1977) 'On qualitative differences in learning IV — Effects of motivation and test-anxiety on process and outcome' *British Journal of Educational Psychology*, 47, pp. 244–57.

GIBBS, G. (1981) *Teaching Students to Learn*, Milton Keynes, Open University Press.

HODGSON, V. (1984) 'Learning from lectures', in MARTON *et al*, see below.

LAURILLARD, D. (1984) 'Learning from problem-solving', in MARTON *et al*, see below.

MARTON, F., HOUNSELL, D.J. and ENTWISTLE, N.J. (1984) *The Experience of Learning*, Edinburgh, Scottish Academic Press.

MARTON, F. and SALJO, R. (1976) 'On qualitative differences in learning II — Outcome as a function of the learner's conception of the task', *British Journal of Educational Psychology*, 46, 115–27.

NEWBLE, D.J. and JAEGER, K. (1983) 'The effect of assessments and examinations on the learning of medical students', *Medical Education*, 17, 25–31.

PASK, G. (1976) 'Styles and strategies of learning' *British Journal of Psychology*, 46, 128–148.

PEEL, E.A. (1971) *The Nature of Adolescent Judgement* London, Staples Press.

POLLITT, A.B., HUTCHINSON, C., ENTWISTLE, N.J. and DE LUCA, C. (1984) *What Makes Exam Questions Difficult?* Edinburgh, Scottish Academic Press.

RAMSDEN, P. and ENTWISTLE, N.J. (1981) 'Effects of academic departments on students' approaches to studying' *British Journal of Educational Psychology*, 51, 368–383.

SALJO, R. (1976) *Qualitative Differences in Learning as a function of the Learner's Conception of the Task* Gothenburg, Acta Universitatis Gothenburgensis.

SCHRODER, H.M., DRIVER, M.J. and STRENFERT, S. (1967) *Human Information Processing* New York, Holt, Rinehart & Winston.

SELMES, I. (1985) *Approaches to learning at secondary school: their identification and facilitation.* Unpublished Ph.D. thesis: University of Edinburgh.

SNYDER, B.R. (1971) *The Hidden Curriculum.* New York, Knopf.

SUTHERLAND, P.A.A. (1982) 'An Expansion of Peel's describer-explainer stage theory', *Educational Review*, 34, 69–76.

The Psychology of Teaching Educational Psychology

Guy Claxton
University of London Chelsea College

How to Examine Teacher Training

The primary goal of teacher training must be to make good teachers, or less ambitiously, to get people to the point where they can, on their own and in the course of working as a teacher, learn within a year or two to become good teachers. Any component of a teacher training course that is not clearly and effectively aimed towards this goal can at best play only a minor and supporting role, and this role and its rationale must, if the students are not to reject it, be carefully explained. I would argue that any component that is presented as being of major importance, either explicitly, or implicitly through the amount of time and weight of assessment that is devoted to it, yet is not effective in enhancing the student teacher's everyday insight or competence, is indefensible. When students perceive ineffectiveness in such a component, they reject it, either actively (by complaining about it) or passively (by forgetting it), (for example Lacey, 1977). This rejection of a component says nothing about its potential worth in other, perhaps more academically oriented, contexts. It says that either the offering is untimely, in that it fails to engage with the students' own priorities: or it is presented in a way that is inappropriate to their current levels of understanding; or it is in fact irrelevant. What we do in teacher training may be ineffective because it is the wrong thing to do, or because it is the right thing done at the wrong time or in the wrong way. Thus given that the most important goal of teacher training is the enhancing of competence, and given that this is what the student teachers overwhelmingly *want*, we need to ask of every putative ingredient of the course:

- is it aimed towards this goal?
- if not is it defensible?
- is it the *most* effective and economical way of achieving its purpose?
- is it present in the right amount?
- is it presented at the right time?
- is it presented in the right way?

It is these questions that I shall address to the psychological component of teacher training courses (especially the Post Graduate Certificate in Education or PGCE).

The Impact of Psychology

Although the Leicester survey (Bernhaum, 1982) shows that psychology is by no means universally disparaged, for some students at least psychology could well be the most disappointing of the so-called 'foundation disciplines' because it seems to promise most. Philosophy, sociology and history are clearly cerebral. They ask that students *think about* the social, historical and intellectual context or content of what they are doing, and this request can be defended with varying degrees of subtlety and success. But psychology is 'about people' and it is not unreasonable of students therefore to expect it to speak much more directly to their own priorities: their needs to be able to communicate and control, enthuse and motivate, to create and orchestrate a harmonious and happy environment within which they and their pupils can feel that their time spent together is time *well* spent. Unless they are carefully warned to the contrary students may come to psychology with high hopes and find, in the event, that the anticipation that it will *make a difference* is not fulfilled. Some students find our offerings *interesting,* and they may work hard and write good essays. But while we may be pleased or relieved when this happens, we cannot accept it as sufficient justification for the inclusion of psychology in the course, because intellectual familiarity or even facility is not the point. More commonly, unfortunately, students go away having learnt the name Piaget, and that this Piaget is important, dead, and had a theory about stages. The examination papers and many of the essays that I have marked for years consistently reveal knowledge of this order. Why is it that psychology too often leaves only a faint smear on memory, a slightly bitter taste in the mouth, and as much effect on spontaneous competence as a passing face leaves in a mirror? Is it that the students are ungrateful and 'unmotivated'? Do we 'teach' it all right but they, through their own perversity, ignorance or shortsightedness fail to 'learn' it? An analysis of such psychological crudeness cannot, I'm afraid, be acceptable to psychologists: so clumsy an exoneration will not wash. School-teachers are prone to use similar sleights-of-hand and we rightly teach our students to reject them. So we have to examine our own duties and offerings in the light of our primary goal, using the questions listed above to help and guide us.

What Do We Do?

Despite local moves to replace it, the typical psychological input to a teacher training course remains the *lecture*, the typical methods of assimilation are *discussion* and *further reading* and the typical product an *essay* or *exam answer*. The lectures consist of 'courses' or 'topics' such as Classroom Interaction, Mixed Ability Research, Punishment, Learning, Adolescence, Motivation, Prejudice and the Multi-Ethnic School, Counselling, Special Education Needs or Child Development. Students are asked or required to listen to these, and may also be asked to take part in seminars about them, select one or two to write in detail about, or to recapitulate them, after a delay of up to nine months, in an examination room. Why? The most prevalent (though for obvious reasons usually unvoiced) rationale is that of tradition and manpower. We've got people who are paid to know about and to teach these things. We've always taught them to the PGCEs (or BEds or whoever), so we will continue to do so. To question this expediency is uncomfortable, but it must be done, especially in the light of recent government papers such as 'Teaching Quality' (1983), which appear to downgrade the role of the foundation disciplines; of the general consensus that the PGCE year is 'far too short', and therefore everything it contains must be prepared to defend its inclusion; and of students reactions, (for example, Bernbaum, 1982).

The next line of defence is very often to assert that 'Students need a "firm grounding in" learning theory' or that 'No-one should be able to go through teacher training without learning something about Piaget (or Bruner or Ausubel or Gagné or the classic research of Hutchinson and Hutchinson [1967])'. Such assertions are however neither self-evidently true nor clear. They fail to locate psychology within an overall approach to teacher training. They say it is good but not what it is good *for*. They often fail to take heed of the way these contributions are received year after year. They do not say what a 'solid grounding' or a 'basic grasp' or a 'firm understanding' means, nor concommitantly how they are appropriately assessed. And perhaps most fundamentally, they do not distinguish between knowing, understanding, believing and mastering — that is between the different kinds of psychological *impact* that is required or produced.

The Pedagogy of Teacher Training

At the bottom of this unsatisfactory rationale lies an untenable assumption: that once something is known it is known for all purposes. Specifically it is supposed that when something is understood, or understood 'properly', then it will, or should, automatically affect every aspect of a person's psychological functioning to which it is potentially applicable. Understanding is *sufficient* to produce appropriate changes in belief, attitude, judgment, perception, feeling and habit. Indeed it almost seems to be assumed sometimes that intellectual understanding is *necessary* for these other changes to come about: that the only way to a person's competence is through their cognition. Of course when this is made explicit people will agree that the most important part of students' learning happens through their experience, on the job, on teaching practice. Yet we act, on occasion, as if psychology (and the other disciplines) were self-evidently vital.

The fact is that understanding is neither a necessary nor a sufficient condition for an expansion of competence. On the one hand people often get better at things without knowing why or how. On the other they often stay stuck with ways of working that don't work despite knowing, agreeing with or even believing sound advice about how to improve. 'Experiential knowledge', that part of a person's cognitive apparatus that controls their perception and action, their sense-ability and response-ability, is mostly developed and modified through immediate experience. 'Verbal knowledge', that which we are taught or which we figure out, is sometimes extremely resistant to being unpacked and dissolved back again into the spontaneous solution of problems like how to get across the concept of a 'mole' or what to do with Dianne. The frequent immiscibility of verbal and experiential knowledge is a profoundly important issue, both practically for anyone who is trying to teach for a change of competence, and theoretically for psychology as a whole. And it has been too little acknowledged by teachers and researchers alike (Claxton, 1984).

The pedagogy that is used to transmit psychology in teacher training has been largely borrowed without question from other more academic forms of teaching and learning, specifically from the standard *modus operandi* of the traditional university department. There is nothing wrong with this pedagogy: applied to the training of scholars in zoology or philology or even psychology it is appropriate and effective. But in teacher training our primary aim is *not* the production of scholars. Our students need to become practitioners first and pundits second. Only to the extent that a good teacher is also an educationalist are we justified in committing our students' time and energy to the researching and comprehension of educational issues. If they *wish* to, and some students do, then there may be an argument for providing the opportunity. But if they do not, and the majority don't, then we have to be very clear how much of our educational studies, despite being a perceived irrelevance, really are 'for their own good'. Other university courses that are also trainings — medicine or engineering, for example — have moved further in this respect, it seems to me, than has education, and indeed are beginning to provide us with alternative models of the teacher training process as a whole (for example, Dreeben, 1970).

Learning to Teach

There are many different specifications of what a Good Teacher is. There must be, for it is a matter of values as well as of pragmatics. But despite disagreements about the ideal *product*, there would be general agreement that the *process* of learning to teach requires changes in beliefs and attitudes, feelings and self-concept, perception and action as well as in knowledge. It is inevitably a complex and personal business. Tacit though firmly held beliefs about the value of one's subject or the nature of school are challenged in the classroom if not in the seminar room. Attitudes to children and to authority are uncovered that one would rather had not been. Feelings of anxiety have to be dealt with one way or another, the constant imminence of failure in school being particularly threatening for those, like graduate student-teachers, who are most unused to it. Self-doubts arise as one finds oneself, *in extremis*, acting in ways that one has forsworn. Perception has to develop to the point where one can 'read' the mood of a class. 'Are they fed up with me, or just fed up?' is an important discrimination to be able to make. And one's spontaneous initiatives and responses, one's habits and actions are often found wanting.

If we were to boil this down, we might say that the student teachers' job is to discover a repertoire of ways of being in school that are simultaneously *comfortable* and *effective*, and it is our job to help them. Their problem, especially those learning to teach in schools rather different from the ones in which they spent their own school-days, is that much of what comes naturally, what feels comfortable, isn't effective; and much of what is effective (which they either begin to discover or are told) doesn't feel at all comfortable. 'Learning to teach is not just learning a job: it is learning a new way of being yourself', as I said, somewhat piously, on the cover of *The Little Ed Book* (Claxton, 1978), and this requires an interim process of experimentation with ways of being that feel alien or phony or 'out of character', or which are actually unsuccessful. It is a time of acting and anxiety not unlike adolescence, and is not surprising in the light of this that many of our students tend to display the simultaneously dependent and hostile attitudes that an understanding parent must learn to absorb. Students' frequent response to educational studies, and therefore to psychology shows this ambivalence. On the one hand we are asked: 'Tell us what to do. You're supposed to know. Help us.' And on the other our best attempts to do so (often, admittedly, not terribly good) are often met with just that apathetic or dismissive resistance that the students themselves will find so hard to take from a bottom-band fourth year.

So if learning to be a teacher is not like learning to be a scholar, it is not like learning to be an engineer either. The expertise of the engineer is (very largely) acquired: that is, the 'person' of the student is relatively little involved. They have to be keen enough and bright enough, but their likes and dislikes, their attitudes and values are not much at stake. They can stay who they were, and add something. The student teacher is much less likely to be able to keep him or herself divorced from the learning experience. The questions 'Will I cope?' and '*How* will I cope?' loom large, and may for a time rattle even a confident-seeming student quite deeply. Thus — and this is the crunch — students are asking for something *that cannot be told*. The changes that they wish to happen quickly and painlessly are at the level of attitude, values, feelings and habits. They want, not surprisingly, spontaneous success, self-acceptance and self-confidence and they want it now! And taught knowledge, however wise, however well-researched or well-communicated cannot deliver that, and should not promise it.

A psychologist of education might at this point be tempted to heave a (well camouflaged) sigh of relief and give up. After all, if (a) we cannot teach them directly what they want to know, and (b) they are going to be upset with us whatever we do (projecting onto us as authority-figures their anxieties about themselves), then why bother? Such a conclusion is too easy, of course. We can learn to see the ambivalence for what it is and ride it. And we need to look more closely both at the *actual* effects of tuition and instruction in the context of teacher training, and at alternative, perhaps less direct but more suitable, ways of deploying our psychological knowledge and expertise. Before we decide on what treatment, if any, is required, we need to pursue the diagnosis a little further, and have a look on the pharmacist's shelves to see what remedies are available.

The Relationship of Teaching to Learning

It will help us to understand what we are doing in teacher training if we make explicit the relationship between teaching and learning. The people we are training ought to be clear about this, and so ought we. A common and accurate parallel for the relationship is like that between feeding and eating. Eating — chewing, swallowing, digesting, etc. — is what a person does for themselves in order to turn input in one form into another form that is compatible with, and therefore assimilable by, the body. Learning — attending, practising, chewing over, etc. — is what a person does for themselves in order to turn information or experience in one form into another form that is compatible with, and therefore assimilable by, the mind. And as nobody else can eat for you, so nobody else can learn for you. Learning is the final, personal, active step in the process of assimilating knowledge and experience. What other people *can* do is arrange the conditions of learning so that learning happens faster, better, more deeply or more reliably. They can wait on you, print full-colour menus to excite you, order (in both senses) the courses for you, and even cut the stuff up for you and transport it to your mouth. These may be helpful. They may even, for certain learners learning certain things, be necessary. But the final act of learning cannot be forced. And if the teachers, misunderstanding the limits of their role, try to shove the facts down the learner's throat; if they mistake the learner's needs or appetites; if they demand a certain rate of chewing and swallowing; if, like a drunken zoo keeper, they confuse two species and give each the wrong diet; then teaching becomes literally a subversive activity, subverting, undermining and misdirecting the natural strategies of assimilation of the mind. It is not a learning-amplifier but a learning-suppressor; not a help but a hindrance.

Because learning is an organic matter, not a mechanical one, it cannot be engineered. The surgeon may 'suggest' a graft: it is up to the body whether it accepts it. The gardener may 'train' a plant, but it is up to the plant to do the growing and flowering. Or rather, a kind of learning *can* be engineered, but only at the cost of fragmenting the learner. Pre-formed fibre-glass branches can be bolted to a living tree. Artifical adult limbs could be fitted to children who are not growing 'fast enough'. Food can be forced down the throats of sated beasts. Learners can be trained to remember things that they do not understand. But the price is confusion, discomfort and a high chance of rejection. The teachers who prefer grafting to training will find their work hard graft indeed.

This of course is common-place in the psychology of education: as Cole and Scribner (1974) said, 'widely acknowledged and just as widely ignored'. By paying only lip-service to the organic nature of learning in our lectures, we send out of our courses many new teachers who continue to misunderstand the nature and limits of their responsibility. They blame either themselves or their pupils for failures of the latter to learn when blame is simply inappropriate. Like temperamental chefs, they read every left morsel as a rejection or a failure, and either malign the offending diner or indict themselves. If my job is to *make* you learn, then there is something 'wrong' with either you or me when you do not. I cannot let it be. If all teachers understood deeply that the most they can hope to be is good and faithful servants, and that this is a matter not of ideology, of choice, but of psychology, of inevitability, then schools would be transformed instantly. Freed of misguided recrimination and abortive pressure, the force feeding would stop, learners would redis-cover their appetites, and teachers their original interest in the culinary arts.

These considerations apply reflexively to our work as teacher trainers. If we fail to punch home such simple, powerful, psychological truths sufficiently strongly, we also, in the *way* we teach, through the medium, convey the mechanical, outside-in model of growth, rather than the organic, integrated, inside-out one. We take personalities of all shapes and constitutions and attempt to laminate them with teacherly ideas and skills. We too believe that a teacher can be *assembled* out of knowledge and practice rather than fertilized or *developed* by them. We expect our tuition and advice to produce growth, not just to sustain or guide it. So we too misconstrue our power and, expecting too much, become disappointed with ourselves and impatient with our students.

Before we go on to look at some of the ways in which psychology could be more useful in teacher training, let me summarize the two principal arguments we have developed so far.

1   *What and how you teach must depend on who you are teaching, and what you are teaching them for.* You cannot teach psychol-

ogy in the same way with equal effectiveness, to 'A' level students, third-year psychology undergraduates, nurses, social workers, psychotherapists, 'people who want to understand a bit about what makes us tick', and teachers. The appropriate contents and optimal pedagogies are different, and psychology is uniquely equipped as a discipline to use itself to transmit itself.

2   *Knowledge — tuition, instruction, advice — does not produce development*. If, as we have seen, learning to teach is a process that demands development rather than just lamination, then the role of formal knowledge in that process has to be re-examined. By development, let me emphasize, I mean a natural elaboration of personality and perception, attitude and ability which supplants what was there before without overlaying it, as a leaf supplants a bud, so that the organism remains integrated and harmonious while becoming more sturdy or competent. The accumulation of knowledge, especially of advice, achieves a sort of learning, but at the expense of integrity, so that the learner becomes many-centred, split between identifying with what they did do, what they thought they would do, what they ought to have done, and what they forgot to do. This splitting is debilitating unless it is handled with great care, and unless everyone involved understands what is going on.

Teaching for Believing

We have said that a student teacher must grow in beliefs and values, in personality and feeling and in sensitivity and competence, as well as in understanding. Let us look at what is required in each of these broad areas, how we as teacher trainers might best deploy our psychology to support and facilitate that growth, and what role, if any, might formal tuition and instruction play. We shall take first the domain of beliefs, attitudes and values, by which I mean those positions that are capable of articulation *and to which the student has a personal commitment*.

All students when they arrive at a teacher training course have a personal theory about education, schools, children, teaching and learning; what is important and what is not, what is essential, what is normal, what is needed, what is right (Hanson and Herrington, 1976; Mardle and Walker, 1980). They have their own intuitive, largely tacit, largely unexamined set of beliefs, attitudes and values that are more or less idiosyncratic, partial, simplistic, archaic and rigid; and which they have unconsciously taken as being necessary and/or desirable. Because of their investment in this theory (so manifest in the recurrent non-discussions of 'seminars') they are loath to give it up, and yet it will not serve them well. What people believe is much more important than what they 'know' (that is, those ideas they hold without giving them their assent or commitment) because they create the guiding maps of 'How It Is' and 'How It Ought To Be' against which the believer checks and judges their experience (Kelly, 1955). These judgments dictate the amount of attention paid or credence given to experience and therefore they influence, in an indirect but very significant way, the rates and domains of a person's learning. (This is an extremely crude summary of a complicated argument developed in Claxton [1984]). When belief and experience conflict, as they often do during a student teacher's life, it is therefore important that *a priori* adherence to the belief is suspended, and that it be submitted to scrutiny, for if it is not, a real growth in competence is sacrificed for the transient and self-defeating satisfaction of 'being right'. (This process is well described by the 'dissonance theory' of Festinger [1957].)

How are students to be helped to inspect and adapt this incoherent mish-mash of experience, hear-say, prejudice and myth? Not, it must be obvious by now, simply by the giving of knowledge, for it is only rarely and by luck that ideas received in this dead-pan way connect with and inform the underlying level of belief. More commonly they make as much impression on a person's held beliefs as water on a duck's back. Odd droplets adhere: most runs off: little is absorbed. Yet knowledge *does* have a role in the more complicated but necessary process which involves (a) eliciting students' preconceptions and bringing them to the surface; (b) showing them that their values and assumptions are questionable, that alternatives exist, and that their original view may be replaced or re-espoused; (c) supporting them in this enquiry, preventing them from rationalizing, defending or escaping, and intimating that, whether they eventually change or not, to assemble their own wardrobe of values and ideas out of the jumble-sale heap of reach-me-downs they have been living with, is a worthwhile activity. The point is not that they should be able to profess more fluently, but that the map they have gives them a sense of orientation and direction in their careers. 'How can I go forward when I don't know which way I'm facing?' asked John Lennon. It's a good question, and a satisfactory belief system tells you which way is forward *for you*, when a choice exists. To formulate such a plan is useful pragmatically for it provides stability and purpose in a job where it is all too easy to flounder in the daily chop of chores and niggles. A boat wallows less when it is under way.

Appropriate techniques here include presenting alternatives concretely, fairly and without judgment. Without an external evaluation to accept or resist students are more likely to look for their own. For this reason formal discussions or seminars are often not the best forum. The search for 'my' point of view gets subverted by the search for 'the' point of view — the 'right' solution — and, often by the assumption, by some group members at least, that 'my' point of view is 'the' point of view, and that my job is only (and generously) to help you to see sense. Attempts to argue things out with oneself in writing may well be more fruitful. People are often scared to expose what they truly believe, or to fumble with their uncertainties, in public. An essay written 'for my eyes only', or for the view of one other sympathetic friend or tutor is safer, and therefore more profitable. Extensive reading, critical analysis of the key concepts, and the like are not required: too rational an enquiry diverts attention from its essentially personal nature. The so-called 'open critical' approach, advocated by Tomlinson (1981), in which students are asked to construct their own *intellectual* evaluation and synthesis of the conflicting theoretical stances to which they have been introduced, is not apt at the level of teacher training. They have neither the time, the inclination nor the need for such disembodied stuff.

The function of knowledge, facts and argument here are (a) to demonstrate that other positions are possible and not patently absurd, (b) to suggest some that might be worth thinking about, and (c) to use the pick of new ideas to break up the crazy-paving of students' preconceptions, so that productive thought can take the place of glib defence. (Annoyed with students at the end of one term for their reluctance to engage with this enquiry, I graffiti-ed on their noticeboard: '"Most people would die sooner than think ... Most people do." Bertrand Russell.' One student, getting the drift, replied below with '"Incest More Common Than Thought in U.S." Headline in St. Louis Times.' We might combine the pointedness of the first with the lovely ambiguity of the second to create 'Rationalization More Common Than Thought in Teacher Training.')

In 1968 David Ausubel gave us a good maxim: 'The most important single factor influencing learning is what the learner already knows. Ascertain this and teach him accordingly.' We zealously pass this on to our students and in the very act of doing so ignore it, for we teach them as if they knew either nothing or all the same 'something'. Rarely do we bother to elicit students' deeper values and beliefs, to get a feel for their structure, diversity and ramifications. So it is only by chance that our teaching *fits*. Instead we pass out pieces of a jig-saw puzzle that may be on an entirely different subject and scale to the one in their heads, and all they can do, at best, is 'collect' them. This superficial type of remembering and understanding, by the way, is encouraged by the prospect of a written examination on Educational Theory, and is antithetical to the personal exploration advocated here.

Much has been written about the process of 'attitude-change' and much remains to be investigated. The way in which tuition affects belief is one of the most intriguing, intricate and ignored problems in psychology. It is related to the allied problem of how words in the form of instructions, maxims, advice and the like are involved in the development of perceptuo-motor competence. It is this that student teachers want most. It does not need selling to them, in the way that a good belief system does. And it is to this that we now turn.

Teaching for Competence

Competence breaks down into three other Cs: control, communication and confidence. What student teachers want is the ability to create an atmosphere, a context within which they can teach, when that context is not already created by the class as a whole. That is *control*. It is of no value in its own right (though some belief systems, different from my own, assign it a value) yet it is for many teachers in many schools, a *sine qua non*. When a congenial climate is established, teachers then need to be able to *communicate* — to present lessons that are interesting, that are seen to have a purpose and a point, that are challenging without being intimidating, that are timed and sequenced appropriately, and so on. This is primarily the responsibility of 'methods' and teaching practice tutors, rather than of those in the foundation disciplines. Yet psychology has useful guidance for all concerned. The final wish of every student is that their competence becomes smooth and reliable and *confident:* that they can get over feeling self-conscious and indecisive and anxious as soon as possible. I shall leave this topic to the next section and deal with the other aspects of competence further here.

Especially if they are going to work in tough schools, student teachers are right to doubt their abilities to communicate and control. Teaching today demands a degree of flexibility and improvization, an ability to read situations with speed and accuracy, and a repertoire of responses, that make the skills of an international scrum-half or a John McEnroe look ordinary. Teachers need to be able to think of good ways of putting things, to tell when to push and when to ease up, to spot young people's idiosyncratic signals of threat or overload, to be able to negotiate effectively with colleagues and pupils, many of whom they don't understand and some of whom they don't like, to cope with the inevitability of making the wrong decision or of being unprepared ... the list of desiderata is a long one. Furthermore it is of little importance that one can understand or explain what one is doing. The crucial thing is to get it right, to do what works, in a split second in the heat of the moment. And the best means to this end — indeed the only means — is practice, practice and more practice, as any virtuoso in any field from ice-dancing to writing, from snooker to trumpet-playing will tell you. Norman (1982) recently estimated, from talking to such skilful folk, that it takes a minimum of 5000 hours practice to achieve mastery. Our students typically get twelve weeks of teaching practice, five days a week, say three hours a day actually teaching: a total of about 200 hours. This analysis, impressionistic though it is, supports my belief that we cannot aim to send out whole, complete, perfect teachers at the end of a PGCE year. What we can and should do is aim to produce people who have the ability and aptitude to continue learning to teach, who have the openness and enthusiasm to keep on experimenting, failing, succeeding and growing. More of this, too, in the next section.

What we need in this area, to help us instruct in such a way that we accelerate perceptuo-motor learning, is a psychology of coaching, but as yet it is very unformed. We need to know the ways in which the Word can be made Flesh, but unfortunately although St. John tells us that it happened, he doesn't tell us how. Let me make a few remarks about the benefits and pitfalls of instructing and advising. Some instructions connect with the level of experiential knowledge, of spontaneous action, instantaneously and effortlessly. 'Stop picking your nose.' 'Look out for a number fourteen bus.' And so on. Such instructions access ways of seeing and behaving that are already well-formed and well-practised. Others — 'Don't worry'; 'Try not to think about it' — seem almost impossible to act on. The programmes for carrying them out do not (and very often cannot) exist. But the interesting ones for our purposes are the ones in the middle: the ones that take a while to 'sink in.' 'Avoid confrontations.' 'Don't shout.' 'Try and get a bit more pace into your your lessons.' 'The "light touch" might be more effective with those kids.' And all the rest of the useful tips and maxims and bits of feedback with which tutors kindly bombard their students. What is their effect? How does instruction work?

True to our earlier analogy we must start by saying that, as information does not directly affect belief, so instruction does not of itself create a development of competence. It may guide, direct, facilitate or support such a change, but it does not make it. Instruction can affect experiential growth but not effect it. In the space available here I shall have to leave this as an assertion, unjustified except by the frequent failure of advice to take root, and simply use it rather than defend it. (The argument is presented more fully in Claxton [1984].)

Coaching, the attempt to enhance competence through verbal directions, as in the end-of-lesson chat or the changing hands of written feedback, can be helpful in two indirect ways. First the coach can direct the learners' *awareness* and their *experiments* towards areas that are likely to prove fruitful. Thus the learning comes through experience and practice, but the selection of the most useful and timely experiences is influenced by instruction. 'Keep your eye on the ball' is the most ubiquitous director of attention, paralleled by 'Don't turn your back on a difficult class' in school. Likewise 'Just swing naturally: don't try to hit the cover off the ball', or 'Make sure your instructions for the experiment are really clear' direct students towards *acting in ways that demonstrate their own effectiveness*. The growth in competence comes from doing and noticing what works — what is effective and comfortable. Useful instruction increases the probability of trying out things that do work.

The second role of instruction is in providing interim *standards* against which to judge performance when the natural consequences are unforthcoming or ambiguous. Many skills do not produce a satisfactory experiential pay-off — the harmonious class, the sweet melody, the leg glance — until they are well advanced: that is until a variety of component abilities and sensitivities are accumulated and integrated. At points during this process one cannot tell whether one is getting better. Instruction provides a temporary guide by saying 'If you follow me you will get where you want to go in the end, even though you can't see it now.' This function of instruction is sometimes called *discipline*.

If we combine these two effects of instruction into another horticultural metaphor, we might say that the relationship of instruction to learner is like that of pea-stick to pea. The pea-shoot provides the growth; the stick provides support and direction which is in the pea's (as well as the gardener's) best interests. If this analogy is borne in mind there is little danger of the relationship between instructor, instruction and learner going wrong. When the relationship is misunderstood by either gardener or plant, however, then teaching damages and perverts development. For example, the gardener may think that because one stick is useful, the more sticks the better. Teacher trainers are often only too willing to surround their students with a palisade of insights and tips whose net effect is to intimidate and confuse. One can only focus one's attention or one's experiments on very few things at once. Too much good advice is worse than too little for one ends up not knowing which to follow. As Michael Flanders and Donald Swann wrote in their song about the off-spring of a match between the clockwise-spiralling honeysuckle and the anti-clockwise columbine:

> Poor little sucker, how will it know
> When it is climbing which way to go?
> Left? Right? Or, what a disgrace —
> It may go straight up and fall flat on its face!

While it is sometimes true that we don't know which way to turn *for* advice, at others we don't know which way to turn *because* of advice.

The second pitfall occurs when either gardener or pea, or most commonly both, believe that instruction ought to create growth, and therefore if it is not acted on immediately, or quickly, there is something wrong. Teacher begins to feel exasperated and impatient; students to feel inadequate and either guilty or resentful; both may fall into the trap of blaming either themselves or the other ('Why can't I do what I'm told' or 'He's a useless teacher' versus 'Perhaps I haven't been clear enough' or 'He just doesn't listen to what I tell him'). And recrimination takes energy and awareness away from the actual data of experience. When the small shoot is made to *feel* small, its inclination is to curl up, and growth is suspended.

The third problem occurs when the gardener is too sure he knows best. Peas are easy, because they all want to go in the same direction — up. But 'up' for student-teachers can mean many different things, and rightly so. If being a good teacher means finding a style that is not only effective but which feels comfortable and natural and satisfying, then the entering personality will be the foundation for the teacher that exits. Thus students must be allowed to experiment with advice and to reject it if it does not 'feel right', if its direction isn't 'up'. A perverse gardener who insisted on training his peas round croquet hooks would be doing them a disservice and diminishing his crop.

The fourth trap to mention here is that of slavery. Both Bruner (1960) and Hawkins (1973) have pointed out that teachers are the servants of learners, yet they serve by temporarily borrowing some of the learners' self-determination. When the teachers' job is done, this responsibility must be handed back. More like a sapling than a pea, I suppose the learners are helped to grow to a point where they can support themselves, and if they remain bound to the stake, then it turns into an impediment to further development. Bruner put it:

> Instruction is a provisional state that has as its object to make the
> learner or the problem solver self-sufficient. Any regimen of

correction carries the danger that the learner may become permanently dependent upon the tutor's correction. The tutor must correct the learner in a fashion that eventually makes it possible for the learner to take over the corrective function himself. Otherwise the result of instruction is to create a form of mastery that is contingent upon the perpetual presence of the teacher.

And Hawkins says, speakng of the relationship between teacher and learner:

> A reasonable general account of the relationship is, therefore, that the teacher is one who acquires authority through a compact of trust, in which the teacher seeks to extend the powers of the learner and promises to abridge them only transiently and to the end of extending them. The teacher offers the learner some kind of loan of himself or herself, some kind of auxiliary equipment which will enable the learner to make transitions and consolidations he would not otherwise have made. And if this equipment is of the kind to be itself internalized, the learner not only learns, but begins, in the process, to be his own teacher — and that is how the loan is repaid.

Finally, it will be clear that 'do' instructions are more helpful than 'don'ts', for the former will lead the learner towards first-hand experience that will enable them to appropriate (or reject) the essence of the instruction; they are invited to suck it and see. But if the instruction is a prohibition, the learner is thereby stopped from discovering how it tastes. If you cannot do that which is prohibited, you must remain without first-hand knowledge about why it isn't a good idea. (Of course in some contexts, prohibitions are necessary and benign. Young children must be taught that the consequences of approaching the fire or the kerb are dire — though even here the learning is largely experiential, the admonition being supported by real consequences that are painful but non-lethal. But in school, with the exception of the science laboratory, such physical dangers are rare, and flat forbidding rarely needed.)

In sum, instructions are helpful when they are presented one or two at a time, in a context of patience and practice; when they are clear, unequivocal, simple and positive; and when the learner feels free to reject or outgrow them.

Guy Claxton

Teaching to Learn

Under this final heading I want to talk about the role of personality and feelings in the process of learning to teach. My belief, as I have said, is that learning to teach is about discovering a repertoire of ways of being in school that are comfortable and effective. If a teacher's life is spent either being incompetent, or being competent and not liking it, then that life will be debilitating rather than satisfying; draining rather than enriching. The numbers of teachers in both categories are non-negligible. However I have also said that the solutions to this problem are bound to be diverse, and that this search for a personal, unique style should be encouraged. The implication for us as teacher trainers is that we are required to focus less on the details of how to teach, or at least to be more tentative in our offerings, and more on facilitating the search, on freeing and oiling the mechanism by which people learn to teach. We must recognize that from the pupils' point of view good teachers come in many shapes and guises, some of them quite unlikely, but that one of the important things they all have in common, as the surveys have shown (for example, Stubbs and Delamont, 1976) is that 'you know where you are with them.' You cannot know where you are with someone who is not at ease with themselves. Failure and self-doubt make people unreliable and mean.

How then can we help people to learn how to learn to teach? And do we need to? What reason is there to believe, as I have implied, that the very machinery of learning is jammed or rusted? Psychology — particularly clinical psychology and psychotherapy — again provides us with both diagnosis and cure. Very roughly the diagnosis goes like this. (a) Human beings need to decide, when something new and strange occurs, whether they are going to approach, investigate and learn about it, or whether it is better to avoid or defend. Is it a challenge or is it a threat? If I judge it to be a threat, I am saying it is more likely to blow up in my face than I am to be able to understand and master it. (2) The feeling of not being sure whether something is a challenge or a threat is called *anxiety*. The feeling of being threatened is primarily *fear*. (3) Threats include threats to self-image as well as to body. Many of the common threats are psychological rather than physical. (4) To the extent that a person is invested in being competent, consistent, clear, 'cool' and in control, to that extent the experiences of being incompetent (failing), inconsistent (unpredictable), unclear (confused), uncool (anxious or afraid), and out of control (floundering) are perceived as threats. (5) The types of learning and experimentation required of the student teacher virtually guarantee that such experiences will occur. (6) The rate at which the student teacher develops, therefore, is determined by the extent to which they can tolerate feeling anxious and unsure. If these feelings are taken as threats, students must defend rather than learn. (7) The mechanisms of defence involve physical avoidance (dropping out; being ill) and psychological avoidance (denying their need to learn; rationalizing and justifying; blaming and projecting; repressing or exaggerating their feelings; etc. etc.).

The cure is implicit in the diagnosis. First it may help to *explain* these things to students. Despite what I have said about the limitations of tuition, one of the ways in which it can be helpful is when it legitimates aspects of one's own experience that have been half-buried. The lecture that I give on this subject every year is always appreciated because I am acknowledging an important, felt part of students' experience that has for many of them not been spoken about before. It is a release to know that these feelings and defences and choices do exist; that other people have them; that they have names and explanations. It doesn't matter whether the account is perfect or even believed. Simply to know that an account exists is liberating.

The second and much more crucial part of the cure is to increase students' tolerance for stress and anxiety. It is difficult to stay put and stay open to the experiences of not being liked ('When's our other teacher coming back?') or appreciated ('You don't wear very nice clothes, do you Miss?' 'This is boring'); of making constant errors of judgment about people ('It *really* wasn't me, Sir') or about teaching ('We did that last year'); of not knowing what to do, where to go, who has the key to the stock-cupboard, how to deal with thieving, almost everybody's *name,* and of not knowing whether its best to keep asking or to keep quiet; of being observed and criticized by teachers and tutors as well as the kids; of being harassed and tired and sometimes downright miserable. It *is* a tough job to learn, for most people, and it is easy to retreat into bitching and blaming and not really telling the truth to anyone, perhaps not even to oneself, about how it is going. Yet understandable though they are, these retreats and evasions prolong the agony. The more one can allow oneself to be incompetent, the quicker competence comes.

Many techniques exist in humanistic, clinical and behavioural psychology and psychotherapy for helping people expand their tolerance for being uncomfortable. There are techniques of imagination and visualization; of desensitization, meditation and relaxation-training; of role-play and psychodrama. There are exercises to get people to be able to share their experience more accurately with others, and to listen with greater attentiveness and acceptance to them. There are ways of anticipating anxiety-provoking situations and of experimenting with them that are much more significant than merely discussing them. These and other methods serve to expand the domain of experiences with which students feel able to experiment when they are back on the job, and thus to accelerate the rate at which they learn, and reduce the time that it takes to master the basic skills of communication and control.

Conclusion

This chapter has explored some of the aims and processes of teacher training and examined how psychology might be more fruitfully applied to their facilitation than heretofore. I have argued that psychology is not just a 'foundation discipline', a body of knowledge to be absorbed, along with philosophy, sociology and history. Rather it is the meta-discipline that can and should inform the pedagogy of teacher training, whatever particular skills or beliefs are at stake. Yet we have not so far realized our potential. Psychology of education does not seem to be a self-actualizing venture.

For this potential to be released certain changes of perspective are required. We need to attend to and connect with the pre-existing knowledge, habits and attitudes of the students. We need to be clear about the *variety* of learnings that will be demanded of them, both by ourselves and by the unsettling experience of being a tyro in school. We need to acknowledge that much of our value can be at the level of helping people to learn how to learn to teach, rather than at the level of *telling* them what to do. And finally we need to expand our compass so that we include within our repertoire of offerings psychological techniques as well as psychological knowledge or theory.

If psychology were to ransack itself for ways of helping the student teacher develop his or her competence more speedily, effectively and painlessly, it would find them. But until it does our reports must continue to read 'has aptitude but lacks application', and 'could do very much better'.

References

AUSUBEL, D. (1968) *Educational Psychology: A Cognitive View*, New York, Holt, Rinehart and Winston.
BERNBAUM, G. (1982) *The Structure and Process of Initial Teacher Education*

Within Universities in England and Wales, University of Leicester.

BRUNER, J.S. (1960) *The Process of Education*, Harvard, Harvard University Press.

CLAXTON, G.L. (1978) *The Little Ed Book*, London, Routledge and Kegan Paul.

CLAXTON, G.L. (1984) *Live and Learn: An Introduction to the Psychology of Growth and Change in Everyday Life*, London, Harper and Row.

COLE, M. and SCRIBNER, S. (1974) *Culture and Cognition: a Psychological Introduction*, London, Wiley.

DREEBEN, R. (1970) *The Nature of Teaching, Schools and the Work of Teachers*, Scott Foresman and Co.

FESTINGER, L. (1957) *A Theory of Cognitive Dissonance*, New York, Harper and Row.

HANSON, D. and HERRINGTON, M. (1976) *From College to Classroom: The Probationary Year*, London, Routledge and Kegan Paul.

HAWKINS, D. (1973) 'What it means to teach', *Teachers College Record*, September.

HUTCHINSON, D. and HUTCHINSON, M. (1967) There is no such paper. (It represents every teacher trainer's individual favourite bit of 'vital' knowledge or research).

KELLY, G.A. (1955) *The Psychology of Personal Constructs*, New York, Van Nostrand.

LACEY, C. (1977) *The Socialization of Teachers*, London, Methuen.

MARDLE, G. and WALKER, M. (1980) 'Strategies and Structure: some critical notes on teacher socialization', in WOODS, P. (Ed.) *Teacher Strategies: Explorations in the Sociology of the Classroom*, London, Croom Helm.

NORMAN, D.A. (1982) *Learning and Memory*, San Francisco, Freeman.

STUBBS, M. and DELAMONT, S. (1976) *Explorations in Classroom Observation*, London, Wiley.

TEACHING QUALITY (1983) HMSO Cmnd 8836.

TOMLINSON, P. (1981) *Understanding Teaching*, London, McGraw-Hill.

Training Intelligently Skilled Teachers

Peter Tomlinson and Roy Smith
School of Education, University of Leeds
College of Ripon and York St. John

Introduction

In this chapter our focus is on the implications of modern skills psychology for teacher education and the role of psychological theory within it. We preface this choice of psychological resources by offering some principles for intelligent selection of theory and follow it by mentioning some problems and possibilities for implementing suggestions from skills psychology, including brief reference to some current work of our own.

The current background to these ideas contains at least four discernible strands worthy of mention. First, the traditional role of psychology in teacher education as bringing theoretical insights to be taught prior to practice and usually quite separately from it is being increasingly questioned, especially as regards the practical relevance of traditional content. We share this concern, though it would be a pity if the more developed forms of recent psychology should be denied any influence on teachers' thinking because of educational psychology being associated with a particular range of ageing and inappropriate paradigms.

Second, in conjunction with the above trend, there have been increasing calls to end the one-way traffic conception of 'pure theory' illuminating practice, and instead to develop an understanding of teaching and learning processes that will start from and be based in the classroom context. Such an 'instructional science' (Desforges), 'educology' (Biggs), 'psychopedagogy' (Stones), as it has variously been called, would foster a two-way interaction between education and psychology which would be to the benefit of both. This trend is surely to be welcomed, as long as it does indeed constitute an intelligently eclectic approach drawing on a wide range of ideas, rather than eschewing 'theory' and then labouring mightily perhaps only to achieve the psychological equivalent of re-inventing the wheel.

A third strand relates to the increased concern at political levels in Britain at least, for accountability and teacher effectiveness. The central aim of teacher education, we are being reminded, is to produce intelligently effective teachers.

The fourth theme is partly an expression of the third, namely a concern to situate teacher training in real school settings and to involve experienced teachers in such training and assessment. However appealing to 'commonsense', the effectiveness of such arrangements is hardly a foregone conclusion. Their appraisal and certainly their implementation will require bases of established understanding. In what follows we will briefly explore one such base, namely the modern psychology of skill and its associated models of the person. However, having announced a preference for intelligent eclecticism, we ought to spell out the principles that have allowed us to settle on this particular focus amongst the possible resources we might have employed.

Some Principles of Intelligent Eclecticism

The minimum prerequisites when seeking to illuminate a practical endeavour would seem to be (1) a relatively clear, if interim, conception of the aims and nature of one's applied concern and (2) principles for the intelligent selection of 'theoretical' resources to be applied.

(1)   An adequate conception of what we are aiming at in teacher preparation, namely effective teachers, will allow that teaching involves an interaction of many elements and factors (*cf.* Tomlinson, 1985) typically in classrooms containing thirty or more pupils, that the teacher plays a variety of roles within teaching activities which are, in traditional psychological terms, relatively complex, and all this with currently increasing limitations on the various sorts of needed resources. So we share the emphasis of those proponents of an instructional science who point out that traditional educational psychology has dealt more with learning theories than teaching realities. It is not inconsistent with this to hold, however, that pupil learning is the prime aim and consideration in education, being logically prior to the concept of teaching in the sense that teaching is *defined* as activity designed to promote learning. Hence an adequate educational psychology or instructional science might not only illuminate what goes on in successful teaching. It might also make clear why, given what is understood about the possible processes of instruction and learning in a particular subject area, the resources and

demands of a given situation make successful teaching unlikely because of the limits and pressures they impose. Ways in which teaching is conceived depend on the concepts, vocabulary and assumptions brought to it. This means that as new concepts and ways of viewing competence, learning, motivation, etc. from psychology and other sources are developed, so should there be continual revision of the ways of thinking about the teaching aims and processes to be illuminated. A range of evidence would suggest that such revisions are unlikely to occur quickly, smoothly, or in unison amongst the cross-section of colleagues we operate with in teacher education. But one can at least recognize one's starting point and encourage openness to new perspectives: it is suggested below that the psychology of skill offers some useful contributions towards something of a reconceptualization of some perennial issues in teacher training.

(2)   We hesitate to pursue explicit principles for intelligent educational application of psychological sources if only because those we are inclined to offer seem obvious to us and, given the venerability of the theory-to-practice tradition, lest we appear arrogant in prescribing egg-sucking techniques to our skilled grandparents. Nevertheless, some of the latter seem to have been sucking for some time now without much success and to have rejected some of what they have extracted from the theoretical eggs. To stretch the metaphor even more uncomfortably, what seem to be needed are not so much egg-sucking algorithms as heuristics for selecting one's eggs in the first place.

The most basic, if general, requirement is surely to adopt what one of us (Tomlinson, 1981) has termed an open-critical stance: open to the potential of any particular resource, but critically attentive to the scope, consistency and validity of its message for the aspects of teaching we wish to illuminate. It is perhaps paradoxical, but no less importantly true, that whilst the 'pure discipline' scholar may regard broader reflection as a luxury irrelevant to normal scientific investigation, the applied worker disregards the philosophy and history of his discipline at the peril of naive applications and wasteful reinvention.

This open-critical approach tends to imply an eclectic use of various types of insight, but we may also suggest some tentative *heuristics for an intelligent eclecticism*. We should stress that these are indeed only heuristics, rules of thumb to guide us, other things equal. Given always the need for critical evaluation of what is being considered, we are suggesting that one should:

(a)   Seek the closest match between the units and level of analysis of the psychological theory and the applied issues under consideration: in other words, maximize the degree of relevance on the basis of our existing awareness of the topic/issues in question.

(b) Go for subsuming paradigms. That is, prefer approaches that can take account of other ideas, for example, as sub-aspects or special cases.

(c) Go for recent, dominant paradigms, on the assumption that progress occurs in thinking within a field over time. This criterion may to some extent lead to the satisfying of the previous one.

(d) Insofar as there are competing paradigms, go for particular ideas generated and specific findings replicated across a variety of approaches. Whilst being alert to the possibility that different processes may produce similar products, remember also that similar concepts and phenomena can be dressed up in very different terminological clothing depending on the designer's psychological paradigm: one man's small step may be another's optimal mismatch, one person's stroke another's reinforcement.

(e) Insofar as one encounters competing hypotheses and findings within or across approaches, one should remember the potentially complex, interactive nature of classroom processes: different means may achieve the same outcomes for different pupils or teachers, for the same persons on different occasions, in different settings and subjects, and so forth.

The Psychology of Skill

Where does all this lead us when we look towards psychology in the context of teacher training? The more specific the issue, the less use our broad principles, but at the level of psychological paradigms and schools of thought, we would argue that the situation is relatively clear.

Generations of student teachers have been introduced, however superficially and summarily, to psychological approaches and models of the person associated with behaviourism, gestaltism, even psychoanlysis and 'humanistic' psychology, not to mention psychometrics and the sort of mentalistic cognitive psychology associated with Piaget. It is therefore surprising that the paradigm which has dominated the central experimental domain of academic psychology over the last quarter century (at least in this country) does not yet appear to be presented with the status of a discernible approach in British educational psychology (though its findings do appear under specific topic headings such as perception and memory). We are referring to what may be called the *psychology of information-processing skill* (IPS), sometimes simply called *cognitive psychology*.

Historically, the IPS paradigm came to prominence in this country during and after the second world war, when psychologists turned their attention to the processes underlying skilled human competences in such areas as flying aircraft, using radar tracking apparatus, and the like. The approach was highly experimental but not external in conception; it dealt in hypothetical views or models of 'what was going on inside the head/body' of a skilled operator, but tried to make such models precise and testable through experiment. Following in the steps of Head and Bartlett, the post-war pioneers of the IPS approach were such people as Colin Cherry and Donald Broadbent in Britain and Paul Fitts and George Miller in America. The concepts they employed in their new approach came from the modern information sciences, at first communications engineering and later cybernetics and computer science. Thus at first one had a cognitive or information-processing approach to understanding skilled human performance and its acquisition; but with time an inevitable specialization of focus developed, so that one can now talk of information processing (with respect to, say, visual perception or memory) without reference to skill — though not the other way round (*cf.* Legge and Barber, 1976; Schmidt, 1982).

We would argue that the IPS paradigm satisfies the first three criteria outlined above as selection heuristics, and that it is consistent with the last two. This claim cannot be backed thoroughly in the confines of the present short chapter and there exist a number of introductions to the psychology of skill to which readers may care to refer (for example, Legge and Barber, 1976; Welford, 1968). However, given that our main purpose here is to probe the reflexive implications of psychology for its own possible roles and forms of presentation in teacher education, we do need to briefly indicate the major features of the IPS approach and its twin focuses, namely the nature of skill and its acquisition and the model of the human performer and learner.

Skills (for instance, driving a car or playing tennis) are purposeful activities, effectively executed with apparent ease, speed and smoothness, though on investigation they are seen to typically involve a systematic and coordinated organization of subprocesses: the skilled performer has 'got it all together', 'has timing', and thus achieves his or her goals in ways that are smoothly and flexibly adapted to the contingencies of the situation. The latter may vary considerably in difficulty: in relatively *closed* skills, such as playing snooker, things are more predictable and under the potential control of the performer than in relatively *open* skills such as tennis, driving or horse riding, where many more independent factors require more constant adaptation. Correspondingly, the model (or class of models) of the person which grew out of the study of skill acquisition and performance sees things in relatively non-reductionistic and complex terms: the person is seen as purposive, able to anticipate, perceive, store, recall and manipulate information in generating skilled performances, in which action is adapted to aims and circumstances. But the experimental study of human performance also confirms a number of less obvious features.

One of these is the availability of at least three levels of awareness: focal/conscious attending, pre-attentive/out-of-the-corner-of-the-eye type awareness, and unconscious/subliminal processing (see Tomlinson, [1981] for references). Another is that the focal/conscious form of dealing with information appears to be extremely limited in its capacity and speed, processing events serially, that is, one at a time. These severe limitations on information processing can be alleviated by dealing with more than one incoming event at a time — in parallel but unconsciously — and this seems to be one of the major features and functions of skill acquisition. In skill acquisition, processes which were initially achieved separately through painstaking conscious control gradually become automatized and integrated through suitable practice to a stage of proficiently skilled performance. Here many constituent subprocesses are being achieved in a simultaneous and organized fashion, though with little, if any conscious control. But even after reliably accurate performance capacity is attained, the speed and integration of skilled performance continues to improve gradually, even with relatively simple, closed skills, over many years of practice.

Skill acquisition requires various things, of which repetition or practice is the most well-known. But it is important to stress that there is more to it than simple repetition: skills are not just habits, though they share the feature of automaticity. Rather, skills involve the automatising of relatively flexible adaptations, integrating awareness and action. Especially in the early stages of skill acquisition the performer needs some idea of what to do and what to expect, and, on trying to carry out the relevant action, requires information on the outcome that can be compared with the intention. To be effective, this feedback or knowledge of results needs providing in such a way that it can be related to existing plans for action. This usually means that feedback needs to be relatively direct and immediate.

Before considering educational applications of the IPS approach the critical strand of our open-critical approach obliges us to admit that, like any other, the IPS paradigm has its limitations. For example, motivational considerations are not, in one sense, a central concern of this approach. By this we mean that the IPS school has not tended to focus on the most obvious aspects of motivation from a common sense point of view, namely the range of particular goals and preferences displayed by persons. On the other hand, this approach is highly relevant to an understanding of motivation (in the sense of the regulation of action). After all, skills involve actual activities that are related to goals: the IPS approach sees the person as essentially active and relatively complex. For instance, it yielded early attempts to conceive of action in cybernetic terms (Miller, Galanter and Pribram, 1960), and more recently the psychology of emotion has been framed in cognitive process terms (Mandler, 1975). And this is not to mention recent developments in cognitive social psychology, including theories concerning the attribution of personal causation and the effects of this on action (*cf.* Eiser, 1980). Not only does the IPS approach look compatible with other psychological approaches which might be of use in understanding teaching and teacher training, it may also yield precision and further perspectives to such views. For example, it has been argued that a psychological skill approach can usefully illuminate notions about personal identity and self-esteem, which are such an important aspect of any teaching/learning situation (Tomlinson, 1981, chapter 7).

Certainly the IPS paradigm appears to have relatively wide applicability: it is some time since Sir Frederick Bartlett (1958) showed how thinking itself could be considered as 'higher order intellectual skill' and more recently the field of social skill training has been pioneered and established in this country by Michael Argyle (for example, 1978) and others. Although it is recognized that people may be quite flexible regarding which aspects of a situation they perceive and use, it turns out that the general human tendency is to process events in a relatively concrete way. Thus, for instance, Wason and Johnson-Laird (1972) found that successful performance on deductive reasoning tasks depends largely on the contents of the task as opposed to its logical structure. Skill training and enhancement therefore require an analysis that is not merely *logical*, indicating the various constituent subtasks required in overall performance, but also *psychological*, that is, giving an indication of what the performer must take account of and ways in which they may actually go about this. There may be various ways in which the same item of information can be picked up at a given point in the execution of a skilled process, and there may be various sequences that are useful (different ones, perhaps, for different individuals) for acquiring and integrating the subskills involved in an overall competence (think once more of driving, for instance).

This latter point about flexibility of training approach may deserve some emphasis, given that in educational circles the writer most frequently associated with the term skill is perhaps Robert M. Gagné. In keeping with his behaviouristic background, he tends to stress analysis of skills into component subskills and instructional approaches which build from parts to whole (*cf.* Gagné, 1977). However, whilst the IPS approach recognizes the need to analyse complexity into manageable subunits, it also respects the interplay and integration of such constituents in the overall competence by practising together those subskills that have an interdependence (Stammers and Patrick, 1975).

An even more basic point may bear emphasis at this juncture, since Gagné's approach seems to have contributed to a rather unfortunate notion amongst some educators that to regard something as a skill is to regard it, by definition, as trainable. Various views of skill can be found (*cf.* Stanton, 1982) but there does seem to be a common-sense tendency to make the further assumption that skills are not only trainable, but trainable solely by repetition or practice. It must be stated firmly that IPS psychology makes no such assumption. The situation has rather been that, having chosen to study skilled activities in a scientific way, a relatively precise conception of their nature emerged from experimental investigation, together with an awareness of features which affect the acquisition of such competences. As we have seen, the IPS notions of skilled action and the skilled performer are not one-dimensionally simple and its view of skill acquisition involves more than practice. To construe a given competence from a skills point of view is therefore to look at the nature of the information processing it comprises, what integration of awareness and action, of subskills with each other, are required. This opens up the possibility of enhancing the acquisition of such competence to the extent that one can analyse the skill and apply the basic principles of skill acquisition intelligently to that case. It perhaps needs stating that the more open the skill in question, the more difficult this will be: there are not a few competences we may recognize as skills, but which we are unable to train, even with the aid of IPS analyses — though it may be worth trying.

With these important qualifications, the key features of skill enhancement remain the need to *practise the processing of relevant information* (that is, practise aspects of the actual performance capacity being acquired rather than, say the skills of 'just' talking about it) under *sufficient and close enough guidance* to support the learner's efforts, especially in the early stages, and with as *concrete and direct feedback as can be assimilated* in order to inform further practice correctively. Under such conditions human beings can generally achieve competences so skilled they don't even look as if they have been learned (for example, many social skills, bicycle riding, etc.) and exceptionally they can acquire competences that appear downright impossible to the rest of us (for example, Olympic gymnasts, concert pianists, magicians, etc.). But without guidance and feedback-supported practice, reliable acquisition of complex, open skills such as teaching remains at best a pious hope and at worst a defensive assumption based only on the uncritical performance of classroom habits whose relationship to pupil learning and even to immediate classroom management remains accidental.

What does all this suggest regarding the nature of teacher education and the role of psychology within it? Certainly that there are no simple, magic solutions to perennial problems. The explicit IPS recognition, even in general terms, of the multifaceted nature of typical skilled human action implies that simple, concrete recipes are no answer when it comes to subtle, complex issues such as we find in teaching. Nor might an IPS approach necessarily suggest anything brand new by way of concrete strategy that could not possibly have been discovered from other angles (though the idea of the RAP technique described below was very much stimulated by taking IPS notions into our classroom work). What it can do at least is to offer a range of principles and insights which may guide our thinking about issues in teaching and teacher education, which may yield concrete tactics and which can act as a framework for appraising and enhancing the effectiveness of particular ideas and practices. In what remains, we offer some broad implications of the IPS approach for teacher education and some specific comments on particular issues in this field, some of which are dealt with at more length and depth in other chapters of this volume.

Some Implications for Teacher Preparation

(1) The context of skill learning

Since what we are centrally aiming at in teacher education are *people who can teach effectively in real settings*, then there must be *substantial provision for the acquisition of actual teaching skills through practice in the real settings of school and classroom and in close approximations to such settings* (for example, microteaching). It is essential, however, that we have not only the practising of the actual activities of teaching in context, but that we respect the principles of skill acquisition by *providing suitable guidance and feedback*. Traditional block teaching practice has too often resembled a push into the deep end whose main function appears to be *an assessment* of whatever the student can come up with — rather than a systematic opportunity to acquire teaching competence under suitable circumstances. The growing emphasis on school-based courses, noted earlier, is surely to be welcomed from this viewpoint. These courses have obvious advantages, such as extending the period over which skill acquisition may take place in real settings and enhancing the perceived relevance of the appropriate theoretical offerings from the training institution. However, a 'passive immersion theory of learning' is as inadequate with respect to school-based experience, however long the immersion, as it is to other aspects of instruction: activity, guidance and feedback are also basic requirements. The IPS emphasis on limited human capacity and the complementary selectiveness of active perception and learning is echoed firmly, if, generally in the old teachers' dictum that twenty years' classroom experience can sometimes be the equivalent of one year repeated twenty times, if the conditions of learning from such activity are not met. The feedback and guidance stressed by the IPS approach as necessary for skill acquisition, especially in its early stages, are feedback and guidance for, and therefore adapted to, particular individuals. For however social human nature may be, it is the individual who acquires competence through suitable learning interaction. This means that in comparison to traditional practices, there needs to be considerable personal attention and support for each student teacher, as an individual, whether from training institution tutors, school staff tutors, other colleagues, or preferably all of these in coordination. School-based courses do of course offer tremendous possibilities for this, though we should not pretend that it will not require considerable shifts from traditional stances, roles and resource deployment, both in schools and training institutions. This brings us to a second broad point.

(2) Skills in the trainer

A further emphasis of the IPS approach concerns the *relatively specific nature of competence*. One implication of this is that *skill in teaching pupils cannot be assumed equivalent to skill in teaching teachers to teach pupils*. As we saw above, the IPS paradigm yields important principles and findings regarding the requirements of skill acquisition, which, when applied to teacher education, imply a need for active training in realistic settings such as the school. This reminds us of the current emphasis, noted at the beginning of this chapter, on involving experienced teachers in teacher training at various phases of that process. We are very much in favour of this type of move, but subject to important qualification. There is indeed likely to be much valuable 'craft knowledge' embedded in experienced teachers' skilled activities, as McNamara and Desforges (1979) contend; but, as these authors also say, it needs 'objectification', that is, explicit articulation and critical/empirical assessment as a basis both for general application and communication. Unfortunately, as we pointed out above and as Doyle (1979) also recognizes, IPS research confirms that the more skilled an activity, the more automatised and inaccessible to conscious reflection its constituent processes generally become. Experienced teachers are therefore likely to be better at 'doing teaching' than at 'teaching teaching'. This is surely one of the factors influencing teachers' apparent reticence to involve themselves in the induction of probationary colleagues.

At any event, whilst welcoming recent recommendations that experienced teachers should make a contribution to initial teacher training and assessment, the above points make it clear that simply bringing them into such processes and giving such opportunities is only the beginning, and far from the achievement of the desired effect. If a simple 'learning by immersion' theory is inadequate, then it is also naive to operate on the basis of a 'learning by infection' view, whereby the experience of practising teachers (assuming one can discern the competent ones anyway) somehow transfers naturally to students through more contact between them.

Sooner or later, an adequate and relevant conceptual framework is required for the articulation and effective communication of guidance and feedback in the intelligent training of intelligent teaching skills. We share Doyle's view that IPS notions provide a natural and useful candidate for this function: in our experience, such views seem particularly accessible and welcome to teachers when situated in reflection and analysis of their actual teaching activity.

(3) *Training for skill within strategic classroom interaction*

However, as we stressed earlier, IPS psychology does not *define* skills as trainable, as some current educational usage seems to assume. Still less does it assume that practice is the only important factor in successful training. It seems important to underline this, if only to maintain *an intelligent and balanced approach* to the sorts of classroom-based training we have been arguing for. Specifically, we would wish to head off any attempt to seize on particular teacher actions and train them through drilled repetition in rote fashion as 'good habits': for as we said earlier, skills are flexible competences, not rigid motor habits.

Like any complex skill, teaching involves a hierarchy of constituent and alternative subskills, some of which (for example, constant visual scanning of the classroom, clear speech) seem likely candidates for a simple-but-always-essential category which it would be desirable to establish firmly. But even these are subskills that are never performed in *exactly* the same way on any two occasions and which are not separable (even if they are distinguishable) from the teacher's skilled activity as a whole, which is adapted towards pupils' cooperation and achievement in a constantly varying classroom situation. Thus, on occasion even such generally useful ploys as scanning might be temporarily counterproductive, so that a skilfully adaptive teacher wouldn't be scanning at that point. Indeed, whilst skills psychology would certainly not forget the detail level, it would also recommend attempts to enhance the skilful deployment of relatively complex sorts of teaching *strategy*. These would include not just attempts to *respond* to classroom contingencies but also, as is typical of skills, to *anticipate and strategically influence in advance* the direction of events. Such skills are going to call upon a range of expressions and implementations and the impossibility of 'training' them in a rote-repetition fashion will be obvious even to those who haven't read a word of IPS psychology. They will also require a correspondingly sensitive awareness of broad tendencies and possibilities in classroom, a sensitive 'classroom knowledge', implicit or explicit, as a basis for flexible responding and anticipation.

(4) Towards skilled training: The RAP innovation as illustration

Finally, a range of approaches is possible in the attempt to enhance teaching skills, whether general or specific. Whether in school classroom or training institution microteaching laboratory, one may range from the more open-nondirective style in which the tutor 'follows' the student teacher's activity and intervenes only to the extent that he appears to need it, through various intermediate possibilities, to an opposite extreme which is more directive. In that case one might set up an explicit taxonomy of aspects of teaching skill and organize training around a specific coverage of them. Even here, however, there will be a variety of possible orders of approach: broad strategy gradually differentiated into specific subskills for instance, as opposed to a Gagnéan build-up from the subskill specifics to the broader strategies. Success may well depend, amongst other things, on the personality and preferred teaching style of the tutor, learning style of the student, subject matter being taught, pupils and schools resources involved, to name but a few. The skills approach lends us some relatively clear general principles to apply, but does not yield, or lead us to hope for, the sorts of concrete recipe some people's versions of the term make them expect — or worse, assume. To develop more specific insights into the training of teaching skill, one will have to gain some intelligent experience in precisely that field, as our earlier point about the specific nature of competence implied. This brings us to a final set of remarks concerning such implementations.

Implementing skill acquisition principles in teacher training will sooner or later involve particular *techniques and technologies*. For notwithstanding the qualifications we have just been making, a skills approach does pin us down to respecting the learner's current resources with respect to the skill in question and his limited capacities regarding the acquisition and establishment of the skill. Namely, the guidance offered must be relatively specific and comprehensible, so that it can be related to the activity in question as the trainee perceives and performs it. Likewise, the feedback needs to be relatively direct and immediate, so that it can be related to subsequent efforts via correction of one's previous attempt. Information-processing capacity limitations and human learning characteristics confirm that in most cases not everything can be grasped or learned at once. Thus a process of skill acquisition will take time, even when enhanced by application of the above insights.

Different types of skill allow of varying degrees of difficulty in such application, and some have yielded more enthusiasm than others for investigating the implementation of skills acquisition principles in specific forms of technique. It must be admitted that teaching skills appear to be amongst the more open and difficult areas and that this field has not seen such explicit application of the IPS approach as certain other areas, from which it might learn. One thinks, for instance, of flying instruction, where there has been a great deal of systematic research into traditional aspects of training, such as verbal guidance, as well as experimental evaluation of the use of creative technological innovations like flight simulators, which can reduce the complexity of the eventual task in ways that allow the gradual build-up of subskills. Whilst flying aircraft is in many ways much simpler than classroom teaching, it is nevertheless a relatively open skill and its similarities and contrasts with teaching, along with approaches to its training, may illuminate some possibilities in teacher training.

Thus, for instance, in teacher training the technique of microteaching (for example, McIntyre, MacLeod and Griffiths, 1977) fulfills some of the complexity-reduction functions of the simulator in flying instruction, for microteaching involves teaching small numbers of pupils relatively specific topics over short periods. A videorecording of the teacher's activity provides feedback as a basis for improving the next attempt. Various problems remain, nevertheless. One is that the amount of information to be taken into account even in five minutes of teaching can easily overwhelm human capacities of perception and memory. This implies difficulties that appear specific to communication activities like teaching, which would be 'de-natured' by certain standard approaches to skill enhancement. Further reducing the size of class and the period of time would be getting dangerously far from the competence eventually intended, though this break-down and build-up approach has been used by workers such as Perrott (1982). The other possibility, that of providing more effective guidance, raises the difficulty that one cannot have overt communication to a trainee who is himself engaged in a skill involving overt communication to someone else, without such interruption changing the whole activity and probably disrupting it.

It would appear that the provision of guidance and feedback in enhancement of teaching competence may most usefully rely for directness, concrete specificity and unobtrusiveness on modern audiovisual technology. Once again, though, we must insist that an intelligent use of such technology must be informed by a psychology of skill sensitively applied to classroom realities. Too often, in our experience, the audiovisual experts pay too much attention to the conventions of their medium, whilst on the other hand, too many psychologists in education have kept away from the practicalities of skill enhancement.

Having said this, it must be admitted that videotape recording constitutes a massive advance in the provision of *feedback* (*cf*. McIntyre *et al*, 1977) and one would hope to see its use become more widespread in teacher training. On the other hand, the provision of *guidance and support* has until recently lacked any such efficient and unobtrusive means. Thinking about this problem whilst supervising teaching practice, however, it dawned on us that the audiovisual technology that might fulfill the requirements is the radiomicrophone. For, like any other skill in its early phases of acquisition, teaching requires the novice to remember, think, react to and anticipate more than he or she can hold in mind: guidance before the lesson, even very concrete suggestions just before a ten-minute microteaching session with seven or eight pupils, has a very good chance of getting lost before being implemented, or forgotten after its first and only application. More is going on in the typical classroom than the unskilled novice can consciously process, for by definition such a novice has not yet automatised and economized scanning, classroom circulation, strategic anticipation, let alone forms of flexible reactions that would comprise effective teaching. One needs to be able, therefore, to 'get through directly' to student teachers during their actual teaching activity, but without interrupting or disrupting it.

We have therefore recently been investigating a technique we label *radio-assisted practice* or RAP. This uses miniaturized radio microphones and receivers to enable unobtrusive communication from tutor to student teacher during the latter's actual teaching activity (Smith and Tomlinson, 1984). The preliminary findings confirm our major expectations based on skills psychology, namely that (a) such a technique is indeed *immensely powerful* by virtue of its immediacy and can therefore allow effective concrete support — all our experimental students welcomed it and wanted more — but also that (b) RAP requires considerable *sensitivity and higher-order tutoring skill* precisely by virtue of its power. The obvious need for an effective but economical *vocabulary* for such communication during ongoing teaching also appears to be a very powerful means of introducing the conceptualisation of classroom events and, thereby, at once a bridge to and criterion of relevant theory. Thus the RAP work illustrates the typical contribution of IPS approaches: they provide positive and well-grounded suggestions, together with qualifying principles for intelligent application that will avoid simplistic 'pseudo-remedies'. In the RAP case, a good deal of useful research needs to be undertaken to investigate its strengths and problems in various aspects of teacher training, as well as the sorts of training tutors might need to use it effectively.

This brings us back finally to the role of psychology as taught theory in teacher education. Our consideration of the psychology of skill has led us to emphasize the role of practical initiation as opposed to theoretical instruction. However, to leave the contrast thus formulated would indeed be oversimple. We have underlined the essential role of guidance and feedback in skill acquisition and the fact that the more open the skill, the wider the range of aspects the skilled performer must be able to represent and deploy in flexible manner. The same is doubtless true of the meta-skills of training teachers: as with all skills, one has sooner or later to have some idea of what one is doing, and in this case it includes having a psychology of skill. Thus experienced teachers may have much to bring to the training of student teachers, but the skills of teaching teaching are not quite the skills of teaching subjects or first-order competences, such as mathematics. But this is not to say that a skill-based psychology of instruction needs to be taught abstractly or separately, whether to students, teachers or teachers-turned-trainers. There are a variety of indications that cognitive learning is likely to be enhanced by relating it to the familiar and the meaningful, so that starting from attempts at actual teaching activity, whether in real settings or microteaching sessions, gives a concrete basis and a touch-stone of relevance. And as we pointed out more specific techniques such as the RAP approach require economical communication, including a common vocabulary, and hence a conceptualisation. Here, then, is an opportunity for the teacher-educator to introduce a psychology in an implicit way which will enable him to raise issues and alternatives whose perceived relevance is assured. Not that we are ruling out any sequence other than practice-then-theoretical reflection. Rather, we are saying that across all the varying kinds of sequence and degrees of structure one might utilize in the psychopedagogical component of teacher education there must be practice, with suitable guidance and feedback, there must be reflection and alternative construing, and that crucially, the practice and the construing must never be allowed to stray very far from each other.

References

ARGYLE, M. (1983) *The Psychology of Interpersonal Behaviour,* (4th edition) Harmondsworth, Penguin.

BARTLETT, F.C. (1958) *Thinking: An Experimental and Social Study,* London, Allen and Unwin.

DOYLE, W. (1979) 'Making managerial decisions in the classroom', in DUKE, D. (Ed.) *Classroom Management,* 78th Yearbook of the N.S.E.E., Part 2, Chicago, University of Chicago Press.

EISER, R.L. (1980) *Cognitive Social Psychology,* London, McGraw-Hill.

GAGNÉ, R.M. (1977) *The Conditions of Learning,* (3rd edition) New York, Holt, Rinehart and Winston.

LEGGE, D. and BARBER, P.J. (1976) *Information and Skill,* London, Methuen.

MANDLER, G. (1975) *Mind and Emotion,* New York, Wiley.

MCINTYRE, D., MACLEOD, G. and GRIFFITHS, R. (Eds.) (1977) *Investigations of Microteaching,* London, Croom Helm.

MCNAMARA, D. and DESFORGES, C. (1979) 'The social sciences, teacher education and the objectification of craft knowledge', in BENNETT, N. and

McNamara, D. (Eds.) *Focus on Teaching: Readings in the Observation and Conceptualisation of Teaching*, London, Longman.

Miller, G., Galanter, E. and Pribram, K. (1960) *Plans and the Structure of Behaviour*, New York, Holt, Rinehart and Winston.

Perrott, E. (1982) *Effective Teaching*, London, Longman.

Schmidt, R. (1982) *Motor Control and Learning*, Champaign, Ill., Human Kinesics Publishers.

Smith, R.N. and Tomlinson, P.D. (1984) 'RAP: Radio-assisted practice. Preliminary investigations of a new technique in teacher education,' *Journal of Education for Teaching, 10*, pp. 119–34.

Stammers, R. and Patrick, J. (1975) *The Psychology of Training*, London, Methuen.

Stanton, R. (1982) *Basic Skills*, London, Further Education Curriculum Development Unit.

Tomlinson, P.D. (1981) *Understanding Teaching: Interactive Educational Psychology*, London, McGraw-Hill.

Tomlinson, P.D. (1985) 'Matching teaching and learning: The interactive approach in educational psychology', in Entwistle, N.J. (Ed.) *New Directions in Educational Psychology I*, Lewes, Falmer Press.

Wason, P. and Johnson-Laird, P. (1972) *Psychology of Reasoning*, London, Batsford.

Welford, A.T. (1968) *Fundamentals of Skills*, London, Methuen.

3

Challenges for Teachers and Trainers

Introduction

The four papers in this section are concerned with some of the biggest challenges in teaching. Charles Desforges looks at the problems of truly helping pupils to understand what and how they are learning, problems which are rooted on one hand in approaches to learning and teaching and on the other in classroom conditions. Peter Evans takes a careful look at the issues in teaching slow learners and in so doing shows how they apply in teaching children both with and without special educational needs. David Fontana takes up the challenge of the widely expressed educational aim of promoting the personal development of pupils, and provides echoes of themes in earlier chapters on the student's development as a teacher. Lastly Hazel Francis looks at the challenges of curriculum development which face both the teacher and the trainer and which demand professional collaboration and evaluative attitudes.

Training for the Management of Learning in the Primary School

Charles Desforges
University of East Anglia

This paper is concerned with identifying those aspects of psychology and psychologically based educational research which might be used with teachers and trainees to assist them in improving the management of learning.

Since time is always at a premium in the educational process, the problem of making selections from the vast domain of psychology and psychological based educational research is immediately presented. Much of the paper is therefore concerned with identifying the grounds on which selections might proceed. This entails some appraisal of the teacher's job and of the nature and content of pertinent psychological work.

Psychologists have always had a great deal to say to teachers about how to foster learning (Bain, 1879; Broadbent, 1975; Bruner, 1966; Gagné, 1965; James, 1899; Piaget, 1971; Skinner, 1968; Thorndike, 1913; Wertheimer, 1945). The advice in these texts usually takes the form of descriptions of models of intellectual growth together with prescriptions on how to design ideal environments to enhance progress to higher forms of intellectual processing. Authors of these texts have been confident that their advice was useful, perhaps even essential, to the conduct of the classroom teacher. Lloyd Morgan (1894) for example, was of the opinion that 'many of the practical problems which school life presents cannot be satisfactorily solved except in the light of such truths as the science of mind reveals'. More recently, Gagné and Briggs' (1979) text was intended to 'describe an intellectually consistent basis for practical procedures'.

Whilst advice to teachers has been given with considerable confidence, it has become clear to many authorities that psychology has had little impact on educational practice. Glaser *et al* (1977), for example, observed that. 'At the present time, cognitive psychology's findings and techniques have not significantly influenced teaching practices, instructional processes nor the design of conditions for learning' (p. 495). Ausubel and Robinson (1969) note that despite favourable responses on the part of teachers to psychology courses, 'the behaviour of these same teachers observed later in the classroom, has typically shown distressingly little influence of the principles and theories which they had presumably learned' (p. iii). With specific reference to educational research, Elliot Eisner (1983) has observed in his own School that 'it has become increasingly clear to me that research findings, and even the theories from which they are derived ... hardly ever enter into the educational deliberations of the faculty regardless of the area about which the faculty deliberates ... colleagues in the School of Education say that they use research in their teaching and planning but find it extremely difficult to give any examples of how it is used'. And as a final example of the perceived lack of impact of psychologically based prescriptions for the improvement of teaching, Cockcroft (1982) recognized that '... we are not saying anything which has not already been said many times and over many years' (p. 72). The persistence of the advice is stark evidence of its lack of impact.

If these observations are accepted then producing more of the same kind of advice to teachers is clearly going to be equally unprofitable for them.

There are a number of ways of accounting for this lack of impact. It could be that the basic psychology is unsound — that teachers attempt to use it but find the theories and perspectives to be invalid. It could be that psychologists are simply poor teachers; that material is never taught effectively so it is never used. Alternatively it could be that teachers (including teachers of psychology) are generally idle and prefer to use old habits and uninformed techniques to occupy their pupils or students. Whilst there is probably some element of validity in each of these accounts they seem unconvincing. There are simply too many committed teachers to permit a general account of their performance in terms of a lack of will, reflection or knowledge. It is more likely that psychology is not used in teaching because it is not useable under the circumstances in which teachers operate. Prescriptions for the design of ideal learning environments often contain detailed analyses of the performance limitations of learners but take no account whatsoever of the performance characteristics of teachers. This is akin to designing aeroplanes on sound aerodynamic principles but in ignorance of the forces of gravity. Any attempt to use psychology in teacher education must take serious account of teachers' conditions of work and the nature of their jobs.

Before considering this issue in more detail however, it is important to note that psychologists have learned to be much more cautious
about the status of the knowledge generated in regard to mental life in
general, and teaching and learning in particular. Few psychologists
nowadays would claim to know, 'truths of the science of mind'. On the
contrary, many eminent workers express bitter disappointment with the
fruits of psychological labour (see, for example, Neisser, 1978; Newell,
1974; Dominowski, 1974). With special reference to education we begin
to see what we do not know and to know what has not worked.

This may be illustrated by reference to research on effective
schools. Comparisons of effective and ineffective schools have consistently found schools with similar demographic composition that differ in
pupil achievements. Rowan *et al* (1983) assert that such research 'has
done much to revive the optimism of practitioners, that schools can be
organized to enhance instructional effectiveness'. The same authors,
however, show that research on 'effective schools' has 'several conceptual and methodological shortcomings which call into question its
utility, both as a model for future research, and as a source of findings
that can guide school improvement and practice'. These shortcomings
include (1) measures of effectiveness that ignore the variety of school
goals and hence are selectively invalid; (2) contrasted groups research
designs which show factors which correlate with school effectiveness but
which provide little information about causal relationships among
variables; (3) methods for identifying effective schools are known to be
unstable over short lengths of time. In Rowan *et al*'s own study only ten
per cent of schools could be judged effective for two consecutive years
and only five per cent were effective for three consecutive years. They
conclude, 'selecting a sample of effective schools for a longitudinal study
is extremely difficult'. And yet longitudinal studies would almost
certainly be necessary to develop models of causal relationships and
models of effective change which could guide school improvement.
Thus, on a strict and cautious interpretation of educational research, it
would be dishonest to proffer advice on how to convert an ineffective
school into an effective one. This is but one example of enthusiasm
generated by early research in a field being tempered by caution
emanating from later and more sophisticated research in the same field.

Attempts to apply Piagetian psychology to education have taught
some to be similarly cautious. The early excitement sparked by the
recognition that Piaget's constructivist theory of intellectual development was consistent with strongly held educational ideals, led to the
view that his theory provided a substantive scientific base for the design

of educational programmes and techniques. Work on the development and evaluation of these programmes is vast and proceeding apace. One certain achievement of this work is that it has revealed important gaps in our knowledge in areas crucial to the management and improvement of learning. For example, (1) the relationship between operational development and progress in curriculum subjects is unclear; (2) the effects of familiarity with the content of particular problems on the deployment of cognitive operations are known to be important but are not understood; (3) the processes of transition from task to task or cognitive stage to cognitive stage are not understood; (4) cognitive processes, that is the selection, processing and representation of mental events involved in specific tasks are not known. The point here, is not to dismiss Piaget's work. On the contrary, it is to emphasize what has been learned from the careful use of his work and more importantly, to emphasize what we do not know. Unfortunately what we do not know in this domain looks very much like what a practitioner might need to know in order to optimise learning.

Examples of cautionary tales could be obtained from almost any field of educational research or cognitive psychology as they pertain to classroom learning. Perhaps we have learned that fools rush in where angels fear to tread. Unfortunately, in the business of managing children's learning, someone has to tread. In helping to prepare teachers for this ground, psychologists will have to be somewhat less than angelic. Careful selections however might make them something better than fools.

The Teacher's Job

With particular reference to primary school teaching, the teacher's main impact on children's learning is in the classroom and takes place through the effects of the tasks assigned. Thus, whilst learning is a covert, intellectual process it takes place in a complex social setting.

Recent research (see Doyle, 1983, for a review) has shown, and professional observations (see HMI reports on primary schools) confirm, that a large amount of school work is structured around text books and printed material. Much teachers' demonstration and explanation consists of presenting material contained in text books. Analyses of these commercial materials show that they are often unwittingly complex and confusing (Anderson, Armbruster and Kantor, 1980; Gammon, 1973; MacGinitie, 1976; Beck and McCaslin, 1978). In selecting tasks from such materials, teachers place a strong emphasis on practice (Bennett *et al*, 1984; Durkin, 1981) and a very high level of mismatching between tasks and children's attainments is evident (Anderson, 1981; Bennett *et al*, 1984; Jorgenson, 1978). It appears that, progressive educational philosophies notwithstanding, the teacher's main pedagogic input takes the form of 'chalk and talk'; contact with individuals is minimal and diagnostic work virtually nil. Exchanges between teachers and individual pupils are mainly confusing for the children and frustrating for the teacher (Bennett *et al*, 1984). The teacher's work might best be summarized by Bloom (1976) who observed that 'the teacher appears to spend so much of his effort in managing the students rather than in managing the learning'. It is clear that teachers, at least in reference to children's cognitive life, operate as technicians who merely deploy resources and monitor, usually in very crude terms, learning outcomes.

Whilst these behaviours seem significantly less than ideal, the above account of teaching appears to be so generally valid (Sirotnik, 1983) as to stand in need of explanation rather than condemnation. More to the point here is that this is the task for which teachers must be prepared and be prepared to improve on.

Psychology and Psychologists in Teacher Training

Any attempt to use psychology in this context must proceed in recognition of the limitations of psychological knowledge, of the lack of impact of the past efforts and of the enduring nature of teachers' practices. Additionally, it must be recognized that classrooms are not going to go away. Architectural changes and the introduction of microprocessors notwithstanding, there will always be several children assigned to each adult and these represent the basic parameters of the class. Perhaps one final, but crucial, guiding principle is that the central objective is to assist in the production of a teacher — not a social scientist. Thus the psychologist must engage the student in those activities which help them to do their job.

With these very extensive preliminary comments in mind, attention is now turned to identifying aspects of psychology useable to teachers.

Aspirations and Reality

It would be unfortunate if teachers were allowed to influence children's learning with no more than commonsensical conceptions of what we might aspire to in fostering learning. Psychology has much to say on this matter of aspiration. There is a huge literature on the nature of learning under different conditions. This provides illustrations of imitation, social modelling, rote, invention, construction, discovery, consolidation and practice. Of course this literature is already presented to student teachers. Unfortunately it frequently appears in the form of debates about *the* nature of learning (discovery versus reception for example). However, we are beginning to learn that learning is multi-faceted; that learning can and does take all these forms and that each form has a role to play in the development of intellect and the acquisition of knowledge. An alternative current mode of presenting versions of the work of, for example, Bruner, Piaget or Skinner, is as models of classroom technologies practicable under everyday conditions. This they are not; and when students find out they are not they discredit psychology and those who teach it. Such literature however, can provide case study materials showing the power of particular environments to produce particular attainments. This work would not help the teacher in the immediate conduct of the job. Its purpose rather would be to help form conceptions of what the job might become.

These aspirations ought immediately to be contrasted with the picture, developed from psychological research, of contemporary classroom realities and attempts to understand them. Again, a large amount of contemporary work is available for selection (see for example, Doyle, 1983; Desforges *et al* 1985; Bennett *et al*, 1984; Jackson, 1968; Woods, 1980). Much is now known about how teachers and pupils adapt to classroom life and students may be provoked to contrast these realities with aspirations and examine the problems thereby posed.

Clearly this contemplation might again not be useful in the direct conduct of teaching. Indeed such reflection might be counterproductive to the job. It is introduced here on the precept that there is more to doing some jobs than doing the job.

The Technician in the Classroom

It was suggested earlier that teachers manage learners rather than learning: they deploy resources, monitor their use and assess products in very basic ways. Whilst these activities may not be sufficient to the conduct of the management of learning they are certainly necessary. Psychology has a role to play in ensuring that these activities are undertaken in the most effective manner possible.

Psychologists have considerable expertise in the design of assessment instruments and an important component of teacher training should be the development of skills in the design of criterion referenced and tailored tests together with the inculcation of skills pertinent to the interpretation of such tests.

The most common mode of teaching seems to be direct instruction. As suggested earlier, this typically takes the form of demonstrations of procedures and algorithms and arrangements for their practice on set piece tasks. Whilst direct instruction is known to have serious limitations on the development of higher order learning (see Doyle, 1983, for a review) it is not without merit (Resnick and Ford, 1981) and can be done to better or worse degrees. The student can be taught how to present model lessons, demonstrations and exercises which capitalize on the advantages and minimize the disadvantages of this mode of teaching. It must be emphasized here that the literature on the effects of direct instruction is of little use to the classroom technician. Rather, mentors should use their knowledge of the literature to assist the student to gain basic skills in teaching. This entails psychologists teaching students how to design pertinent and particular lessons and tasks rather than giving advice in the form of general principles.

The business of managing learners would also be enhanced if teachers were introduced to and made adept at behavioural techniques. Frequent use of such techniques in the normal classroom might call into question the quality of the teacher's provision, but all teachers need a repertoire of emergency skills of which behavioural techniques seem the most well founded in psychology (Wheldall and Merrett, 1984).

The Technologist in the Classroom

A highly prized aim for pupils in schools is that we equip them to be rationally autonomous. There can be no less an aim for student teachers at whatever their level of professional development. If direct instruction in basic skills produces automata in children it is likely to have the same effect on student teachers. To go beyond these limitations as teachers must be equipped to understand children's learning in their own classrooms to diagnose their misconceptions, identify zones of development and comprehend their own impact on pupils' cognition. If they are to use commercial materials as an important source of tasks they must be able to identify confusing or redundant aspects of those materials and to design alternatives. This is a very tall order indeed, since it requires that the teacher understands what actually goes on in the name of learning in the classroom and can design alternative forms of behaviour to move this closer to aspirations. This notion has been described as the 'self monitoring teacher' and, conscious of the demands of accountability, many local education authorities have developed check-lists to aid their teachers in this form of development. Examination of these check-lists reveals that they have an *ad hoc* nature and are huge in scope. The check-lists appear to be catalogues of good intentions and are unlikely to contribute to the development of serious professional thinking: more to the point here, is that they contain no evident psychological perspective.

Making a psychological contribution immediately presents a serious problem. In many important respects, what goes on in the name of school learning is largely unknown (Desforges, 1982). We are thus, with our students, at the frontiers of knowledge. Whilst in recent years a number of social scientists have made interesting contributions to understanding teachers' classroom behaviour (Jackson, 1968; Smith and Geoffrey, 1968; Doyle, 1979; Woods, 1980) the utility of this work to teachers is limited in several respects. First the work is framed in theoretical perspectives drawn from sources other than the classroom. Secondly, the emphasis is on the social exchanges in the classroom rather than dealing, in any detail, with cognitive content. Finally, results and explanations in this research are, necessarily, set out as general propositions. In contrast teachers have to operate in the context of particular events. For these reasons, merely informing teachers of this work would be as futile as informing them of the work of Piaget or of the literature on time-on-task.

The particularity of the teacher's work emphasizes the fact that what teachers must be brought to understand are the cognitions of their pupils and their impact on them. It appears that teachers know very little indeed about children's confusions, about how they interpret tasks and about their strategies for tackling assigned work (Jackson, 1968; Bennett *et al*, 1984). In the latter study it was observed that teachers frequently knew when children were confused but they rarely knew precisely where the confusion lay. In one instance, for example, a child was given some shopping problems to work on. The teacher intended her to look up the prices of items on a work card, to work out how much she had spent on buying one or two items and to calculate her change from a given amount. The problems involved prices including half pence. The child was obviously very confused and got all the problems wrong. She seemed unable to read the price cards, added up prices wrongly and appeared unable to calculate the change. She used plastic money to help her and worked only with half pence coins. At one stage she had forty-five of these on her desk. The teacher recognized the child was in trouble and assumed that she did not know what the word 'change' meant. Later, in an interview between the child and a research worker it was established that the girl could read the prices, that she could add up quantities and that she could work out change. The problem was that she had assumed that everything had to be done in half pence coins and the sheer load on her attention in dealing with the large quantities involved led her into wholesale confusions. The girl had made this assumption, it seemed, because on the two previous days she had indeed had to work converting pence to half pence and had been told to use only half pence coins. Evidently she had carried this instruction over. These misinterpretations were found by Bennett *et al* to be commonplace and almost wholly unrecognized by the teachers. Similarly, children's strategies for working tasks were found to be beyond the teachers' ken. For example, one teacher gave a child tasks intended to provide practice in the concept of 'ten'. Sums of the type: 15 + 16 were set out on a work card. The child in question laid out fifteen counters and sixteen counters and then counted the lot. This strategy did not involve any use of the concept of ten and subsequent questioning showed that the child had little grasp of this concept. The child's strategy, unbeknown to the teacher, was subverting her intentions for the task. Under the conditions in which teachers work their blind spots are hardly surprising.

To improve on this situation, the teacher must be equipped to deal with particular cases. Clearly, in this respect, detailed knowledge of curriculum content is essential but not sufficient to ameliorate children's problems and capitalize on their strengths. Teachers must be taught how to explore children's interpretations of classroom materials as they are used in classrooms.

Until fairly recently psychologists knew very little about these matters. A great deal was known about performances on particular tasks as presented under laboratory conditions. But even these performances were not well understood — witness the persistent re-interpretation of performance on Piagetian tasks for example. More recently however, detailed studies of children's classroom learning are beginning to emerge.

The first steps in this direction took the form of attempts to examine children's performance on typical classroom tasks. The work of Driver (1982) and of Hart (1981) working on the CSMS project are examples of this sort of work. Detailed analyses of responses to APU tests offer opportunities to observe children's typical performances and common errors and offer some hypotheses for understanding these misconceptions.

However, these studies do not face up to the complexities of classroom learning and cannot indicate the origins of children's misconceptions. More valuable studies which analyse children's strategies for dealing with teachers' tasks as they operate in situ are now available. One can quote, for example, the work of Francis (1982) on children's reading, Baroody and Ginsburg (1982) and Erlwanger (1975) on coping with maths tasks, and an examination of the presentations at recent AERA conferences show such work to be rapidly developing.

It is amongst this work that psychologists will find their closest correspondence to the teacher's job. They will also find the intellectual and empirical tools to help teachers improve their professional practice. It is not being suggested that this literature be taught as such (although it could be argued that young teachers would gain more from reading Erlwanger than reading Piaget). Rather, it is suggested that in this literature psychologists show that they have learned a lot about how to tease out children's thinking and learning strategies in the complex circumstances of the classroom and it is these lessons which teachers must learn if they are to manage learning.

To summarize this section it has been suggested that recent literature on children's classroom learning could be used as a quarry of ideas from which psychologists could design tasks for student teachers. These tasks would be aimed at directing the students towards increasing their capacity to understand children's responses to learning tasks. The student would be taught skills (mainly of the form described as 'clinical interviewing' or 'critical exploration') and would not necessarily be directed to read the material referred to above.

The Social Organization of Learners and Learning

The previous sections have focused on interactions between teachers and individual children. However, it was recognized earlier that the classroom is a complex social organization and it has been shown that this has important consequences for managing learning. These factors pose at least two major types of problem for the teacher. First, how to manage the class to permit time to interact with individual children? Secondly, how do interactions in the class as such operate on learning and how can one manage these to optimize the quality of the learning environment?

In order to maximize their time with individual children teachers must learn to solve the problem of profitably organizing the rest of the class. Whilst there is a number of well known ways of approaching this problem (for example, using groups, using parents, peers or other aides) what works in a particular instance depends so much on particularities. Most teachers appear to learn holding-behaviours (in other words, means of occupying some children) but, as suggested already, these are less than profitable for all concerned. And psychology appears to have little more to offer here. Examination of research on learning in groups reveals general conclusions which are no more than commonsense (Webb, 1982). The results merely set out alternative forms of action. Once again the teacher is placed at the frontiers of knowledge. So little is known about how groups work in the absence of teachers or of what children learn in these settings. It is one thing to exhort teachers to allow children group discussions on, for example, maths problems (*cf*. Cockcroft, 1982), it is another thing to be convincing about what children get out of these situations. Indeed some of the latest US research is only just beginning to frame key questions and useable perspectives in this respect (Noddings *et al*, 1983; Easley and Easley, 1983). Noddings for example, asks 'What do individuals gain in small groups mathematical problem solving?' She observed that 'A major problem for researchers interested in the development of individual intellect through small group processes is *quite what to look at*'. If that is where we are at, there seems to be little, as yet, to say to teachers; except, that is, to pose this very important question and to attempt, with them, to answer it.

The implication here, as in earlier sections, is that the substantive psychological literature in this area will not help the teacher to do the job. What will help is to learn to pose classroom relevent questions and to acquire or invent the skills necessary to answer them.

Quite apart from the teachers' deliberate efforts to group children to particular ends, it is now well known that classroom social processes have considerable influence on pupils' learning (Doyle, 1983). In particular, social interactions in the classrooms are used by children to help them identify what the teacher rewards and hence what they will strive to deliver. On the other hand Doyle notes that '. . . performance on tasks is often evaluated publicly (and) teachers are often under pressure to adjust standards and pace to the level at which most students can accomplish tasks' (1983, p. 186). Thus pupils and teachers reciprocally interact to define important characteristics of work in the classroom. The general lesson from this is that teachers must learn how these subtle accountability processes work and to 'handle them creatively' (Doyle, 1983, p. 186). Easily said, this, not easily done. The social negotiation of work pace and standards is a crucial issue in the management of learning. Yet, as with other issues, psychologists have, as yet, little concrete to offer. The role of the psychologist thus lies not in presenting pertinent literature but in providing the student with the skills necessary to observe these processes in her own classroom and, in conjunction with their students, to develop and monitor the effect of productive alternatives.

Summary

In training teachers to manage learning the very difficult nature of the teacher's work must be acknowledged. Additionally, the limitations of knowledge generated by psychological research must be recognized.

A skill rather than knowledge curriculum should be developed to focus first on identifying problems and issues related to learning and the teacher's impact on these; secondly to gain detailed knowledge precisely specifying problems and thirdly to generate suitable teaching behaviours to ameliorate the problems.

Teachers would thus be trained to be creators rather than consumers of pedagogic knowledge with particular reference to their own classrooms. In this work psychologists have an exciting role to play. Whilst there appears to be little useable substantive psychological knowledge to transmit, psychologists have made considerable progress in identifying key questions, developing classroom relevant perspectives and generating a corpus of skills pertinent to the task in hand. The way ahead seems to be for psychologists and teachers to work in conjunction in a form of research based teacher education.

References

ANDERSON, L.M. (1981) 'Student responses to seatwork: implications for the study of students' cognitive processing', Paper presented to AERA, Los Angeles.

ANDERSON, T.H., ARMBRUSTER, B.B. and KANTOR, R.N. (1980) *How Clearly Written are Children's Textbooks?*, Urbana, Centre for the study of reading, University of Illinois.

AUSUBEL, D.P. and ROBINSON, R.G. (1969) *School Learning: An Introduction to Educational Psychology*, New York, Holt, Rinehart and Winston.

BAIN, A. (1879) *Education as a Science*, London, Kegan Paul.

BAROODY, A.J. and GINSBURG, H.P. (1982) 'The effect of instruction on children's understanding of the "equals" sign, Paper presented to AERA, New York.

BECK, I.L. and McCASLIN, E.S. (1978) 'An analysis of dimensions that affect the development of code breaking ability in eight beginning reading programmes', Pittsburgh, Pa., Learning Research and Development Centre, University of Pittsburgh.

BENNETT, S.N., DESFORGES, C., COCKBURN, A.D., WILKINSON, B. (1984) *The Quality of Pupil Learning Experience*, London, Lawrence Erlbaum Associates.

BLOOM, B.S. (1976) *Human Characteristics and School Learning*, New York, McGraw Hill.

BROADBENT, D.E. (1975) 'Cognitive psychology and education', *British Journal of Educational Psychology*, 45, pp. 162–76.

BRUNER, J. (1966) *Toward a Theory of Instruction*, Cambridge, Harvard University Press.

COCKCROFT, W.H. (1982) *Mathematics Counts*, Report of the Committee of Inquiry into the Teaching of Mathematics in Schools, London, HMSO.

DESFORGES, C. (1982) 'In place of Piaget: recent research on children's learning', *Educational Analysis*, 4, 2, pp. 27–42.

DESFORGES, C., COCKBURN, A.D., BENNETT, S. and WILKINSON, W. (1985) 'Understanding the quality of pupil learning experience,' in ENTWISTLE, N.J. (Ed.) *New Directions in Educational Psychology*, London, Falmer Press.

DOMINOWSKI, R.L. (1974) 'How do people discover concepts', in SOLSO, R.L. (Ed.) *Theories in Cognitive Psychology*, Chicago, Loyola University.

DOYLE, W. (1979) 'Making managerial decisions in classrooms', in DUKE, D.L. (Ed.) *Classroom Management*, Chicago, University of Chicago Press.

DOYLE, W. (1983) 'Academic work', *Review of Educational Research*, 53, 2, pp. 159–99.

DRIVER, R. (1982) 'Children's learning in science', *Educational Analysis*, 4, 2, pp. 69–79.

DURKIN, D. (1981) 'Reading comprehension instruction in five basal reader series', *Reading Research Quarterly*, 16, pp. 515–44.

EASLEY, J. and EASLEY, E. (1983) 'Group learning in a Japanese school and the American ideal of individualism', Paper presented to AERA, Montreal.

EISNER, E. (1983) 'Can educational research inform educational practice?' Paper presented to AERA, Montreal.

ERLWANGER, S. (1975) 'Case studies of children's conceptions of mathematics', *Journal of Children's Mathematical Behaviour*, 1, p. 157.

FRANCIS, H. (1982) *Learning to Read: Literate Behaviour and Orthographic Knowledge*, London, Allen and Unwin.

GAGNÉ, R.M. (1965) *The Conditions of Learning*, New York, Holt, Rinehart and Winston.

GAGNÉ, R.M. and BRIGGS, L.J. (1979) *Principles of Instructional Design*, New York, Holt, Rinehart and Winston.

GAMMON, E.M. (1973) 'Syntactical analysis of some first grade readers', in HINTIKKA, K.J.J. *et al* (Eds.) *Approaches to Natural Language*, Dordrecht, Holland, Reidel.

GLASER, R., PELLEGRINO, J.W. and LESGOLD, A.M. (1977) 'Some directions for a cognitive psychology of instruction', in LESGOLD, A.M. *et al* (Eds.) *Cognitive Psychology and Instruction*, New York, Plenum Press.

HART, K.M. (1981) *Children's Understanding of Mathematics: 11–16*, London, Murray.

JACKSON, P. (1968) *Life in Classrooms*, New York, Holt, Rinehart and Winston.

JAMES, W. (1899) *Talks to Teachers on Psychology: And to Students on Some of Life's Ideals*, London, Longmans.

JORGENSON, G.W. (1978) 'Student ability-matieral difficulty matching: relationship to classroom behaviour', Paper presented to AERA, Toronto.

MacGINITIE, W.H. (1976) 'Difficulty with logical operations', *The Reading Teacher*, 29, pp. 371–5.

MORGAN, C. LLOYD (1894) *Psychology for Teachers*, London, Arnold.

NEISSER, U. (1978) 'Memory: what are the important questions?' in GRUNEBERG, M.M., MORRIS, P.E. and SYKES, R.N. (Eds.) *Practical Aspects of Memory*, London, Academic Press.

NEWELL, A. (1974) 'You can't play twenty questions with nature and win', in CHASE, W.G. (Ed.) *Visual Information Processing*, New York, Academic Press.

NODDINGS, N., GILBERT, K. and LEITZ, S. (1983) 'What do individuals gain in small group mathematical problem solving?' Paper presented to AERA, Montreal.

PIAGET, J. (1971) *Science of Education and the Psychology of the Child*, London, Longmans.

RESNICK, L.B. and FORD, W.W. (1981) *The Psychology of Mathematics for Instruction*, Hillsdale, N.J., Lawrence Erlbaum Associates.

ROWAN, B., BOSSERT, S.T. and DWYER, D.C. (1983) 'Research on effective schools: a cautionary note', *Educational Researcher*, 12, 4, April, pp. 24–31.

SIROTNIK, D.A. (1983) 'What you see is what you get — consistency, persistency and mediocrity in classrooms', *Harvard Educational Review*, 53, 1, pp. 16–31.

SKINNER, B.F. (1968) *The Technology of Teaching*, Englewood Cliffs, N.J., Prentice Hall.

SMITH, L.M. and GEOFFREY, W. (1968) *The Complexities of an Urban Classroom*, New York, Holt, Rinehart and Winston.

THORNDIKE, E.L. (1913) *Educational Psychology*, New York, Columbia University.

WEBB, N.M. (1982) 'Student Interaction and Learning in Small Groups', *Review of Educational Research* 52, 3, pp. 421–45.

WERTHEIMER, M. (1945) *Productive Thinking*, New York, Harper.

WHELDALL, K. and MERRETT, F. (1985) 'Training teachers to be more positive: the behavioural approach'. In BENNETT, N. and DESFORGES, C. (Eds.) *Recent Advances in Classroom Research*, Monograph of the British Journal of Educational Psychology.

Charles Desforges

Woods, P. (Ed.) (1980) *Teachers Strategies,* London, Croom Helm.

Woods, P. (1984) 'Pupil strategies', in Bennett, N. and Desforges, C. (Eds.) *Recent Advances in Classroom Research,* Monograph of the British Journal of Educational Psychology.

Psychology and Special Educational Needs: Pygmalion Revisited

Peter Evans
University of London Institute of Education

This chapter is concerned with the role of aspects of psychology in the education of children with special educational needs and its significance in the training/education of teachers. On considering this chapter in the light of other chapters in this volume it will, I hope, become clear that there is no great divide between the general approaches that have been taken by the various authors. Certain references and quotes may be taken from the context of chapters concerned in the main with non-handicapped children and incorporated quite happily into this one doing no violence to them in the relocation. That this is possible is indicative of the consistency that psychology can bring to thinking concerned with the education and development of children and it makes the introduction of the first point that must be made that much easier.

Understanding the Nature of Special Educational Needs

The title of this chapter incorporates the term special educational needs and one might be forgiven for concluding that there are two categories of provision that must be distinguished, namely education and special education. This view must be dispelled immediately in favour of the notion of a continuity of educational needs that are presented by children in schools. They may be presented by any children at any particular time in their years at school and while the term special education has, in the UK, typically been used to refer to those experiences especially provided for children with perceived problems in learning, this is not true of all countries; and in the USA for instance the term is often used to include gifted children. It is important to stress at the outset that, just as all education is concerned with providing access to a preferred curriculum, special education is concerned with providing access to the same curriculum with the same overall goals but modified in the light of the nature of the problems. These modifications will vary to an extent commensurate with the nature and severity of the difficulties but require knowledge, sensitivity and flexibility on the part of the teacher and an adaptable policy on the part of the school as an organization. The required adjustments may be quite trivial (for the teacher but not for the child) such as making sure that children with hearing loss can hear the teacher and other pupils, or more substantial involving careful consideration of curriculum adaptation, teaching method and classroom organization.

Just recently, with the implementation in 1983 of the Education Act (1981) this notion of continuity of special educational needs (SEN) has been given legislative approval with the recognition that the existence of SEN cannot be isolated from the provision supplied. Thus with regard to children who are of school age special educational needs are defined as follows:-

A child has 'special educational needs' if he or she has a learning difficulty which calls for special educational provision to be made.

Learning difficulty exists if a child:
(a) has a significantly greater difficulty in learning than the majority of children of the same age; or
(b) has a disability which either prevents or hinders him or her from making use of educational facilities of a kind generally provided in schools within the area of the local authority concerned, for children of the same age; ...

In the process this legislation eliminates the previous categories of children (for example, maladjusted, educationally subnormal, partially sighted etc.) with the recognition that the identification of a child's apparently primary handicap cannot be used meaningfully to describe fully an appropriate education for that child. This view develops quite naturally and consistently from recent changes in the conceptualisation of children with SEN from one which emphasized within child factors as being the major 'cause' of educational problems to a more psychologically developmental model emphasizing the interaction between the child and the environment over time. This point will be elaborated further at a later juncture.

Given the diversity of the nature of human beings, families, education systems, the environment in which we live, our cultural beliefs etc., and accepting the interactive model referred to above, it would probably come as no surprise to discover that the estimates of the proportion of children who require special education are quite large and are usually considered to be in the region of fifteen to twenty per cent of school aged children (Warnock, 1978). These figures are not exceptional and they agree quite well with estimates from other Western countries. Since only about two per cent of children with SEN are in special schools the figures make the point that all teachers at both primary and secondary levels of education will come across some children who will have SEN for some, if not all, of their school experience. Recently in recognition of this the DES committee on the supply and education of teachers (ACSET) have taken the unprecedented step of recommending that all teachers in initial training must compulsorily have some component of their course which covers SEN.

In what ways, then, can a knowledge and application of psychology and its methods prove useful to teachers and trainee teachers both in conceptualising and attacking the problem? There are three pieces of general advice that span several hundred years that have always impressed me and which are quite central and should serve to focus our thinking. The first is the famous dictum of John Adams, (Adams, 1897) which is also remarked by Margaret Sutherland in this volume, and that is 'if you want to teach John latin then you need to know both John and latin'. The second is the equally famous tenet of Ausubel: 'if I had to reduce all educational psychology to a single principle I would say ascertain what the child already knows and teach him accordingly' (Ausubel, 1968), that is, know John and John's knowledge of latin better. The third piece of wisdom is probably less well known but comes from no less an authority than Richard Lovell Edgeworth of the Birmingham Lunar Society (a society founded at the end of the 18th century for philosophical discussion and technological innovation, which had members such as Erasmus Darwin, James Watt and Joseph Priestley). Edgeworth, who was also a close friend of Rousseau, argued that education should be based on an understanding of the child's mind and should be treated as an experimental science in which conversation was noted down and analyzed (Edgeworth and Edgeworth, 1798).

Taken together these views stress that teachers should know the children they teach, their personal idiosyncrasies and their knowledge of the areas that are to be learned; and the last view in particular advises us that this should be achieved through close observation and analysis of one aspect, at least, of the child's behaviour. This last point immediately raises the question of which behaviours should be observed and, since it is not possible to observe all of them, some choice is required. Since it is the teacher who is most involved then he or she must make a decision about what to look for first, and this of course necessarily requires, albeit implicitly, that the teacher entertains some hypotheses concerning particular children and their learning. One of the first priorities of teacher training, therefore, is to develop awareness in trainee teachers that they do hold ideas and attitudes about what children are like and how they learn, and that these views will influence the judgments they make concerning the interpretation of their pupils' learning and behaviour. It is, therefore, essential that these hypotheses or attitudes become educated by what we know about the processes involved in learning and the influences which affect behaviour, so that the judgments that teachers make may become as objective and constructive as possible.

In the area of SEN the importance of the accuracy of these observations and the insight which may follow cannot be underemphasized since the educational decisions which follow, and which may have long lasting effects on the child, will be based very largely on the expressed views of the teacher based on his or her observations and experience of the child.

The behaviours that are most likely to alert teachers to the fact that there may be problems fall into two rather different categories. The first might be reflected as poor classroom behaviour, and could take the form of either overly disruptive or excessively taciturn or sullen behaviour, while the second is manifested in the children's *lack* of learning vis à vis their classroom peers. Thus these two major sets of problems present two sets of issues. The first group may be perfectly capable of learning but seem to want to do anything else while the second group may appear reasonably well adapted but have real difficulties in learning anything substantial. Both problems may of course occur together and by the time the children reach secondary school age the two problems may be so inextricably linked that it becomes a difficult if not impossible task to sort out which is the 'cause' of the other, and from the point of view of the class teacher such an attempt may be totally futile. What is needed, then, is the identification of current difficulties in the form of a model which implies practical action, not a seeking of obscure origins.

Returning now to the question of the interactive developmental model of SEN, Wedell (1980) has proposed a useful conceptualisation of the issues in terms of a compensatory interaction model. This model analyzes the progress of the child by weighing the balance of resources and deficiencies of the child against the balance of resources and deficiencies in the environment that the child experiences, for example, quality of parenting, organization of the school. This balance is experienced by the child over the course of development and its natural corollary, that of time. Good progress is achieved with good resources of both child and environment experienced over time. Poor child but good environmental resources, good child resources with poor environmental resources, and poor child and poor environmental resources continued over time, all lead to uncertain progress, with the largest proportion of children who will appear to teachers as being in need of special education being included in the last of the three conditions. Thus whether they are seen to have special needs or not will depend largely on the quality of the environment which is provided over the duration of the child's schooling.

The model presented above emphasizes the transaction between the child and the environment over time, and this in principle supports the idea of SEN being both a relativistic concept as reflected in the 1981 Education Act, where learning difficulties are identified relative to the child's peers and in consideration of the current curriculum, as well as one which stresses the notion of a continuum between children who may be considered to have SEN and those who may not. The extent to which extra resources need to be marshalled (and thus special provision needs to be made) depends at least as much on what the school is already offering as it does on the kind of problems that the child is currently presenting. Teachers who are well geared up to making the appropriate curriculum delivery adjustments as soon as they identify the need are automatically providing teaching which in another school with a different ethos or from another teacher who is less adaptable might require special provision to be made.

The transactional model therefore places great emphasis on the role of the child's teachers in the amelioration, and indeed causation, of any difficulties that the child might be having and this in turn requires that the teachers can identify and accurately assess difficulties when they arise, and crucially that, as a result of the assessment, appropriate teaching follows, It is exactly these skills which require development in trainee teachers, as well as in those with more experience.

Identification and Assessment — Understanding the Teacher's Role

The identification and subsequent accurate assessment of children who require additional help is obviously a key issue and in this regard teachers in classrooms make up the thin red line and are the people who have to come to decisions, not only about when to provide extra help themselves for children, but also about when and where to go for assistance. That is to say they must recognize when their competence to deal with certain problems is exceeded. In order to cope with this issue adequately teachers must feel confident about what they can and can't manage and feel relaxed and unthreatened about seeking advice. Individual teachers are going to sit in different positions at this particular crossroad and the particular decision that is made will depend on a complex array of factors that are partly to do with the personality and particular skills and interests of the teacher and partly to do with the school organization in which the individual is working and the support system that is provided both within the school and the LEA. The learning of skills that develop self-awareness and confidence and the ability to cope with large organizations are clearly areas in the psychological domain which are crucial for all concerned.

However, to return to the question of the identification and assessment of children with SEN that is relevant to the classroom teacher, it is necessary to re-introduce the important point discussed earlier of the continuity between children with special needs and those without when viewed in the light of a compensatory interaction (CI) model. Teachers represent the main medium through which children have access to the curriculum and the continuity notion implies that the greater the child's difficulties then the greater the role the teacher must play in providing access to the curriculum for that child; the teacher has to know John and latin that much better. However, this immediately raises questions concerning how and in what ways are John and latin to be better understood and this is an issue to be addressed in a later section.

The CI model with its emphasis on the child's environment does not only include the school environment but also the wider social experiences that the child is having. The involvement of parents in the education of children with SEN has proved to be extremely effective, and parents are becoming increasingly more involved in discussions concerning the education of their children. Because of this teachers are having to consider more closely their own position in involving parents not only in the personal development of their children but also in their education. Thus there is an increasing need for such teachers to be developing counselling skills that will enable them to interact effectively with parents towards mutually agreed goals.

In the next sections some of the issues raised above are elaborated more fully. They are discussed for convenience under the headings of problems with learning and problems with behaviour although it has already been intimated that the two areas may well be closely related.

Problems in Learning

There are three significant questions that are frequently asked concerning problems in learning. Why is the child not learning? What form does this not learning take? What can I do about it? All of these questions contain key psychological issues relating to for example, learning, cognition, motivation, conation, emotion etc., which may relate to the child's confidence, his or her learning styles, the knowledge he or she brings to the situation and so on. The problems presented are complex but not immutable, and a suitable and adequate response from a school cannot be simple. It will have to involve the school in a consideration of its organization and general aims so that all of its pupils may benefit to their furthest extent. Moreover any reorganization is bound to involve the classroom teacher, who will also have to reconsider both the general and specific aspects of his or her classroom work.

Thus, in my view, there are two distinct but complementary approaches that must be taken in considering answers to the questions raised above and that may be seen as a rather simplified version of the ecological/systems approach advocated by, amongst others, Bronfenbrenner, (1977) and Apter, (1982). The first is a top down analysis which raises questions relating to such issues as the examination structure, the content of the curriculum, and the method of its presentation, in rather general terms. For example, presentation in modular form with summative assessments at the end of short modules may be contrasted with the more usual format of examinations at the end of a one or even two year course of learning. With particular reference to the less able child it has recently been proposed that the assessments should take the form of profiles which present the child's achievements in a positive light across a wide range of curriculum areas. The organization of the school and how teachers are distributed within it are also significant issues which bear on such questions as maintaining continuity across years and teachers and the value of team teaching in contrast to teachers operating in isolation. Adequate consideration and adjustment of these factors may enable the resources of the school to be marshalled in the most effective manner. The implementation of such a plan has of course psychological dimensions, for example concerned with management strategy; but these will not be elaborated here since this is not the central theme of this chapter, but aspects of this problem are discussed by Norwich in this volume. It goes without saying, however, that to have contented and motivated teachers and pupils it is necessary to have the appropriate organizational structure with clear aims and objectives as well as a commensurate reward system.

The second approach to the questions raised above is from the bottom up. Here I focus on the classroom and how the individual teacher is going to tackle the problems that arise. This may be achieved by emphasizing the analysis of what it is that is slowing down the child's learning and, by implication, what measures may be taken. In order for theory and practice to relate to each other it is also useful if the analysis is made in terms of variables that the teacher can in fact manipulate in order to bring about successful learning.

However, before developing this aspect further, there is another issue which is of particular relevance to children with SEN. Not all curriculum areas are of the same type. Some, like geography or history, introduce children to bodies of knowledge, to facts and issues and ways of thinking about these areas of knowledge. To some extent they may be considered to be rather arbitrary, but nevertheless they introduce the child's mind to certain cultural beliefs which are well reinforced and rehearsed and take on a certain naturalness as they become common sense. However, there may be less of a sense in which these areas are basic or for which there is an inherent aptitude. As Thorndike (1982) has put it, in the language of trait theory, there is something strange in the idea of a 'trait of history ability'.

Other areas of the curriculum may not be seen quite in this way: language for example is one. It has been argued that there are innate propensities for the acquisition of language (for example, Lenneberg 1967). Music is another candidate. How does one account for the precocious skills of Mozart or for the idiot savant who can reproduce any piece of music after one or two presentations but cannot reproduce sentences given to him in his own native language (Sloboda *et al.*, 1985)? To what extent is text recognition a natural and sophisticated development of the visual perceptual system, and to what extent is reading an integration of this and language development allied with a comprehension of the environment? These last curriculum areas are representative of those which depend heavily on the interplay between psychological ability and educational experiences, and the slow development of these areas raises questions that by their very nature have psychological implications. Furthermore language and reading, for example, are areas of the curriculum with which children with SEN very often have significant problems. Because of their generality and wide significance across the curriculum an understanding of the processes involved is absolutely fundamental for all teachers. So in understanding John and latin teachers must in the context of reading, for example, understand the many ways in which reading can develop, understand the approach that John is taking and how that fits into the overall goal of the development of reading skills. Finally of course they must understand where John is on this trail. This last point makes reference to Ausubel's principle mentioned earlier, while to understand the approach that John is taking requires the teacher to listen closely to his reading or language skills, thus assessing his ability and level of understanding and teaching in the mode advocated by Edgeworth.

If children are failing to learn in any curriculum area the teacher is challenged to decide how to restructure the work and also how to relate it relevantly, and at the right level, to the child. One way of approaching this problem is to require the teacher to think carefully about what it is that he or she wants the child to learn, that is, to make an analysis of that area of the curriculum, so that it can be related to what the child already knows and where in the teacher's overall teaching plan that particular piece of learning fits. However, this strategy of its own may not be adequate to ensure that learning takes place for all children, and the problems become accentuated for children with learning difficulties as those difficulties become more and more severe.

What, then, is the most constructive position to take with regard to this further problem? One obvious starting point is to consider the literature that has attempted to provide some understanding about how learning processes may be facilitated. It would appear that a number of generalizations may be made. First, children who find themselves in this position, for whatever reason, are frequently lacking in confidence and self-esteem. They may have experienced failure for many years and clearly what is required for them are feelings of success in the school situation. Secondly, children may have approaches or strategies to their learning which are either irrelevant or severely degraded; and thirdly, and this is probably a corollary of the second point, they have difficulties in making appropriate generalizations or they fail to transfer their learning to new situations.

These last two problems in particular appear to become greater as children demonstrate ever increasing difficulties in learning and this analysis would indicate that teachers would be advised to plan their work for such pupils with these kinds of considerations in mind. For example work can be planned and presented in order to provide clear and obvious (to the child) features for success. Since learning is likely to be slow, and in order to maintain confidence on the part of both the pupil and the teacher, it is useful to record progress, monitoring closely how the child is approaching or attacking the problem with regard to what knowledge is brought to the task and what strategies are being used. Finally, teachers should build into their work not only approaches which actively encourage the development of factual matters but also approaches that allow the child to develop for him or herself ideas and concepts and so encourage transfer of learning. While this may sound like good teaching practice that might be adopted in any setting, and that is a perfectly sensible position to take, for children with learning difficulties the difference comes at the level of detailed planning that must quite deliberately be carried out. But again, from an educational perspective these points further emphasize the importance of thinking about special needs provisions within the continuum model.

Monitoring Progress and the Significance of Observation

Thus far the topics of identification and assessment have only been mentioned in a previous section and their importance noted as significant areas of concern for teachers. The issues involved figure strongly in the Warnock Report (1978) and in the official thinking about that knowledge which all teachers should have. But the omission of a full discussion has been intentional for it is hoped that in what has been said above the reader will see that seeds of the identification and assessment processes have already been sown.

Assessment, for the teacher, is perhaps better conceptualised as the monitoring of pupil progress, for herein lies much of what is required for the identification of children with SEN. Teachers identify children who have learning problems by the children's attitude to their work and their success at it. If both or either of these factors are leading to children steadily falling behind their peers to such an extent that a more detailed intervention becomes necessary then that in itself is an identification process and would form for example the first stage of assessment as described in the Warnock Report (1978). Of course teachers can only recognize these failings if they are monitoring progress adequately and understand enough of the learning process to be able to make appropriate and accurate observations.

The position that has been taken above emphasizes questions concerned with what approaches to take when children fail to learn, and how this lack of learning is to be interpreted and responded to by teachers in their classroom work. In order to advance the argument let us assume that the curriculum questions have been resolved — the top down analysis has been successfully carried out — we know our latin and we are convinced of its relevance and general presentation but there is still a lack of progress; what next? Here we need to concern ourselves further with the details of the presentation of the material and most importantly with establishing the child's actual level of knowledge.

What is needed is real evidence from the performance of the child in the curriculum area of interest that the child actually knows what the teacher is assuming the child knows. This is a particular problem in the context of children with learning problems, and experience in the classroom informs us that more often than not teachers assume that these children are more competent than in reality they are (for example, Hunt and Kirk, 1974). Thus in this arena the adage 'observe then teach' (Stevens, 1968) carries great significance, but the observations must be focused quite precisely on the questions that the teacher wants answered in the particular curriculum area. Hence the value of the scientific empirical approach advocated by Edgeworth in understanding the child's mind. In many cases a focus on such matters may well resolve the problem in a satisfactory way, but it must be recognized that many children have immense problems in aspects of learning where many of us have none. Smith (1982) refers to the individual learner as being a creative organizer of learning material, and I have no argument with that general view, but for children with learning problems this creative process may be somewhat constrained. Inhelder (1943) for example refers to such children as being 'viscous', or apparently lacking the spontaneous organizing ability shown by children without special needs, and furthermore this conclusion is well supported by other more recent literature such as Torgesen and Licht (1983). Thus it is up to the teacher to understand John, to be able to gain access to his learning processes, to make overt his covert strategies, figuratively to turn his mind inside out and to compensate for his difficulties in the presentation of the teaching materials.

Thus, for example, the literature that has shown that children with learning difficulties have problems applying strategies to their learning, thus failing to remember their work (for example, Bray, 1979), may be taken to indicate that the teacher might supply these strategies. The child might be helped to organize his or her own efforts through the use of activities such as rehearsal, mnemonics, imagery, organizational strategies, practice in other situations, and problem-solving (Glidden, 1979). Furthermore, research in the area of skills (referred to by Tomlinson in this volume) would suggest that the automatization of learning, or the process whereby new learning becomes automatic or even subconscious, is also likely to be slowed down for children with learning difficulties, thus leading, quite directly, to further problems that require the teacher to take care in the planning of practice on tasks in order to compensate for the slowness of this process.

One productive way of presenting work to help overcome such difficulties has been suggested by Haring *et al* (1978). They have proposed a hierarchy of learning that has proved useful in organizing the teaching plans developed for children with SEN that encourages both the acquisition of basic skills and also the transfer of the learning. The first level in this hierarchy involves the acquisition of the appropriate and accurate skills and is described as the period between the first appearance of the desired behaviour and the reasonably accurate performance of that behaviour. The second level is the development of fluency or proficiency which allows for new skills to be developed so that they may be used in meaningful ways. At this level, accuracy of response is important but it may not distinguish between learning that is newly acquired in contrast to that which is well rehearsed. Thus the term fluency implies the speed at which, for example, reading takes place or at which the scales on the piano are played and is an important measure or indicator to consider. The third level is that of generalization and here it is important to know whether the learning that has taken place can transfer to other situations. For example if a child has learned how to add single digit numbers, can he or she still do it accurately and fluently if the problems are presented in a different format, say horizontally as opposed to vertically, or if embedded in a context with subtraction questions? The fourth and final level involves the application or adaptation of the skills. Essentially this level involves understanding the function of the learning so that it may be modified and applied to new problems. One example of this idea in practice would be the use of new learning in problem solving situations where the idea behind what has been taught must be extracted and utilized.

To efficient and competent learners such as trainee teachers these levels of learning just presented may seem unnecessarily detailed, and the planning of work for pupils with learning difficulties that takes them into account may appear formidable. However, unless an approach which gives careful consideration to issues such as these is accepted in educational provision, it is most likely that many children will continue to fail quite unnecessarily because of deficiencies in the environmental resources. Such deficiencies may include the teacher showing a lack of sensitivity to the child, a lack of thought concerning the presentation of the curriculum area, a lack of knowledge about the learning processes involved and finally a lack of skill in observing relevant aspects of the child's behaviour with reference to the learning of that particular curriculum area.

Of course knowing John also means knowing not only about his cognitive processes and skills but also about his interests and motivations so that these may inform the selection and presentation of the teaching materials. This aspect of teaching is, I believe, a highly creative one. The teacher is placed in the front line of curriculum development and is required to make day to day decisions on the details of the content and planning of work for individual children. It is a highly complex, intellectually demanding task that gives teachers great responsibility. To some extent such work frees teachers from the rigours of teaching to a syllabus as part of a curriculum laid down by the school or other body, but this freedom brings with it the necessity of increasing the skills of accurately observing and interpreting children's behaviour in the light of current knowledge, not only of learning processes but also of the particular interests of the child. The creative skills of putting all of this together with the curriculum area of interest in a presentable package to the child must also be carefully nurtured in training, and protected in everyday practice. In this way children may experience success in a meaningful manner thus developing self-esteem and confidence and an understanding that their efforts can lead to control over at least some of their learning through being able to attribute success to their own work and skills (Seligman, 1975). Furthermore the child can also see that the teacher is able to engage him or her in a meaningful educational dialogue, that is to say, the teacher can understand the child's learning problems and can adapt to them. Through this process the teacher will become an agent through whom the pupil can develop what has been called effectiveness motivation (Stott, 1978) and *ipso facto* will be a 'good' teacher.

It has not been my purpose here to explore the ways in which such good teaching may or may not be possible in the currently prevailing conditions in our schools, but rather to have made a particular psychological analysis of the needs of children with learning difficulties and to present this as a challenge that must be met by the educational system and by teacher education within it in the delivery of adequate provision.

Behaviour Problems

Of all the issues that concern trainee teachers most the question of behaviour problems is perhaps paramount. Disaffected children are frequently experienced in all schools by all teachers and clearly teachers need to develop strategies which allow them to maintain an appropriate balance between control, discipline and repression which will allow for a creative and enjoyable classroom atmosphere for all participants.

Working from the top down approach many educationalists see the problems in terms of an irrelevant curriculum which leads to boredom and frustration in the children, or in terms of a process of labelling which is intended to explain deviant behaviour through the development of expectations by teachers of likely poor behaviour and work. These views have developed alternative conceptual frameworks from those positions which would hold that difficult behaviours can best be understood through an analysis of within-child factors. Thus the psychodynamic framework, which would not deny the role of experience in creating the problems, may nonetheless see them in terms of the faulty dynamics of personal psychology. Treatment may then, for example, focus on encouraging the child to understand the realities of the world he or she experiences. The more environmental or sociological argument would suggest that children can best be treated through changes in society's attitudes to them via its officially appointed change agents in education, that is, teachers and other local authority appointees. The problem, however, is really more complex than this. Attempts over the years to define behaviour problems and maladjustment have floundered because of the heterogeneity of the symptoms, the lack of clear relationships between perceived causes and perceived effects, and the manner in which these behaviour problems and emotional disturbances vary with age and circumstances. One way of making a rather simple distinction is to distinguish between conduct or behaviour problems on the one hand and personality disorders on the other, although more complex models have been proposed (for example, Rutter *et al* 1969).

While all of these views have something to offer in our understanding of the problem, and an appreciation of the difficulties is clearly important for teachers in the identification process, in my view and continuing with the pragmatic approach taken in this chapter, the most appropriate unit of analysis on which to focus is the interaction between the teacher and the child in the context of the classroom and of the particular aspect of learning. Using this approach unruly behaviour may be seen to have its causes in several different arenas. The curriculum itself may be irrelevant, the teaching of that particular curriculum area may be inadequate, the school may not care enough about the personal concerns of the children in it, the teacher's own attitude may be inappropriate or the teacher's own style may be antagonistic and the organization of the classroom itself may be problematic. These six possible causes do not exhaust the potential set but they do serve to point out some of the areas of possible difficulty.

These six areas of analysis noted above all have situational and inter-personal components. It follows from this that teachers and schools must closely consider themselves and the extent to which they may be making the major contribution to the behaviour problems that they are experiencing. This process itself requires reflection, and as objective an analysis as may be possible of the situation and the attitudes that are held. This new self-awareness must then be adequately translated into practice in the classroom. However, if viewed appropriately the exercise may not be as threatening or as daunting as it might at first appear provided that the level of analysis is essentially on the commerce between the teacher and the child. Work that has been carried out on observing teacher-child interactions, with respect to the existence of unruly behaviours, (and on many other aspects of psychological research for that matter) has shown that one of the main concerns is that of obtaining observations that are reliable. Obtaining reliability is in large part a question of defining adequately the criterion of the occurrence of the behaviours. If the criteria are vague then sometimes behaviours will be counted as having occurred and sometimes they will not and thus inconsistency will arise. If the criteria are too narrow then the reliability may be high but the occurrence may be so rare that it becomes trivial and perhaps more significant behaviours may be missed. Thus the first lesson to be learned is that teachers should clarify in their own minds what they mean by their perception of naughtiness. This does not mean that all teachers should have the same view; different people have different tolerances and this is an important lesson that we all have to learn, but it is essential that an individual teacher is clear about what he or she thinks so that his or her reactions to the children become consistent. This consistency may be manifested in two forms, the first is the interpretation of the children's behaviour (does it fall into a category that I consider to be naughty?) and the second relates to the teacher's reaction (am I sending out different and potentially conflicting signals, thus creating uncertainty in the child?). Finally it is extremely important that these actions and reactions are documented by the teacher in some objective way since this has the effect not only of monitoring the pupil's behaviour but also of acting as a constant reminder to the teacher of criteria and his or her consistency in interpreting and maintaining them.

Thus the suggestion is that teachers should clarify in their own minds what is acceptable behaviour and communicate this to the children. Indeed this may act as a point of discussion for a negotiated agreement out of which the class might devise a small number of rules that they will attempt to adhere to. There are two important qualifications to this, the first is that there should not be too many rules and clearly these should apply to the most significant behaviours that are creating the difficulties. The second is that there must be consequences contingent on these rules being kept or broken, since this feature of the teacher-child interaction has been shown to be effective in many studies in changing behaviour (for example, Lovitt, 1978).

However, in my view there is a further important qualification which is not often stressed but which needs to be made, concerning the consequences that are made contingent on the child's behaviour. Obviously these consequences are going to be mainly in terms of praise or rebuke. All teachers, as do all human beings, use these strategies either implicitly or explicitly much of the time and they have much to do with the setting of the emotional climate of the classroom. Thus there will be a kind of ambient level — or a usual level of the praise/rebuke balance — that children will learn to adapt to. Individual teachers will vary with respect to this balance (Evans, Beveridge and Halil, 1985). An appreciation of this point is extremely important, since if praise is going to be perceived by the child as something special then it must exceed the ambient level in a noticeable way. Indeed the same point may also be made for rebukes. We can all remember the teacher who was always shouting and in order to make some disciplinary point had to shout even louder! This analysis is of special significance if teachers wish to use the technique of ignoring children in order to reduce or eliminate some undesirable behaviour for it is only likely to work if it occurs against a general background of praise (Solnick *et al*, 1977). It is contrasts, or the relationships between events, that have the highest salience, and not their absolute values. Thus teachers need to learn to modulate their actions appropriately, monitor their own performance and be continually self-reflective.

Children with behaviour problems may also show learning difficulties that appear not only in terms of a lack of skill in various educationally relevant areas but also show unadaptive behavioural styles such as poor attentional skills, excessive out of seat behaviours, attention seeking, shouting out, boisterous or impulsive behaviour and so on. There is a vast psychological literature that provides techniques for dealing with such behaviours appropriately, some of which may use self-control techniques (for example, Meichenbaum, 1977), some may focus on the improvement of the teaching method with correlated improvements in behaviour (for example, Ayllon and Roberts 1974) while others focus on the establishment of classroom rules and management.

It is not the place here to develop these methods more fully since there is an ever increasing literature which can be readily referred to. However, it must be stressed that there is a real limit to what individuals can do in classrooms, and effective solutions that will generalize to new situations and significantly help children require whole school responses if not whole community approaches (see Apter, 1982; Wall, 1979). Thus as with problems in learning the analysis poses a challenge which goes beyond the training of the individual teacher.

Conclusion

This chapter has centred on two of the major aspects of problems that teachers face in school, namely those of learning difficulties and behaviour problems, although it must be recognized that the two are not necessarily unrelated. Both of these issues have been introduced within a general systems or ecological framework and the compensatory interaction model (Wedell, 1980). Within this model the chapter has focused on an attempt to give a relevant psychological discussion of learning difficulties in the child as well as of the deficiencies in the environment, where one can not be defined totally independently of the other. However, because of the nature of this volume as a whole the psychological issues have been the ones which have been stressed. Furthermore the psychological aspects that have been selected have been those that focus mainly on teaching children who have special educational needs and on teaching where the environment in which the child is functioning must make increasingly more adaptation as the problems that the children present become ever more extreme. I have seen the teacher as needing to be very much a curriculum decision-maker who must be acutely aware of his or her impact on the classroom environment, both in terms of interaction with the children and also in terms of the presentation of the curriculum materials. I have proposed that this is essentially an empirical endeavour in which psychology has a central role and which requires an equal partnership with the various curriculum areas but with agreed overall and mutually understood goals. This particular alliance gains more and more significance as children show ever increasing special needs and lack of relatively normal environmental adaptation.

I hope it is clear from the arguments presented that psychology in some of its various theoretical manifestations has a great deal to contribute to our understanding of such problems and the ensuing action, not only from the point of view of pedagogy but also in an overall conceptualisation of the curriculum when that term means more than just a list of subjects taught or areas of experience.

Finally, perhaps I can end with a slightly light-hearted (and inevitably something of a caricature) but nonetheless beautiful example of the various themes of this chapter which suggests the revisit to Shaw's *Pygmalion*.

It will be recalled that Eliza has desired to speak 'proper' and to be a lady (she manifests special learning needs and also shows disaffection from, albeit a middle class, society and is thus readily identified). She encounters Professor Higgins who is interested in linguistics and speech development and who immediately impresses her not only with his charisma, but also with his phenomenal knowledge of his subject and magical ability of being able to predict peoples' birthplaces. Further he is able to assess accurately her language needs by listening to her and recognizing the disparity between her spoken English and the preferred alternative. Being interested in intellectual challenges Higgins takes on Eliza, determined to pass her off as a lady at an appropriate Garden Party (there are clear goals). Our Professor combines his understanding of the curriculum area of language development with a judicious use of behavioural methods in which Eliza's craving for chocolates is used to good avail in helping to maintain her motivation and new learning. Higgins then monitors her progress not only by listening closely to the changes in her speech but also checking for generalization at the end of session exam, when her new skills are tried out at his mother's house. Finally with further expert tuition, as we know, she passes muster at the Garden Party, and with the personal confidence born of success is able to free herself from dependence on her teacher. Adams, Ausubel and Edgeworth in perfect harmony.

References

Government documents

ADVISORY COMMITTEE ON THE SUPPLY AND EDUCATION OF TEACHERS (ACSET) (1984) *Teacher Training and Special Educational Needs*, London, HMSO.
EDUCATION ACT (1981) London, HMSO.

Other references

ADAMS, J. (1897) *Herbartian Psychology Applied to Education*, London, D.C. Heath and Co.
APTER, S.J. (1982) *Troubled Children, Troubled Systems*, Oxford, Pergamon.
AUSUBEL, D. (1968) *Educational Psychology: A cognitive view*, New York, Holt, Rinehart and Winston.

AYLLON T. and ROBERTS, M.D. (1974) 'Eliminating disruptive problems by strengthening academic performance', in *Journal of Applied Behaviour Analysis*, 7, pp. 71–6.

BRAY, N.W. (1979) 'Strategy production in the retarded', in ELLIS, N.R. (Ed.) *Handbook of Mental Deficiency, Psychological Theory and Research* (2nd edition), Hillsdale, New Jersey, LEA.

BRONFENBRENNER, U. (1977) 'Toward an experimental ecology of human development', in *American Psychologist*, 32, pp. 513–31.

EDGEWORTH, M. and EDGEWORTH, R.L. (1974) *Practical Education 1798*, London, reprinted by Garland Publishing.

EVANS, P.L.C. BEVERIDGE, M. and HALIL, T. (1986) Analyzing teacher/child interaction in the classroom through linear modelling techniques. *Educational Psychology*, in Press.

GLIDDEN, L.M. (1979) 'Training of learning and memory in retarded persons: strategies, techniques and teaching tools', in ELLIS, N.R. (Ed.) *Handbook of Mental Deficiency, Psychological Theory and Research* (2nd edition) Hillsdale, New Jersey, LEA.

HARING, N.G. and LOVITT, T.C. (1978) 'Systematic instructional procedures: An instructional hierarchy', in HARING, N.G., LOVITT, T.C., EATON, M.D. and HANSEN, C.L. (Eds.) *The Fourth R: Research in the Classroom*, London, Merrill.

HUNT, J. McV. and KIRK, G.E. (1974) 'Criterion referenced tests of school readiness: a paradigm with illustrations', in *Genetic Psychology Monographs*, 90 (1st half), pp. 144–82.

INHELDER, B. (1943) French Edn, translated by STEPHENS, W.B. (1968) *The Diagnosis of Reasoning in the Mentally Retarded*, New York, Day.

LENNEBERG, E.H. (1967) *Biological Foundations of Language*, New York, Wiley.

LOVITT, T.C. (1978) 'Strategies for managing naughty behaviours', in HARING, N.G., LOVITT, T.C., EATON, M.D. and HANSEN, C.L. (Eds.) *The Fourth R: Research in the Classroom*, London, Merrill.

MEICHENBAUM, D. (1977) *Cognitive Behaviour Modification*, London, Plenum Press.

RUTTER, M., LEBOVICI, S., EISENBERGE, L., SNEZNEVSKIJ, A.V., SADOUN, R., BROOKE, E. and LIN, T-Y. (1969) 'A triaxial classification of mental disorders in childhood', in *Journal of Child Psychology and Psychiatry*, 10, pp. 41–61.

SELIGMAN, M.E.P. (1975) *Helplessness*, San Francisco, Freeman and Co.

SLOBODA, J., O'CONNOR, N. and HERMELIN, B. (1985) 'A case of extraordinary musical memory,' *Proceedings of the Experimental Psychology Society*.

SMITH, F. (1982) *Writing and the Writer*, London, Heinemann Educational.

SOLNICK, J.V., RINCOVER, A. and PETERSON, C.R. (1977) 'Determinants of the reinforcing and punishing effects of time out', in *Journal of Applied Behavior Analysis*, 10, pp. 415–28.

STEVENS, M. (1968) *Observing Children who are Severely Subnormal*, London,

Edward Arnold.

STOTT, D.M. (1978) *Helping Children with Learning Difficulties*, London, Ward Lock Educational.

THORNDIKE, R.L. (1982) 'Educational Measurement-Theory and Practice, in SPEARRITT, D. (Ed.) *The Improvement of Measurement in Education and Psychology*, Victoria, Australia, Australian Council for Education Research.

TORGESEN, J.K. and LIGHT, B.G. (1983) 'The learning disabled, child as an inactive learner: retrospect and prospects,' in McKINNEY, J.D. and FEAGANS, L. (Eds) *Current Topics in Learning Disabilities*, Norwood, N.J., Ablex Publishing Co.

WALL, W.D. (1979) *Constructive Education for Special Groups*, London, Harrap UNESCO.

WARNOCK, M. (1978) *Special Educational Needs: report of the Committee of Enquiry into the Education of Handicapped Children and Young People*, London, HMSO.

WEDELL, K. (1980) 'Early identification and compensatory interaction', in KNIGHTS, R.M. and BAKKER, D.J. (Eds.) *Treatment of Hyperactive and Learning Disordered Children*, Baltimore, University Park Press.

The Psychologist and Children's Personal Development

David Fontana
University College, Cardiff

If that strange and mythical creature (usually credited with a convenient forte for teasing out human weaknesses and idiosyncracies) known as a visitor from another planet were to visit Britain and take a close look at our educational system, one of the things that would most surprise him would be our extensive neglect at any formal level of what we can best call children's personal development. Doubtless he will correct me if I'm wrong; but I see him as poring through syllabus after syllabus and textbook after textbook, his high and noble brow furrowed with perplexity at this apparent absence of concern with those behaviours which represent the individual's relationship with himself, and which in a deep sense determine the way he feels about life in general and his own life in particular.

Assuming our visitor is a curious person he (it could just as readily be she) might ask the psychologist to explain this omission, on the sensible assumption that since psychology is the study of human behaviour then the psychologist should know about this central and critical area of individual experiencing. Imagine his surprise (to persevere with our metaphor of the visitor from outer space for just a little longer) when he hears from the psychologist that personal development is much too vague a concept for an aspiring science like psychology, and that since in any case it involves questions of value it really falls within the purlieu of the philosopher rather than of the psychologist. On being questioned in his turn the philosopher provides further surprise by suggesting that since philosophers can't agree amongst themselves on what kind of personal development is most desirable or even on the definition of personal development the whole business tends to get left very much to the schools, which brings us back full circle to the gaps in

155

the syllabus already noted by our perspicacious visitor. If he has the energy and persistence to carry his questioning into the school staff-room he like as not receives the answer that personal development tends to be a by-product of all the other good and proper things that appear in the syllabus, and that no-one can expect the teacher to be any more precise about it since experts like psychologists and philosophers persist in being so unhelpful on the subject.

The Meaning of Personal Development

At this point I have to abandon our useful and obliging visitor, and try to show that there is little excuse, on the part at least of psychologists, for this unhelpful stance since psychology has a great deal to offer teachers on the nature of personal development and on how it can best be viewed within the educational context. And here I make the claim that personal development is not simply a generic term for such things as personality development, self-concepts and the like. Rather it is an holistic term that incorporates the nature of an individual's experiences, feelings and attainments together with the concepts and values he attaches to them. If psychologists were not bound by the constraints of a would-be scientific vocabulary they would say it is the experienced *quality* of his psychological life.

One obvious point that emerges from this is that in talking about personal development I am not using the term 'development' in the same way as in language development or physical development or most other kinds of psycho-physical development. It is perfectly possible for a young child and even a small baby to experience a good quality psychological life. Conversely it is equally possible for an adult to experience a bad quality one. So personal development is not a matter of going from immaturity to maturity, rather it is a matter of keeping pace with the new experiences and new demands that the individual encounters as he grows older. As life becomes more complex and more challenging, so the individual has to adapt and grow, but this is less a case of passing through stages à la Freud or Piaget or Kohlberg than of learning how to maintain this quality in the face of increasing assaults upon it from outside. If we doubt this interpretation of 'development' we only have to look at the delight that a child from a favourable background takes in life and in his or her response to life to realize that in a sense however much we grow we are going to be hard pressed to improve upon the quality of this kind of personal experiencing.

This is not to suggest, of course, that personal development is something that takes place independently of the worth placed on us by others and of social development in general, or independently of the acquisition of cognitive and physical skills. At each point it is intimately affected by these variables. But in themselves they none of them can *ensure* satisfactory personal development. We may enjoy good social relationships and good social esteem yet still have unsolved personal problems. Even more likely we may acquire highly impressive cognitive or physical skills yet still find our inner life profoundly unsatisfying. Closely linked as it is to social, cognitive and physical factors, personal development is yet in a very real sense distinct from them, and can only be fully understood by the educator if this distinction is recognized and respected.

It may be apparent by now that what I am edging towards is a simple categorical statement that personal development is essentially a part of — perhaps even the same thing as — psychological health. And just as the physician can produce perfectly workable criteria for physical health (with a healthy child scoring just as highly as a healthy adult) so it should be possible for the psychologist to produce workable criteria for psychological health (with the child again showing the same potential as the adult). This involves questions of 'value' just as the notion of physical health involves questions of value (at what point do we say that health deteriorates into unhealth and, for that matter, why do we consider that this condition represents health while that condition does not?), but there is no special reason why the psychologist should feel these questions present particular difficulties and, more importantly, no special reason why he should feel he has the right to ignore them as being 'unscientific'.

The Nature of Personal Development

What, then, are these workable criteria, and how do they relate to the task of the teacher within formal education? One approach to them which is both unequivocal and likely to find support amongst a significant body of psychological opinion is through the concept of the mature personality. Gordon Allport (for example, 1961), in focusing particular attention upon this concept, suggests that psychological research into individuals revealed as personally mature by autobiographical writings and peer ratings tend to show a range of common traits. These can be summarized as including an extended sense of self (that is, a concern for others and an absence of undue self-centredness), realistic appraisals and judgments of external events, emotional security, warm and non-possessive relationships with others, self-knowledge and self-acceptance, and a consistent and unifying philosophy of life. Allport stresses that, taking account of the more restricted world within which they operate, children can show these qualities as readily as can adults. He further stresses that although very few people show all these qualities in abundance at any one stage of their lives, the possession of any of them to any significant degree is an indicator of burgeoning maturity within the areas concerned.

Granted then that these are qualities of which the teacher should take account when conceptualising psychological health, how does he go about encouraging their development? The problem he faces is that these things cannot easily be taught in a direct sense, in the way in which a subject like mathematics can be taught. Even if we knew the skills such teaching might require it seems probable that, because of the individual nature of the *processes* of personal development in the life of each child, what might prove effective with one might prove ineffective or even counter-productive with another. To take a simple example, if we found that an 'introspective' skill such as meditation was useful for personal development in some cases we would then doubtless find large numbers of children for whom the skill was not only meaningless but impossible to acquire under school conditions. Far from having their personal development enhanced, such children would either become antagonistic to the whole notion of the school's role in this development or, worse still, would come to see themselves as 'failing' in personal development in rather the same way that they fail in other areas of the curriculum.

Personal Development and an Extended Sense of Self

Personal development rather looks, therefore, like something that should be taught through other school subjects rather than something that can be taught in its own right. This emphatically does not mean that the personal development as 'a by-product of all the other things that appear in the syllabus' approach mentioned earlier is the correct one. It means rather that we can have definite objectives within the field of personal development and can deliberately select and manipulate certain areas of the curriculum in order to facilitate their achievement. One obvious example of these areas is provided by Bruner's syllabus entitled 'Man; A course of Study' and used experimentally by Jones (1972) and others as a way of increasing children's awareness of what it means to be human and to tackle the disparate challenges offered by life, constructing and operating value systems in the process.

The basic purpose behind Bruner's syllabus is to focus children's attention upon the *meaning* that life has for individual men and women, thus increasing their understanding of themselves and of others. Since the syllabus involves written work and can also embrace aspects of history and geography it clearly helps achieve a range of conventional curricular objectives in addition to helping the development of both the extended sense of self and the self-knowledge which we have already identified as components in the mature personality. Subjects such as religious education, literature and what are variously known as civics, humanities and liberal studies can also further this development provided their objectives are defined not simply in terms of factual knowledge but also in terms of the potential influence they are designed to have upon children's self and self-other awareness. The point is that the teaching of literature or of any other of these subjects *per se* does not lead to the kind of personal development that we have described. If it did, graduates in English Literature would be identifiably far more advanced in this development than graduates in most other subjects (or than people in the population at large), a state of affairs which is in most cases very far from proven.

It seems likely that the preparation of objectives in accordance with the higher levels of Krathwohl's affective domain taxonomy (Krathwohl *et al* 1964) as part of literature and other humanities programmes would be of significant help in the development of this self and self-other awareness, but it is by no means clear that this or any other taxonomy fully covers the kind of personal change that I am discussing. Much of this change lies beyond the more straightforward business of learning how to handle and react to classroom material in a way which accords with the conventions of the subject that is being taught. Nevertheless the teacher has to have some operational yardstick for assessing the impact of class work upon children's personal behaviours, and Krathwohl's work provides a useful start. In the long term, it requires supplementation by a more extended taxonomy which seeks to develop a precise vocabulary of the affective responses involved in personal growth, especially where this growth involves the sympathy and concern for others which constitute the extended sense of self.

Personal Development and Realistic Appraisals

Moving from the extended sense of self to the realistic appraisals and judgments contained in the second of Allport's personal maturity criteria we find the links with curricular activity much more clear-cut. I am talking here about helping the child acquire the skills and appraisals necessary to comprehend and cope satisfactorily with the particular environment in which he or she has to operate. In a sense this is a plea for relevance (that much used and much misunderstood term) in the school curriculum. Relevance entails equipped the child with knowledge that is of direct and observable use. For many children, this does not mean offering them an academic education geared to higher education, or offering them a set of expectations (vocational and personal) which are doomed to inevitable disappointment. It means providing them with basic literacy and numeracy and a range of skills which will prove effective in the environment in which they will probably have to live and work, while giving them at the same time the foundation for the further development needed should they aspire to move out of this environment or should they be faced with new challenges due to social or economic change. Space does not allow us to discuss these skills, but their determining feature should be that they are linked to the objective necessities of the child's life, and are therefore seen by the child as providing useful tools for living that life more effectively and satisfyingly. They will include not only factual, motor and judgmental skills but also social skills of the kind discussed and illustrated by Argyle (for example, 1981).

Personal Development and Emotional Security

The third of Allport's criteria, emotional security, will obviously depend greatly upon what happens in the child's life outside school (particularly within the home). But the school's contribution is still a highly significant one, and lies in providing assurance to all children that, whatever their abilities, they are valued and respected within the school community. Such respect will necessarily be realized in different ways according to needs. The very fact of equipping the child with realistic skills helps develop the self-confidence that is an important part of emotional security, but to indicate to the child that he or she is valued and respected requires that these skills be presented in a way that protects him or her from the damaging effects of continual failure. The extent to which our educational system is geared to producing failure rather than success is fully documented elsewhere (Fontana, 1984) but it is relevant to repeat that one third of children leave school without a single example of the paper qualifications that our educational system equates with success, while of those who do proceed to GCE Ordinary Level examinations the decision is made in advance that something akin to forty per cent will fail to obtain 'O' Level pass grades. Even amongst those who go on to university only eight per cent will gain the top accolade of success, represented by the first class honours degree, while the remaining ninety-two per cent will have to live with varying levels of comparative failure.

The ways in which we can teach through success rather than through failure are well-known and fully discussed in the literature, but what may be lacking is an awareness on the part of many teachers of the impact of failure upon self-concepts and self-esteem and upon the emotional security that depends in large measure upon these variables. After all, most have experienced a fair degree of success and would rather forget the pain of their own failures. Children who consistently fail and who see the school as rejecting and even despising them have a hard task to develop that sense of self-significance that allows them to tackle and overcome the challenges that life inevitably holds for them. In the end, the overriding consideration in any educational process should be not with whether material has been learnt or not learnt, but with the effect upon the learner that the learning experience has had.

Of enormous potential value in assessing this impact and indeed in helping the individual explore the whole field of self concepts and personal construing are the computer based learning programmes currently under development by Thomas at Brunel University. Using the personal construct theories of Kelly and of Bannister, Thomas has developed the Pegasus Programme (Thomas 1979, Thomas and Aug-stein 1984) which enables the computer to elicit a repertory grid from the child and then, as the judgments attached by the child to the grid elements become apparent, to reveal their implications so that the child can engage in an active interrogation of his or her own construing. The Focus Programme allows the child to re-sort these judgments and to study the implications of these changes, while a further range of programmes actually allows two or more people to converse through the grid programme thus clarifying their personal and inter-personal perceptions. The implications of these and similar programmes for helping children work towards a fuller knowledge of the way in which they view themselves and others, of the implications of these views, and of the further implications of changes in these views, are readily apparent.

Personal Development, Personal Relationships, and Self-Knowledge

The fourth and fifth of Allport's criteria, warm and non-possessive relationships with others and self-knowledge and self-acceptance have been partly catered for in what we have said already. An education designed to increase a child's awareness of and sympathy towards others will in addition help teach the tolerance and acceptance that are part of a warm relationship with them, while the increased understanding of others (and of their needs and rights) which also comes through this education will prompt him or her towards a less possessive attitude. The development of emotional security is another important factor here, since it helps the individual avoid imposing excessive demands upon others as a way of compensating for their own feelings of personal inadequacy.

By the same token an education which helps the child gain self-awareness and the confidence and self-respect that goes with the development of realistic skills will also help towards self-knowledge and self-acceptance. Self-knowledge (or self-insight) implies the ability to observe and evaluate the self objectively and realistically, and in consequence to work towards the elimination of behaviours judged undesirable and the cultivation of those behaviours judged to be of value. Linked closely with this is the development of another important quality stressed by Allport and not mentioned so far, namely consistency of individual behaviour. The mature person, though flexible and adaptable in response to the demands of the situation and to the dictates of a concern for the well-being of others, yet shows an underlying unity to behaviour that makes him or her identifiably the same person whatever the context within which he or she appears, with the same standards and values and the same determination to uphold these standards and values. Such unity depends not only upon the possession of a coherent philosophy of life, which is the last of Allport's criteria and to which we shall pass in a moment, but to the ability to know oneself and to take some responsibility for the shaping and direction of one's own behaviour.

Lest this should suggest the tightly over-controlled person, it must be made clear that Allport equates self-insight with a sense of humour, defined by him as the ability to identify the difference between pretension and performance, in oneself as well as in others, and to laugh at this difference without the laughter leading to any loss of regard for the person concerned. Such laughter therefore comes from understanding, and is never far from sympathy. It stands in sharp opposition to what can be described as a sense of the comic, which takes pleasure in the discomfiture of others, and which can too easily become associated with rejection and cruelty. As such it gives us access to the concept of self-acceptance, that is to the ability to sustain one's self-respect in spite of the awareness of personal shortcomings that comes through self-knowledge. To recognize weaknesses in oneself and in others, and yet to go on offering love to the possessor of these weaknesses is an important indication of that harmony in one's relationships with self and others recognized as a component of the psychological health that we are equating with the mature personality and personal development.

Personal Development and a Unifying Philosophy of Life

Self-acceptance does not, of course, imply complacency. I have already indicated that a consequence of self-knowledge is the opportunity to work towards the elimination of behaviours judged undesirable and the cultivation of those behaviours judged to be of value. Clearly this means equipping the child with the skills necessary for self-evaluation and self-development, and basic to these skills is the realization that the self-examination taught through education is not offered as a stimulus for guilt and for feelings of unworthiness but as a means towards greater personal enhancement and effectiveness. The same applies to the last of Allport's criteria, a unifying philosophy of life. Since such a philosophy implies a code of conduct, a set of morals and values which help the individual evaluate and reflect upon the behaviour of both self and others, it is important that this philosophy is seen not as a means towards the restriction of personal freedoms (though inevitably it will lead at times to the voluntary curbing of certain kinds of behaviours) but as a way of preserving and enlarging those personal freedoms that are consistent with the rights and freedoms of others. The purpose behind a unifying philosophy of life is that it helps the individual identify in a manner which is comprehensible the variables that operate upon and are responsive to individual actions. At its best such a philosophy (which may or may not be religious in conception) provides life with that sense of meaning and purpose that Jung (for example, 1961) sees as such an essential component of psychological health, and whose absence he identifies as overwhelmingly the most important problem experienced by his clients from middle life onwards.

The school cannot, of course, *teach* a unifying philosopohy of life. One of the qualities of such a philosophy is that it brings meaning to each individual in his or her own way and in terms of his or her own unique life experiences, and as such it has to be worked out with the individual's personal participation. Anything less than this becomes not a philosophy of life in the sense in which Allport uses the term but a form of indoctrination in which the individual is deprived of the right of personal choice. But what the school can do is to provide the conditions in which such a philosophy can develop. These conditions involve clear evidence that individual members of staff refer their own behaviour to some such workable philosophy, and are prepared where there is no conflict with the rights of others to tolerate philosophies that differ from their own. They also involve providing the child with ready and comprehensible access to the great philosophies and belief systems of the world, together with those of individual men and women who have triumphed through belief and courage over obstacles and challenges. Religious education and literature lessons are obvious media for work of this kind, but science also contains a vast philosophy which has to do with noble attempts to understand man as well as to understand his environment, and to improve his lot as well as to broaden the agencies of change.

Where work of this kind is at present carried on in schools, it is seen as incidental to other work instead of as a central theme which can carry its own clearly expressed objectives and can have the notion of children's personal change as its overriding aim. In the event of any educator seeing such an aim as too personalized to be of value to society at large it can be emphasized that social change can be (indeed perhaps can only be) brought about through personal change. And this does not refer to the actions of a few particularly gifted individuals but to personal change in and through the lives of the great majority of individuals who attract no special attention to themselves. Children have to grow up into the difficult and dangerous world bequeathed by their elders, and a workable philosophy of life helps them to find meaning in this world and to identify both the areas where change is desirable and possible and the means through which this change can best be effected.

Other Approaches to Psychological Health

It may be thought that by taking the mature personality as a measure of psychological health I have been over-ambitious, and should instead have taken some purely operational definition like the ability to keep clear of the psychiatrist's consulting room. It may also be thought that I have been too solemn, and that by talking about such grand concepts as a unifying philosophy of life I have lost sight of the kind of spontaneous joy which in a sense I was identifying in my opening paragraphs as a sign of psychological health in the child. Cabot (1974) suggested that the psychologically healthy person was one who could play as well as work, and it is obvious that it would be a bad mistake to neglect the ability to take pleasure in non-serious activities in the way in which the child does. Maslow (1954) deplores the fact that in psychology textbooks there are no chapters on 'loafing about', on 'wasting time' and on other such apparently frivolous activities which yet can relax and entertain. Huizinga (1949), in a book which has much to say to modern man, even identifies the decline of the non-serious element in society (anyone who doubts this decline has only to look at the deadly serious nature of much organized modern sport) as a grave indication of a general psychological malaise in Western man. More recently Apter (1982) has drawn attention to the distinction between what he calls the *telic* and the *paratelic* states (in the former of which the individual pursues an activity for the sake of the goals with which it is associated while in the latter of which he pursues the activity for its own sake), and together with Hyers (1985) and Fontana (1982, 1985), has urged the importance of paratelic states for psychological health and deplored their neglect relative to telic states in Western formal education). Other authors (for example, Alvin 1975) have broadened the discussion to include the arts, and have stressed the great importance to psychological health of music and of artistic experiences in general, especially those experiences which both divert and have a deeper meaning which speaks to us of the fundamental nature of the human condition.

All these points are of vital importance, as is Maslow's discussion elsewhere (Maslow 1968) of the need for self actualization and ultimately self transcendence in man, and no paper on personal development would be complete without reference to them. But in a sense they all lie within the areas already covered. The drive to play and to create seems innate in man, and an understanding of oneself and of others implies recognition of this fact and of the fact that individuals should be given freedom and opportunity to express this drive. Similarly an extended sense of self implies the value of co-operation rather than competition (since winners inevitably imply losers), and suggests that organized sport at school level should be concerned with pure enjoyment rather than with set standards which a lucky few are able to reach and the vast majority are not. If the ability to play is declining in our society, this must partly be a function of the seriousness with which the activity is treated at school level, with children encouraged to 'grow out of the playful pleasures of early childhood and to substitute for them a participation in organized sport which brings trophies and something called 'prestige' to the school.

By the same token, the playful pleasures of painting and drawing and making music in early childhood are replaced within the school by rigidly timetabled activities in which standards are set and marks given, prompting an apparently life-long reluctance on the part of the less successful to undertake any sort of subsequent creative endeavour. Again self-knowledge and the extended sense of self implies the ability to recognize the importance of such endeavour in the psychological life of the individual, while emotional security and the acquisition of realistic skills imply the confidence and the techniques to carry on with these endeavours in a form which is personally satisfying and stimulating. Above all perhaps the unifying philosophy of life hopefully implies the ability to respect the endeavours of others, and to recognize the situations in which evaluation is either inappropriate or should be based more upon the fun that these endeavours appear to bring to the individual concerned than upon any arbitrary sets of standards and classifications.

Training Teachers of Personal Development

It is hopefully apparent by now that a basic premise of the present chapter is that just as all teachers in a sense are teachers of English, so all teachers in a sense are teachers of personal development. We have outlined some of the ways in which this development can be taught (perhaps fostered would be a better word), and it remains now to relate this to the broader issue of how teachers can best be prepared for the responsibilities that they carry in this area. There are four main points to raise here.

(1) Clearly the first point is that during the period of initial teacher training the student teacher should be helped to recognize the nature of these responsibilities. No teacher, whatever his or her teaching subject, should conceptualize the teacher's role as encompassing only narrowly specified curricular duties. By virtue of the legal obligations that require them to act in *locum parentis* if nothing else, the task of teachers is to care for children's personal development to the same degree to which they cares for their academic development.

On the face of it I am not saying anything particularly startling here. Teachers have always accepted what is vaguely called a personal or pastoral role vis-à-vis children, in addition to more obvious academic concerns. But the problem lies in the uncertainty which surrounds the extent of this role, an uncertainty for which psychologists themselves are largely to blame. Hitherto they have tended to leave discussion on most aspects of the teacher's role to sociologists, philosophers and adminstrators, and to say little themselves about the obligations which each teacher has towards helping children develop the psychological health which I have been discussing in the present chapter. For the most part psychologists have confined themselves to specific issues related to children's academic progresss and social behaviours to the neglect of broader issues such as the psychological aims of education and the teacher's role in the furtherance of these aims. In consequence educational psychology as a discipline has become associated in the minds of teachers primarily with strategies for helping the minority of children who evidence severe learning or behavioural problems, and little thought has been given to what it has to say about the psychological development of the great majority. And this in spite of the fact that many of the children who go to make up this majority will in adult life form part of the ten per cent of the population who need specialist treatment for mental illness and the much larger percentage who have to contend throughout life with less dramatic but no less real problems of psychological suffering and ill-health.

Within teacher education courses, therefore, students should be helped to grasp the fact that the teacher's role encompasses not blurred commitment to something passed off as pastoral care but a highly specific involvement, within the curriculum as well as outside the curriculum, with crucial and definable areas of children's psychological well-being.

(2)   Once the extent of this involvement has been established, the next point is that teachers should be trained to recognize what is meant by psychological well-being in children. I have already detailed the major variables here, relating them firmly to established criteria on the mature personality, and students should become familiar with these criteria and with the behavioural symptoms with which they are associated. But in addition to matters of recognition, students require practical training in developing the necessary sensitivity to children's psychological states. Role playing exercises are of great importance in this context, and in particular role playing exercises associated with relatively simple but effective psychological techniques for uncovering children's psychological problems and for facilitating discussion of these problems between teacher and child.

Transactional Analysis is one such technique (Barker 1980, Pitman 1982, Simmons 1982), and Neuro Linguistic Programming (Bandler and Grinder 1979, Grinder and Bandler 1982) is another. Neither technique demands psychological knowledge over and above that taught on most initial teacher education programmes, and both give rapid and accurate insights into the more accessible areas of psychological malfunctioning. Tuition in how to administer social skills training programmes (Argyle 1982) is also important. Though aware that many psychological problems in children are related to social difficulties, few teachers are taught how to diagnose these problems and how to offer the necessary practically-orientated remedial measures.

(3)   In addition to specific psychological strategies of this kind, it is also incumbent upon the educational psychology tutor to co-operate with method tutors in order to help students identify ways in which, as teachers, they can use their subject specializations to help promote children's personal development. It is relatively easy to see how this can be done through the teaching of arts subjects — in particular drama, music, literature and religious education — less clear in the case of the sciences (which incidentally present us with something of a paradox since psychology itself aspires to the status of a science rather than an art!) But nevertheless through a concern with the nature of scientific knowledge, together with a concern for the impact of science upon society and upon the individual, the science teacher can play an essential part in work of this nature. The essential pre-requisite is that discussed under the first point above, namely that the science teachers along with colleagues in arts subjects should recognize the responsibilities that they carry in this area, and that teachers of all disciplines should recognize that the school curriculum is not merely a way of helping children learn about the outside world but a way of helping them learn about their own individual self and about the way in which that self relates to, is influenced by and in turn influences the outside world.

(4)   Finally, if teachers are to play a full part in children's personal development, they should be proceeding towards satisfactory development of their own personal lives. Any course in psychology should, in principle, help the individual towards self-understanding and self-management, and the educational psychology component of teacher education courses is no exception. Psychology is essentially a practical discipline, a discipline of doing as well as a discipline of knowing. Often however this practical, self-related aspect of the subject is overlooked, and there is little attempt to use psychology as a way of helping the student teacher identify himself, both personally and professionally, and to establish effective ways of working upon and of resolving problems. This raises broader issues related to the teacher's resistance to professional stress and to negative personal and professional self-concepts, and related to his ability to avoid excessive emotional involvement (of both the over-accepting and over-rejecting kind) with children and with colleagues. But through the action of the educational psychology course, the teacher should emerge better equipped personally as well as professionally to face the tasks that lie ahead.

The very process of learning psychology, and of learning how to apply it to the solution of real-life problems, is the keystone here, but the techniques mentioned under the third point above are also of relevance. Properly structured they lead not only to a greater sensitivity and understanding towards children's psychological problems but also to a greater sensitivity and understanding toward one's own and towards those of one's colleagues.

Conclusion

It is important to anticipate and rebut the possible criticism that I am advocating that the teacher become a kind of amateur psychoanalyst. Such criticism misses the point that, if psychology is effective as a discipline, then it does not require a deep knowledge of psychodynamic structures and strategies to be of practical use in helping people live their lives. We are all psychologists already, even before we take up any training, simply because we are all trying to get to know, to understand, to relate to, and to change for the better other people and ourselves. What is advocated in this chapter is simply that the psychology included in teacher education courses should be designed to help teachers become more effective and caring. In other words that this psychology should be practical, and have as its focus not only the well-trodden field of children's abilities and learning skills, but the equally important and relatively ignored field of their personal development.

Obviously personal development is such a vast area that in one short chapter it has been possible only to touch on the major issues involved. The purpose however has been to show that personal development within education is a proper concern for the psychologist, and that drawing upon the existing work of psychologists a range of advice can be offered to teacher educators as to the nature of this development and the variables that are likely best to encourage it. For the future more attention should be focused on the way that teachers respond to these variables and are able to modify their professional behaviours in the light of them. This in turn will help generate research undertakings aimed at further clarifying the input required by teacher education programmes if students are to be adequately prepared for their tasks in this complex aspect of their work.

References

ALLPORT, G.W. (1961) *Pattern and Growth in Personality*, London, Holt Rinehart and Winston.

Alvin, J. (1975) *Music Therapy*, London, Hutchison.

Apter, M.J. (1982) *The Experience of Motivation*, Academic Press.

Argyle, M. (1981) 'Social behaviour', in Fontana, D. *Psychology for Teachers*, London, MacMillan/British Psychological Society.

Bandler, R. and Grinder, J. (1978) *Frogs into Princes*, Moab, Utah, Real People Press.

Barker, D. (1980) *TA and Training*, London, Gower Press.

Cabot, R.C. (1914) *What Men Live By*, Boston, Houghton Mifflin.

Fontana, D. (1981) 'Reversal theory, the paratelic state and Zen', *Self and Society: European Journal of Humanistic Psychology* 9, pp. 229–36.

Fontana, D. (1984) 'Academic failure', in Gale, A. and Chapman, A. (Eds.) *Psychology and Social Problems*, Chichester, John Wiley and Sons.

Fontana, D. (1985) 'Educating for creativity', in Apter, M.J., Fontana, D. and Murgatroyd, S. (Eds.) *Reversal Theory: Applications and Developments*, Cardiff, University College Cardiff Press.

Grinder, J. and Bandler, R. (1982) *Reframing, Neuro Linguistic Programming and the Transformation of Meaning*, Moab, Utah, Real People Press.

Huizinga, J. (1949) *Homo Ludens: A Study of the Play Element in Culture*. London, Routledge and Kegan Paul.

Hyers, C. (1985) 'Reversal theory as a key to understanding religious diversity', in Apter, M.J., Fontana, D. and Murgatroyd, S. (Eds.) *Reversal Theory: Applications and Developments*, Cardiff, University College Cardiff Press.

Jones, R.M. (1972) *Fantasy and Feeling in Education*, Harmondsworth, Penguin.

Jung, C.G. (1961) *Modern Man in Search of a Soul*, London, Routledge and Kegan Paul.

Krathwohl, D.R. *et al* (1954) *Taxonomy of Educational Objectives: Handbook II, Affective Domain*, New York, David McKay.

Maslow, A.H. (1954) *Motivation and Personality*, New York, Harper and Row.

Maslow, A.H. (1968) *Toward a Psychology of Being*, Princeton, N.J., Van Nostrand, 2nd edition.

Pitman, E. (1982) 'Transactional Analysis: an introduction to its theory and practice', *British Journal of Social Work*, 12, pp. 47–63.

Simmons, C. (1982) 'The use of transactional analysis', *Education Section Review*, 6, pp. 93–6.

Thomas, L.C. (1979) 'Construct, reflect and converse: the conversational reconstruction of social realities', in Stringer, P. and Bannister, D. (Eds.) *Constructs of Sociality and Individuality*, London, Academic Press.

Thomas, L.C. and Augstein, S. (1984) 'Education and the negotiation of personal meaning', *Education Section Review*, 8, pp. 7–36.

Developing Teaching: Psychology and Curriculum

Hazel Francis
University of London Institute of Education

Introduction

Learning to teach involves the trainee in two kinds of curriculum planning — that pertaining to his or her own teaching in school, and that behind the training course. Ways in which psychology might be useful in curriculum design and evaluation can be explored with reference to both; and, because a number of important considerations apply equally to both, the argument below moves rather freely between them.

Whatever else they do teachers must make decisions about what to teach and how. Stenhouse's (1975) idea of the teacher as curriculum developer and researcher is a useful starting point for this essay, since even with fairly strong constraints from government, from examination syllabuses, from local authority and local parental and school policies, the individual teacher still has a considerable degree of freedom. It is this freedom that bears so heavily on the trainee attempting to plan lessons and carry them through, and which contributes to question and discussion amongst teachers and a felt need for in-service training.

Stenhouse (1975, p. 144) summarized his view of the characteristics of the fully professional teacher. These were commitment to development of teaching on the basis of systematic questioning of it, commitment and skill to study one's own teaching, and concern to question and test theory in one's own practice. He envisaged the professional as acting not simply in isolation, but as sharing curriculum research and development with other teachers within the school, and possibly with others in the broader educational field.

This view of the teacher was related to Stenhouse's general approach to curriculum research and development in which he was critical of approaches based on pre-determined educational objectives and emphases on measurement of product. He drew attention to the discipline and tradition-based pool of resource for the curriculum and to the importance of the processes of valuing and exploring in teaching and learning. This, I think, is more interesting and challenging to psychologists than the objectives approach, although much of the debate amongst curriculum specialists has implied that psychologists are particularly inclined to the latter. It is worth seeing how such a limited and mistaken view of psychology has found expression, since the implication could be misleading to teachers, trainers and administrators.

Limited Views of Psychology and of its Value in Education

Three aspects of a tendency to define psychology too narrowly, and then to dismiss it, can be noted, these being reference to behaviourism, mental testing and focus on educational product. Gordon (1981, p. 9) wrote 'The simplistic and muddled assumptions of behaviourism . . . can be seen not only in the reliance on mental testing, but in the behavioural objectives model of curriculum planning and evaluation'. To a psychologist the association of mental testing with behaviourism is surprising in the sense that within psychology they represent very different traditions with different concepts and theories. To the extent that the curriculum objectives model as developed in the US may have drawn upon them it has done so by adopting an 'economics' model of educational provision in which the comparison of measurable outputs has been of crucial interest. It is interesting that writers such as Holt (1981, p. 35–6) recognize this and yet slip, without any adequate historical or theoretical analysis, into confusing behaviourist psychology with economic management thinking and with instructional objectives analysis. The latter, for example, cannot be discussed adequately without reference to Bloom's (1956) account of the origin of the taxonomy of educational objectives in the concerns of college examiners in 1948, not in the work of psychologists, and of the difficulty of relating the taxonomy to theories of learning in psychology. The former seems to be endemic in the American culture, and Eisner (1979) has sketched well the pervasive goal-oriented flavour of American education from Dewey onwards. His view seems to be that psychologists, not always from the strictly behaviourist school, were particularly drawn into this in curriculum development and evaluation in the 1960s.

Since behaviourism stresses observable and measurable acts as providing the data-base for theory one can understand why criticism of the objectives model might attack behaviourist psychology, but the latter is actually more directed towards the conditions under which behaviour changes than to the assessment of end states. Its impact on education is more correctly seen in the development of individualized programmes of learning for a wide range of specific behaviours rather than in curriculum planning in main-stream education. As for educational testing, this is neither the exclusive nor the primary interest of psychologists. As Eisner (1982) acknowledges, such testing is mandatory within the American educational system. There are good historical reasons for confusion, but educational testing should be distinguished from psychometrics in so far as the latter has been developed not only to assess individual differences but also to explore and test theoretical notions pertaining to intelligence and personality.

Altogether it would be a mistake therefore to accept the implied dismissal of psychology which can be seen in criticisms of the objectives model of curriculum design and evaluation. Instead it would be more sensible to consider what positive involvement of psychology in curriculum design is evident or could be usefully developed. There could then be grounds for including psychology in the teacher training curriculum in the light of Stenhouse's model of the teacher.

A search through recent curriculum literature at first looks promising, there being references to the psychology of learning, cognition, child development, the person, and social interaction; but then serious problems become evident. Some of these are to do with the kind of involvement given to psychology. Too often the writers seem to regard psychology as a library resource, something to be used for reference when implementing already formulated curriculum decisions. What is worse, in giving reasons for the selection of topics no case is made for preferring one part of the reference book to another or for the overall pattern of selection. Gordon (1981), for example, judged the nature of intelligence to be worth discussing because different beliefs about it have been associated with educational values. He also referred to the importance, at the classroom level, of taking account of how children learn, of motivation and of cognitive development, but on reading the contributions to his volume, one is struck by the feeling that the reader is being taught simplified psychology rather than being encouraged to use psychology in curriculum thinking. A similar reaction sets in to the volume by Lawton *et al* (1978) which includes such topics in greater detail but gives no disciplined argument as to why they are included, nor as to why they are simply treated as straightforward 'potted' psychology rather than as integral to curriculum issues. Looking at Lawton's own model of the selection of what is to be taught one can begin to see part of the difficulty. In this model philosophical and sociological criteria are used to determine the curriculum selection, and then psychological theory may be drawn upon to assist in working out the actual curriculum sequences and practices. Whether psychological criteria might have a role in the selection process, particularly in curriculum development, and how to choose amongst practical alternatives from psychology, is not asked. It may be said in defence that Lawton intended his model to apply at a national rather than a classroom, or institutional, or subject level, but it is not clear that different models are required for different levels.

An interesting example of the problem in practice can be found in the Schools Council's reports of curriculum development case studies. In Harlen's (1973) account of the development of a project for teaching science to five to thirteen year olds she reported that the terms of reference for the project included 'the identification and development, at appropriate levels, of topics or areas of science related to a framework of concepts appropriate to the ages of the pupils'. She then went on to say that a search through the literature for such a framework of concepts revealed that it did not exist. The assumption appeared to have been that there was a psychology of learning or of cognition adequate for curriculum development but somehow derived independently of curriculum matters. In the event a fairly loose adaptation of the Piaget stages of thinking was adopted, but this was in no sense evaluated in the development. Indeed the actual development appears to be more the writing of a series of materials for use in schools than a complete specification of content and practice. In Patricia Story's (1973) report of the Cambridge School Classics Project in the same volume, it appears that the materials for the project were drafted before any evaluation took place. They were intended to be suitable for pupils aged eleven to twelve and of a wide range of ability, but what is elusive in these reports is the basis on which the materials were selected and drafted. What kind of criteria and information did the writers use to determine the appropriacy of the materials? And did the evaluation suggest any modifications in the light of psychological criteria? Such questions point to the necessity of involving psychology in curriculum development and the difficulty of doing so in an adequate manner.

Problems of Language and Theory in Educational Debate

If there are problems about the adequacy of curriculum theory in its treatment of psychology there are equally quite severe problems related to the language of education. The very nature of the business ensures that terminology to do with child development, learning, thinking, interest and motivation is bound to be used. At the level of everyday language these terms are related and have meaning in so far as they are used to refer to the ordinary experiences of life both in and out of school. In the language of education they are embedded in the network of practices in schools and in philosophical and policy-oriented studies in education. They are part of the language of educational theory. In psychology, however, they are a part of networks of concepts related in theories of development and of learning and thinking behaviours, and they are grounded in particular samplings of behaviour. Their use carries theoretical implications, not always of any utility or relevance for educational practice, but it is not at all clear in much educational writing just what meanings are being involved. One result of this is that references to the possible value of psychology tend to fall short in either a disappointing vagueness or a sampling of psychological theory with insufficient grasp or analysis to relate it to curriculum design.

Unfortunately for teacher training psychology has often been drawn on in just this way. Difficulties in curriculum design for training courses arise both at the level of overall course planning and at the level of using psychology within the curriculum. The psychologist has a dual responsibility to engage in both; but can expect to be treated as a delivery-man, and trainees to be treated as recipients, if psychology is seen as a supply of ready-made goods to be taken from the shelf. Why it should be so treated, especially amongst psychologists, is something of a mystery when it is widely acknowledged that in any scientific enterprise the findings are no more than tested hypotheses still open to further testing, and that the identification of questions and the methods of dealing with them are at least as important as provisional results. It is in the context of a need to affirm this that Stenhouse's approach to curriculum design is so refreshing. He acknowledged a bad press for psychology from some curriculum workers but made a strong claim himself for the importance of the psychology of learning, child development and social psychology. Although he was led into some 'straight psychology' reporting as a result of selecting certain issues, he emphasized curriculum workers' 'need to share the psychologists' curiosity about the process of learning rather than be dominated by their conclusions'. This extends to a good case for the involvement of psychologists and their research practices in teacher education.

Underlying Issues in Psychologists' Engagement
with the Curriculum

To move interest in psychology from findings to curiosity is to bring the thinking of the psychologist to the fore and to stress a discipline of systematic inquiry rather than a body of knowledge. This necessarily invites examination of the philosophies and models behind psychological investigation and it becomes clearer that differences in findings are not arbitrary or inexplicable but rest on different assumptions about the learner, the process of learning and the nature of what is learned. Without some coherence with the philosophical and sociological criteria to which Lawton referred for the selection of curriculum content, it is not possible to know how to turn to psychology for help in working out the curriculum. The way the Peabody language development programme, which was based on a behaviourist model of learning, was rejected by teachers who had been trained to a curriculum built on a child-centred model illustrates the point (Halsey, 1972). In order, therefore, to devise and implement a curriculum it is necessary to be selective within philosophical stances to questions of learning, and to appropriately contain the domain of psychological curiosity.

Crucial considerations will include conceptions of the learner as active rather than passive, not because passivity is ruled out but because activity certainly cannot be, and is moreover generally regarded as desirable, at least within the UK educational system. They will also include views of development as constrained by nature or experience. Clearly educators are most interested in the effects of experience, but there must be some question about the constraints of nature. The extent to which motivation in learning is viewed with or without reference to what is learned is also important, as is the extent to which the learning process is regarded as closed or open. It is legitimate to inquire into learning which is clearly delimited and with a single end, as well as to explore that which opens up a number of possibilities for fresh thinking. The task for the educator is to select wisely in relation to other curriculum decisions. Additionally the manner in which the learning and teaching processes are regarded as structured is important, particularly in relation to the way in which the skill or knowledge to be learned is analyzed. This is a central issue in curriculum development. Further considerations must be the ways conditions of learning at all levels from the classroom to the system are modelled, and how inter-personal relations between learners and teachers are conceived in relation to educational aims of personal development and to conceptions of the role of communication in learning. While these are not exhaustive they are sufficient to indicate that sharing curiosity with the psychologist implies not only the adoption of a general attitude of inquiry necessitating empirical testing of ideas, but also a choice of philosophical and theoretical stance and the development of a nose for questions and methods of inquiry which are appropriate within curriculum design. The implication for teacher trainers is that, if they take the Stenhouse view of the teacher seriously, they should perhaps be in the business of encouraging that attitude and developing that nose both in themselves for their training programmes and in their students for their work in schools. To do this they will no doubt wish to see, and perhaps to use, any reports of how psychologists have engaged with curriculum issues in mainstream education.

Limitations and Promise in Psychologists' Involvement in Curriculum Matters

A very clear chapter on contributions from learning theory was written by Gagné (1971). It traced how psychology has tended to operate at a level of detachment from specific educational contexts. He reviewed Skinner's analysis of learning (which he considered to have only very general applicability in the school situation); his own work, referring to the conditions of learning ranging from classical conditioning to principle learning and problem solving; and also Ausubel's approach to the psychology of meaningful verbal learning, stressing how this really comes to grips directly and specifically with the learning of facts and principles, and is therefore very much related to learning in school. He also treated the learner's contribution to his own learning, and analyzed the differences between individualized instruction and group instruction. A reading of this chapter leaves the impression that psychology needs to meet the curriculum in certain important ways. On the one hand it is possible for the curriculum specialist or subject specialist to analyze what is to be learned in terms of say concepts, and principles and so of the network connecting them, while on the other hand it is possible for the psychologist to give some theoretical coherence to the principles of learning these concepts and principles. Only if the two come together, however, can this be done in relation to the specific materials concerned. Gagné commented that he knew of no textbook or curriculum which had been designed on the basis of psychological principles but he pointed out that there was nothing to stop the individual teacher or pupil from employing them, at least to some extent, within the existing curriculum. This has strong implications for training.

Gagné's own approach (Gagné 1965; 1967) was to make a logical analysis of the learning sequence required for a topic and then to test the derived result, alter it if necessary and retest until an optimal solution was found. Although it is perfectly possible to criticize his focus on performance objectives and the superficial attention to questions of structure within the mathematical topic, it would be a mistake not to recognize that within a broader or different perspective the technique of scalogram analysis in an empirical testing of anticipated orders of psychological or epistemological difficulty might be very useful.

With a different orientation and an interest in developmental and cognitive psychology Bruner (1960) developed an analysis of the process of instruction. He attempted to relate inquiry-based learning to the structure of knowledge in the learner and in the subject to be learned. He first sketched how the original interest of American educational psychologists in the nature of learning in schools had changed over the years.

> The psychology of learning tended to become involved with the precise details of learning in highly simplified short-term situations and thereby lost much of its contact with the long-term educational effects of learning. For their part, educational psychologists turned their attention with great effect to the study of aptitude and achievement, and to social and motivational aspects of education, but did not concern themselves directly with the intellectual structure of class activities. (p. 4)

He argued that work of the last two decades on the nature of learning, and particularly on transfer, had turned interest back to learning in schools, basically because it had been shown that massive general transfer could be achieved by appropriate learning, including learning how to learn. He himself pursued his own particular interest in the question of learning a structured body of knowledge. This led him to discuss readiness, structure and intuition; and he dealt with the issue that is now so familiar of how far one can teach a topic, provided it is appropriately structured, to a child of any age.

In practical terms Bruner was responsible for the development of a project entitled 'Man, a course of study' intended to promote in children an understanding of man, his nature, development and adaptation to environment. Such a curriculum development did not lend itself to the objectives evaluation approach used by Gagné, but a report of the way it was received by teachers and children was produced and an interesting critique can be found in Jones (1968). This can only extend an appreciation of the importance of an inquiry attitude, but it also adds to the repertoire of inquiry techniques and in a way which would presumably please the critics of overly narrow testing approaches by including observation, interview and diary records with cross-checking from different observers. Jones himself wrote from a psycho-analytic point of view and raised a number of concerns about the emotional and expressive aspects of curriculum both in the critique of Bruner's work and in a separate volume (Jones, 1966). His work would presumably appeal to Eisner, who, whilst accepting that cognitive development is the business of education, has been critical of overly-narrow conceptions of cognition and, by viewing it in the light of the various forms of representation and communication open to learners, has effectively asked for epistemological analysis to inform curriculum design (Eisner, 1982).

This raises a question which has been of explicit interest to psychologists for some time and is probably behind the common practice of introducing student teachers to the works of Bruner, Piaget and Vygotsky. Unfortunately, without a nose for the curriculum issues of interest, what is gleaned is a potted version of each with forced comparisons of uncertain value. The fundamental positions of the three differ with respect to the origins and grounds of knowledge. At the risk of dangerous over-simplification it might be said that Piaget saw the growth of knowledge as based in the interaction between the development of the biologically based, maturing thinking powers of the individual and his experiences in his environment. Bruner brought in an evolutionary angle to both the biological basis in the individual and the social basis in the environment. Vygotsky emphasized the impact of the social curriculum on the growing child. Thus the most interesting question for the curriculum designer to ask is not 'What does Piaget, Bruner or Vygotsky say about mathematics (or whatever) teaching to five, ten, or fifteen year olds?' Rather it is, 'If five, ten, or fifteen year olds can generally cope with this aspect of mathematics (or whatever), is this inevitable under any circumstances or does it happen only under a certain broad social curriculum or is it due to the specific way they have been taught in school?' These are questions which can be investigated empirically, and the literature yields some useful hints on how to go about the task. There is the additional epistemological problem, to return to Eisner, of what coping with the task might mean, and again the literature is not lacking in methodological signposts, but this is a good point at which to turn to psychology in the UK for this problem has been addressed to some extent in work in psychology in this country.

In so doing one finds relatively little engagement with the school curriculum. It has already been suggested that this is partly due to the way curriculum decisions have been largely regarded as the province of teachers but it may also be attributed to a relative lack of interest amongst psychologists. Insofar as research which may bear on curriculum design is concerned, as for example research into the thinking strategies and abilities of children when faced with particular problems, the principal target has been to inform straightforward psychological theory of cognitive development, with perhaps a passing suggestion that it may be relevant to education. There are exceptions, however, and it is worth looking at some of those that are addressed to the investigation of learning from realistically complex materials. Inroads are being made by Bennett and Desforges (1984) and Francis (1982) into learning within the curriculum in primary schools, while Peel (1971) Entwistle (1981) and Pask (1976 a, b, c) have reported work in higher and secondary education. These researches share attempts to analyze learning strategies in relation to curriculum task demands.

Peel (1971) reported his empirical testing of hypotheses about the levels of understanding and judgment shown by adolescents in reasoning tasks typical of those they find in various subjects in the school curriculum. He was influenced by the manner in which Piaget had investigated the development of logical reasoning but did not confine himself to this. His work would stimulate Stenhouse's research-minded teacher to a disciplined exploration of the thinking of his or her own pupils in relation to the work designed for them, and thus give a basis for making informed decisions in curriculum design.

Pask (1976a, 1976b) reported a much more complex investigation, unfortunately in terms which are not at all easy to comprehend. His theoretical position is not unlike that of Meredith (1948, 1966) who elaborated a systematic epistemics or study of the forms and instruments of communication on which learning depends and in which knowledge is grounded. Meredith developed a scheme of topic analysis based on a conception of education as the development of public knowledge, a process which requires individuals to forego their fine differences of private experience and to agree on a 'logic' of language and a 'logic' of the dynamics of matter in the physical world. Teaching and learning involves the objective correction of expressions which disagree and thus a careful attention to their form rather than their material expression. In Meredith's view topic analysis, based on this conception of the development of knowledge, would yield instruments, methods and insights for the experimental investigation of educational processes. This theoretical approach did not in fact yield much experimental work, partly because the form in which Meredith expressed it was through geometrical models of epistemic relations.

Pask, however, has recently engaged in experimental testing of similar ideas. His theory (Pask, 1976c) describes learning in terms of 'conversations' between two representations of knowledge, either in the cognitive structures of two people or in the cognitive structure of a learner and the representation of knowledge in curriculum materials. His 'conversation' is not unlike Meredith's conception of establishing agreement in the development of public knowledge. Pask has, however, worked through his own esoteric expression of his theory, to practical realizations of 'conversations' between learners' knowledge structures and carefully analyzed curriculum subject areas. By using a computer to control and record the way a student proceeds through the learning materials and by providing materials through which understanding of necessary concepts can be demonstrated, he has been able to explore the learning strategies adopted in the face of quite complex and realistic demands. His work challenges the teacher not only to explore the way he or she structures the curriculum and the levels of understanding and judgment shown by pupils in relation to different structures, but also to explore the way learners set about the tasks. Do they show the formation of complex hypotheses and the use of analogy described by Pask as 'holist' strategies or do they show the 'serialist' approach of step-by-step learning with simpler, narrower hypotheses? And do they balance these appropriately in relation to the task or do they show handicapping biases? Although Pask concentrated on the learning of the individual student engaging with curriculum materials his theory also opens up the possibility of modelling and exploring the interpersonal engagement of knowledge structures. This would lead to questions relating to strategies of negotiation of agreed meanings in interpersonal communication.

Teaching and Training — Implications of the Stenhouse Model

By now it may be objected that his kind of research enterprise is far beyond the capacity of the teacher in his day-to-day work, and clearly if actual research reports were being demanded this would be so. But the thrust of this paper is not that the teacher should be a research worker, but that he or she should have a research attitude and a nose for questions and techniques that will aid in classroom curriculum decisions. Given the rate at which computers are entering schools the Pask approach may soon be seen to be compatible with classroom practice.

It will also be asked what this approach means in practical terms in teacher training. To this at least four things should be said. First, it cries out for cooperation between the traditional foundation and method tutors in the curriculum design and implementation of training courses. It implies that psychology in the training curriculum should have a real impact at the level of the trainee's preparation and implementation of lesson plans. (Possibly after the event, for example, these could be usefully analyzed with guidance in the light of various psychological questions about the relationships between the instruction, materials, learning and topic.) At this level of involvement the model also suggests some empirical exploration and the trainee could be helped to systematically examine or test some aspect of practice. For the trainer, the problem of selection of materials and methods of training should be tackled consistently and in accordance with the model of the teacher and the model of training he or she has in mind. Selection must therefore be economical, practical, empirically tested, and wise. (Would that psychology texts for teachers could make explicit the criteria for their form and content, rather than displaying potentially useful wares with no clue that there is a big gap between resource and use!) Finally, the model of teacher as curriculum developer and researcher is only one aspect of what it might mean to be a professional teacher, and it should not be used too greedily. Other models have strong claims to serious consideration.

Conclusions

The conclusions to be drawn from consideration of the implications of Stenhouse's view of the teacher for the role of psychology in teacher training can now be brought together. First, psychology cannot be dismissed from curriculum considerations on grounds that certain underlying values and assumptions are incompatible with favoured educational values. The range of philosophical positions within psychology is too great. This range requires that if wise choices are to be made the positions be systematically evaluated in relation to the philosophical and sociological criteria adopted in curriculum selection decisions. This does not imply that particular choices must follow, but that both trainers and trainees should comprehend the grounds of selection. Second, it is not consistent with a view of the teacher as having a research attitude to his or her work to seek to use psychology simply to present findings. Moreover, much of psychological research in education can offer little in the way of findings because it has engaged relatively little with curriculum design. What can be offered is assistance with the development of the research attitude and with sharing a nose for interesting questions and ways of exploring them. Third, it is consistent with the research model of the teacher that the same model be thought of for the trainer. This implies a research attitude and 'nose' in all trainers, including psychologists. Just as the teacher in school is expected to discuss, design, and test the curriculum in partnership with colleagues, so teacher trainers need to work out a training curriculum which is continually under discussion and development. The psychology contribution ought to be understood in terms of whatever underlying philosophical and sociological criteria are adopted, and the grounds for selection ought therefore to be explicit. Psychologists in teacher training need to be engaged in determination of these and to be clear about them and about the implications for their selection of curriculum content and practice. Training institutions will not necessarily come to identical decisions. Finally, although the teacher cannot be expected to analyze and research curriculum development beyond the challenge of his or her own classroom, the trainer has a considerable obligation to be involved in the epistemological analysis required for adequate research and with its implementation in school-based contexts. If training has been wisely implemented the teacher should prove to be an understanding participant in such research and development.

References

BENNETT, N. and DESFORGES, C. (1984) *The Quality of Pupil Learning Experiences*, London, Lawrence Erlbaum Assoc.

BLOOM, B.S. (1956) *Taxonomy of Educational Objectives: 1. The Cognitive Domain*, London, Longmans.

BRUNER, J.S. (1960) *The Process of Education*, Cambridge, Mass, Harvard University Press.

EISNER, E. (1979) *The Educational Imagination*, New York, Macmillan.

EISNER, E. (1982) *Cognition and Curriculum*, New York, Longman.

ENTWISTLE, N.J. (1981) *Styles of Learning and Teaching*, Chichester, Wiley.

FRANCIS, H. (1982) *Learning to Read*, London, Allen and Unwin.

GAGNÉ, R.M. (1965) *The Conditions of Learning*, New York, Holt, Rinehart and Winston.

GAGNÉ, R.M. (1967) 'Curriculum research and the promotion of learning', in TYLER, R., GAGNÉ, R. and SCRIVEN, M. (Eds.) *Perspectives of Curriculum Evaluation*, Chicago, Rand McNally.

GAGNÉ, R.M. (1971) 'Learning theory, educational media, and individualized instruction', in HOOPER, R. (Ed.) *The Curriculum: Context, Design and Development*, Edinburgh, Oliver and Boyd.

GORDON, P. (1981) *The Study of the Curriculum*, London; Batsford.

HALSEY, A.H. (1972) *Educational Priority Volume 1: E.P.A. Problems and Policies*, London, HMSO.

HARLEN, W. (1973) 'Science 5–13 Project', in Schools Council, *Evaluation in Curriculum Development: Twelve Case Studies*, London, Macmillan Educational.

HOLT, M. (1981) *Evaluating the Evaluators*, London, Hodder and Stoughton.

JONES, R.M. (1966) *Contemporary Educational Psychology*, New York, Harper and Row.

JONES, R.M. (1968) *Fantasy and Feeling in Education*, New York, New York University Press.

LAWTON, D. *et al*. (1978) *Theory and Practice of Curriculum Studies*, London, Routledge and Kegan Paul.

MEREDITH, G.P. (1948) 'The method of topic analysis', *Educ. Dev. Assn*.

MEREDITH, G.P. (1966) *Instruments of Communication*, Oxford, Pergamon.

PASK, G. (1976a) 'Conversational techniques in the study and practice of education', *British Journal of Educational Psychology*, 46, pp. 12–25.

PASK, G. (1976b) 'Styles and strategies of learning', *British Journal of Educational Psychology*, 46, pp. 128–48.

PASK, G. (1976c) *Conversation Theory: Applications in Education and Epistemology*, Amsterdam, Elsevier.

PEEL, E.A. (1971) *The Nature of Adolescent Judgment*, London, Staples.

STENHOUSE, L. (1975) *An Introduction to Curriculum Research and Development*, London, Heinemann.

STORY, P. (1973) 'Cambridge school classics project', in Schools Council, *Evaluation in Curriculum Development: Twelve Case Studies*. London, Macmillan Educ.

Postscript

This book began by asking how to teach and by giving some indication of the ways the practices rather than the theories of psychology might prove useful. This question opened up the yawning gap between the psychology needs of trainers and trainees and the kind of academic psychology which can easily be supplied but which apparently makes very little impact. Reasons for the gap and analyses of its nature were developed in the first part of the book. Suggestions for ways of bridging it began to emerge in the second and third, essentially by taking seriously what it means to become a teacher and what it means to provide an education.

In becoming a teacher the need is for a self-constructed, active, practical psychology which will carry the trainee forward in terms of both his or her own learning and personal development and that of the pupils. Psychologists can help with the sign-posts, concepts, principles and supports they find most useful from their expert knowledge of their field, but real help means using these in active engagement with the trainees in their work.

Psychology, it appears, can do more than evaluate principles and practices of teaching in the light of its theories and research methods. It can test and lend its own practices, which span research, counselling, training, and teaching. The authors of this book, in one way or another, are saying that psychologists in teacher training should practice their psychology.

What they are not saying is that psychologists in teacher education and training should all be doing the same thing, only that perhaps it should be the same kind of thing. Courses have their own characteristic curricula and psychologists their own expertise. Nevertheless, psychologists could evaluate the effects of their practices, and since these will vary across courses this might give better-informed options than are available at present. This cannot honestly be done, however, without judgment of the human and educational values that lie behind them. The criteria for selection of psychological input, whether it be information or practice, are not contained solely within the discipline. They include those arising from the collaborative nature of education and those which are generally used to determine what is good.

Bibliography

ADAMS, J. (1897) *Herbartian Psychology Applied to Education*, London, D.C. Heath and Co.

ADVISORY COMMITTEE on the SUPPLY and EDUCATION of TEACHERS (ACSET) (1984) *Teacher Training and Special Educational Needs*, London, HMSO.

ALLPORT, G.W. (1961) *Pattern and Growth in Personality*, London, Holt Rinehart and Winston.

ALVIN, J. (1975) *Music Therapy*, London, Hutchinson.

ANDERSON, L.M. (1981) *Student Responses to Seatwork: Implications for the Study of Students' Cognitive Processing*, Paper presented to AERA: Los Angeles.

ANDERSON, T.H., ARMBRUSTER, B.B. and KANTOR, R.N. (1980) *How clearly written are children's textbooks?* Urbana, Centre for the Study of Reading, University of Illinois.

APTER, M.J. (1982) *The Experience of Motivation*, London, Academic Press.

APTER, S.J. (1982) *Troubled Children, Troubled Systems*, Oxford, Pergamon.

ARGYLE, M. (1981) Social Behaviour in FONTANA, D. *Psychology for Teachers*, London, Macmillan/British Psychological Society.

ARGYLE, M. (1983) *The Psychology of Interpersonal Behaviour* (4th Edition) Harmondsworth, Penguin.

ASHTON, P. (1983) *Teacher Education in the Classroom*, London, Croom Helm.

AUSUBEL, D. (1968) *Educational Psychology: A Cognitive View*, New York, Holt Rinehart and Winston.

AUSUBEL, D.P. and ROBINSON, R.G. (1969) *School Learning: An Introduction to Educational Psychology*, New York, Holt Rinehart and Winston.

AYLLON, T. and ROBERTS, M.D. (1974) 'Eliminating disruptive problems by strengthening academic performance', *Journal of Applied Behaviour Analysis*, 7, pp. 71–6.

BAIN, A. (1879) *Education as a Science*, London, Kegan Paul.

BANDLER, R. and GRINDER, J. (1978) *Frogs into Princes*, Moab, Utah, Real People Press.

BANNISTER, D. (1982) 'Personal construct theory and the teaching of psychology', *BPS Education Section Review*, 6, pp. 73–9.

BARKER, D. (1980) *TA and Training*, London, Gower Press.

BARNES, D. (1977) *Language Across the Curriculum*, London, Heinemann.

BAROODY, A.J. and GINSBURG, H.P. (1982) *The Effect of Instruction on Children's Understanding of the 'Equals' Sign*, Paper presented to AERA: New York.

BARTLETT, F.C. (1958) *Thinking: An Experimental and Social Study*, London, Allen and Unwin.

BECK, I.L. and McCASLIN, E.S. (1978) *An Analysis of Dimensions that Affect the Development of Code Breaking Ability in Eight Beginning Reading Programmes*, Learning research and development centre, University of Pittsburgh.

BENNETT, N. and DESFORGES, C. (1984) *The Quality of Pupil Learning Experiences*, London, Lawrence Erlbaum Assoc.

BERNBAUM, G. (1982) *The Structure and Process of Initial Teacher Education Within Universities in England and Wales*, University of Leicester.

BIGGS, J.B. (1978) 'Individual and group differences in study processes', *Br. J. Educ. Psychol.*, 48, pp. 266–79.

BIGGS, J.B. and COLLIS, K. (1982) *Evaluating the Quality of Learning, the SOLO Taxonomy*, New York, Academic Press.

BINET, A. (1903) *L'Etude Expérimentale de l'Intelligence*, Paris, Schleicher Frères.

BLOOM, B.S. (1956) *Taxonomy of Educational Objectives: 1. The Cognitive Domain*, London, Longmans.

BLOOM, B.S. (1976) *Human Characteristics and School Learning*, New York, McGraw Hill.

BLOOM, B.S. (1979) *Alterable Variables: The New Direction in Educational Research*, Edinburgh, Scottish Council for Research in Education.

BRAY, N.W. (1979) 'Strategy production in the retarded' in ELLIS, N.R. (Ed) *Handbook of Mental Deficiency, Psychological Theory and Research* (2nd Edition) Hillsdale, N.J., Lawrence Erlbaum Associates.

BRESSLER, M. (1963) 'The conventional wisdom of education and sociology' in PAGE, C.H. (Ed) *Sociology and Contemporary Education*, New York, Random House.

BROADBENT, D.E. (1975) 'Cognitive psychology and education', *British Journal of Educational Psychology*, 45, pp. 162–76.

BRONFENBRENNER, U. (1977) 'Toward an experimental ecology of human development', *American Psychologist*, 32, pp. 513–31.

BRUNER, J.S. (1960) *The Process of Education*, Cambridge, Mass., Harvard University Press.

BRUNER, J.S. (1966) *Toward a Theory of Instruction*, Cambridge, Mass., Harvard University Press.

BURT, C., VERNON, P.E., THORNDIKE, E.L., DREVER, J., PEAR, T.H., MYERS, C.H. (1941–3) 'Is the doctrine of instincts dead?' in *British Journal of Educational Psychology*, 11, 3; 12, 1, 2, 3; 13, 1.

BUTCHER, H.J. (1965) 'Attitudes of student teachers to education: a comparison with attitudes of experienced teachers and a study of changes during training courses', *British Journal of Social and Clinical Psychology*, 4, 17–24.

CABOT, R.C. (1914) *What Men Live By*, Boston, Houghton Mifflin.

CHAMBERS, J. and CHAMBERS, P. (1984) 'Teacher educators and teachers', in ALEXANDER, R.J., CRAFT, M. and LYNCH, J. (Eds) *Change in Teacher*

Education, London, Holt, Rinehart and Winston.

CHILD, D. (1977) *Psychology and the Teacher* (2nd Edition), London, Holt, Rinehart and Winston.

CLAXTON, G.L. (1978) *The Little Ed Book*, London, Routledge and Kegan Paul.

CLAXTON, G.L. (1984) *Live and Learn: An Introduction to the Psychology of Growth and Change in Everyday Life*, London, Harper and Row.

CLEGG, A. (1973) *Children in Distress*, Harmondsworth, Penguin.

COCKCROFT, W.H. (1982) *Mathematics Counts*, Report of the Committee of Inquiry into the Teaching of Mathematics in Schools, London, HMSO.

COLE, M. and SCRIBNER, S. (1974) *Culture and Cognition: A Psychological Introduction*, London, Wiley.

CRUICKSHANK, M. (1970) *A History of the Training of Teachers in Scotland*, University of London Press.

DAHLGREN, L.O. (1984) 'The outcome of learning, in MARTON, F. *et al.*, *The Experience of Learning*. Edinburgh, Scottish Academic Press.

DALE, I.R. (1977) *The Structural Context of Teaching*, Open University.

DENSCOMBE, M. (1980) 'The work of teaching: An analytic framework for the study of teachers in classrooms', *British Journal of Sociology of Education*, 1, 3, pp. 279–91.

DENSCOMBE, M. (1982) 'The hidden pedagogy and its implications for teacher training', *British Journal of Sociology of Education*, 3, 3, pp. 249–63.

DEPARTMENT of EDUCATION and SCIENCE (1984) *Initial Teacher Training: Approval of Courses*, DES, Circular No. 3/84 Welsh Office Circular No. 21/84: Annex, pp. 8–9, paras. 11–12.

DESFORGES, C. (1982) 'In place of Piaget: Recent research on children's learning', *Educational Analysis*, 4, pp. 27–42.

DESFORGES, C., COCKBURN, A.D., BENNETT, S. and WILKINSON, W. (1985) 'Understanding the quality of pupil learning experience', in ENTWISTLE, N.J. (Ed.) *New Directions in Educational Psychology: I: Learning and Teaching*, Lewes, Falmer Press.

DOMINOWSKI, R.L. (1974) 'How do people discover concepts', in SOLSO, R.L. (Ed.) *Theories in Cognitive Psychology*, Chicago, Loyola University.

DOYLE, W. (1979) 'Making managerial decision in the classroom', in DUKE, D. (Ed.) *Classroom Management* 78th Yearbook of the NSSE, Part 2, Chicago, University of Chicago Press.

DOYLE, W. (1983) 'Academic work', *Review of Educational Research*, 53, pp. 159–99.

DREEBEN, R. (1970) *The Nature of Teaching, Schools and the Work of Teachers*, London, Scott Foresman and Co.

DRIVER, R. (1982) 'Children's learning in science', *Educational Analysis*, 4, pp. 69–79.

DURKIN, D. (1981) 'Reading comprehension instruction in five basal reader series', *Reading Research Quarterly*, 16, pp. 515–44.

EASLEY, J. and EASLEY, E. (1983) *Group Learning in a Japanese School and the American Ideal of Individualism*, Paper presented to AERA: Montreal.

EDGEWORTH, M. and EDGWORTH, R.L. (1798) and (1974) *Practical Education*, London, Reprinted by Garland Publishing.

EISER, R.L. (1980) *Cognitive Social Psychology*, London, McGraw-Hill.

EISNER, E. (1979) *The Educational Imagination*, New York, Macmillan.

EISNER, E. (1982) *Cognition and Curriculum*, New York, Longman.

EISNER, E. (1983) *Can Educational Research Inform Educational Practice?* Paper presented to AERA: Montreal.

ENTWISTLE, N.J. (1981) *Styles of Learning and Teaching*, London, Wiley.

ENTWISTLE, N.J., HANLEY, M. and HOUNSELL, D.J. (1979) 'Identifying distinctive approaches to studying', *Higher Education*, 8, pp. 365–80.

ENTWISTLE, N.J. and KOZEKI, B. (1985) 'Relationships between school motivation, approaches to studying, and attainment among British and Hungarian adolescents', *British Journal of Educational Psychology* — forthcoming.

ENTWISTLE, N.J. and MARTON, F. (1984) 'Changing conceptions of learning and research', in Marton *et al.*, *The Experience of Learning*, Edinburgh, Scottish Academic Press.

ENTWISTLE, N.J. and RAMSDEN, P. (1983) *Understanding Student Learning*, London, Croom Helm.

ERLWANGER, S. (1975) 'Case studies of children's conceptions of mathematics', *Journal of Children's Mathematical Behaviour*, 1, p. 157.

ETZIONI, A. (Ed.) (1969) *The Semi-Professions and their Organisation*, New York, Free Press.

EVANS, P., BEVERIDGE, M. and HALIL, T. (1986) 'Analyzing teacher/child interaction in the classroom through linear modelling techniques', *Educational Psychology*, in press.

FESTINGER, L. (1957) *A Theory of Cognitive Dissonance*, New York, Harper & Row.

FINLAYSON, D.S. and COHEN, L. (1967) 'The teachers' role: a comparative study of conceptions of college of education students and headteachers', *British Journal of Educational Psychology*, 37, 1, pp. 22–6.

FLOUD, J. (1962) 'Teaching in the affluent society', *British Journal of Sociology*, 13, 299–308.

FONTANA, D. (1981) 'Reversal theory, the paratelic state and Zen', *Self and Society: European Journal of Humanistic Psychology*, 9, pp. 229–36.

FONTANA, D. (1984) 'Academic failure', in GALE, A. and CHAPMAN, A. (Eds.) *Psychology and Social Problems*, Chichester, John Wiley & Sons.

FONTANA, D. (1985) 'Educating for creativity', in APTER, M.J., FONTANA, D. and MURGATROYD, S. (Eds.) *Reversal Theory: Applications and Developments*, Cardiff, University College Cardiff Press.

FRANCIS, H. (1982) *Learning to Read: Literate Behaviour and Orthographic Knowledge*, London, Allen and Unwin.

FRANCIS, P. (1975) *Beyond Control? A Study of Discipline in the Comprehensive School*, London, Allen and Unwin.

FRANSSON, A. (1977) 'On qualitative differences in learning IV — Effects of motivation and text-anxiety on process and outcome', *British Journal of Educational Psychology*, 47, pp. 244–57.

GAGNÉ, R.M. (1965) *The Conditions of Learning*, New York, Holt, Rinehart and Winston (3rd Edition 1977).

GAGNÉ, R.M. (1967) 'Curriculum Research and the Promotion of Learning', in TYLER, R., GAGNÉ, R. and SCRIVEN, M. (Eds.) *Perspectives of Curriculum Evaluation*, Chicago, Rand McNally.

GAGNÉ, R.M. (1971) 'Learning theory, educational media, and individualised instruction', in HOOPER, R. (Ed.) *The Curriculum: Context, Design and*

Development, Edinburgh, Oliver and Boyd.

GAGNÉ, R.M. and BRIGGS, L.J. (1979) *Principles of Instructional Design*, New York, Holt, Rinehart and Winston.

GAMMON, E.M. (1973) 'Syntactical analysis of some first grade readers', in HINTIKKA, K.J.J. *et al.*, (Eds.) *Approaches to Natural Language*, Dordrecht, Reidel.

GIBBS, G. (1981) *Teaching Students to Learn*, Milton Keynes, Open University Press.

GINSBURG, M.B., MEYENN, R.J. and MILLER, H.D.R. (1980) 'Teachers' conceptions of professionalism and trades unionism: An ideological analysis', in WOODS, P. (Ed.) *Teacher Strategies*, London, Croom Helm.

GLASER, R., PELLEGRINO, J.W. and LESGOLD, A.M. (1977) 'Some directions for a cognitive psychology of instruction', in LESGOLD, A.M. *et al.* (Eds.) *Cognitive Psychology and Instruction*, New York, Plenum Press.

GLASS, D. (1961) 'Education and social change in modern society', in HALSEY, A.H., FLOUD, J. and ANDERSON, C.A. (Eds.) *Education Economy and Society*, Free Press of Glencoe.

GLIDDEN, L.M. (1979) 'Training of learning and memory in retarded persons: strategies, techniques and teaching tools', in ELLIS, N.R. (Ed.) *Handbook of Mental Deficiency, Psychological Theory and Research*, (2nd Edition). Hillsdale, N.J., Lawrence Erlbaum Assoc.

GOODE, W.J. (1969) 'The theoretical limitations of professionalisation', in ETZIONI, A. (Ed.) *The Semi-Professions and their Organisation*, New York, Free Press.

GORDON, P. (1981) *The Study of the Curriculum*, London, Batsford.

GORDON, P., PERKIN, H., SOCKETT, A.H. and HOYLE, E. (1983) *Is Teaching a Profession?* Bedford Way Papers No. 15, University of London Institute of Education.

GRINDER, J. and BANDLER, R. (1982) *Reframing: Neuro Linguistic Programming and the Transformation of Meaning*, Moab, Utah, Real People Press.

HALSEY, A.H. (1972) *Educational Priority Volume 1: E.P.A. Problems and Policies*, London, HMSO.

HANNAM, C. (1977) *Young Teachers and Reluctant Learners*, Harmondsworth, Penguin.

HANSON, D. and HERRINGTON, M. (1976) *From College to Classroom: the Probationer Year*, London, Routledge and Kegan Paul.

HARGREAVES, D.H. (1978) 'what teaching does to teachers', *New Society*, 9, pp. 540–2.

HARGREAVES, D.H. (1980) 'Occupational culture of teachers', in WOODS, P. (Ed.) *Teacher Strategies*, London, Croom Helm.

HARING, N.G. AND LOVITT, T.C. (1978) 'Systematic instructional procedures: An instructional hierarchy', in HARING, N.G., LOVITT, T.C., EATON, M.D. and HANSEN, C.L. (Eds.) *The Fourth R: Research in the Classroom*, London, Merrill.

HARLEN, W. (1973) 'Science 5–13 Project', in Schools Council, *Evaluation in Curriculum Development: Twelve Case Studies*, London, Macmillan Educational.

HARRIS, K. (1982) *Teachers and Classes: A Marxist Analysis*, London, Routledge and Kegan Paul.

HART, K.M. (1981) *Children's Understanding of Mathematics: 11–16*, London, Murray.

HAWKINS, D. (1973) 'What it means to teach', *Teachers College Record*, September.

HIRST, P. (1983) *Educational Theory and its Foundation Disciplines*, London Routledge and Kegan Paul.

HODGSON, V. (1984) 'Learning from lectures', in Marton *et al. The Experience of Learning*, Edinburgh, Scottish Academic Press.

HOLMES, E. (1911) As quoted in MATHIESON, M. *The Preachers of Culture*, London, George Allen and Unwin.

HOLT, J. (1969) *How Children Fail*, Harmondsworth, Penguin.

HOLT, J. (1970) *How Children Learn*, Harmondsworth, Penguin.

HOLT, M. (1981) *Evaluating the Evaluators*, London, Hodder and Stoughton.

HOYLE, E. (1983) 'The professionalisation of teachers: A paradox', in GORDON, P. *et al. Is Teaching a Profession?* Bedford Way Papers, No. 15, University of London Institute of Education.

HUIZINGA, J. (1949) *Homo Ludens: A Study of the Play Element in Culture*, London, Routledge and Kegan Paul.

HUNT, J. McV. and KIRK, G.E. (1974) 'Criterion referenced tests of school readiness: A paradigm with illustrations', *Genetic Psychology Monographs*, 90, pp. 144–82.

HYERS, C. (1985) 'Reversal theory as a key to understanding religious diversity', in APTER, M.J., FONTANA, D. and MURGATROYD, S. (Eds.) *Reversal Theory: Applications and developments*, Cardiff, University College Cardiff Press.

INHELDER, B. (1943) French edition, translated by STEPHENS, W.B. (1968) *The Diagnosis of Reasoning in the Mentally Retarded*, New York, Day.

JACKSON, P. (1968) *Life in Classrooms*, New York, Holt, Rinehart and Winston.

JACKSON, P.W. (1977) 'The way teachers think', in GLIDEWELL, J.G. (Ed.) *The Social Context of Teaching*, New York, Gardner Press.

JAMES, W. (1899) *Talks to Teachers on Psychology: And to Students on Some of Life's Ideals*, London, Longmans.

JARRETT, J.L. (1983) Review of H. Judge, American Graduate Schools of Education, *British Journal of Educational Studies*, 31, 3, p. 268.

JONES, R.M. (1966) *Contemporary Educational Psychology*, New York, Harper and Row.

JONES, R.M. (1968) *Fantasy and Feeling in Education*, New York, University Press, (1972) Harmondsworth, Penguin.

JORGENSON, G.W. (1978) *Student ability-material difficulty matching: relationship to classroom behaviour*, Paper presented to AERA: Toronto.

JUDGE, H. (1980) 'Teaching and professionalisation: An essay in ambiguity', in HOYLE, E. and MEGARRY, J. (Eds.) *World Yearbook of Education 1980 Professional Development of Teachers*, London, Kogan Page.

JUNG, C.G. (1961) *Modern Man in Search of a Soul*, London, Routledge and Kegan Paul.

KAY-SHUTTLEWORTH, J. (1843) *Report on Battersea*. As quoted in RICH, R.W. *The Training of Teachers in England and Wales During the Nineteenth Century*, Cambridge, Cambridge University Press.

KELLY, G.A. (1955) *The Psychology of Personal Constructs*, New York, Van

Nostrand.

KRATHWOHL, D.R. *et al.* (1954) *Taxonomy of Educational Objectives: Handbook II, Affective Domain*, New York, David McKay.

LACEY, C. (1977) *The Socialisation of Teachers*, London, Methuen.

LAURILLARD, D. (1984) 'Learning from problem-solving', in Marton *et al. The Experience of Learning*, Edinburgh, Scottish Academic Press.

LAWTON, D. *et al.* (1978) *Theory and Practice of Curriculum Studies*, London, Routledge and Kegan Paul.

LEGGE, D. and BARBER, P.J. (1976) *Information and Skill*, London, Methuen.

LENNEBERG, E.H. (1967) *Biological Foundations of Language*, New York, Wiley.

LORTIE, D.C. (1969) 'The balance and control in elementary school teaching', in ETZIONI, A. (Ed.) *The Semi-Professions and their Organisation*, New York, Free Press.

LOVITT, T.C. (1978) 'Strategies for managing naughty behaviours', in HARING, N.G., LOVITT, T.C., EATON, M.D. and HANSEN, C.L. (Eds.) *The Fourth R: Research in the Classroom*, London, Merrill.

McDOUGALL, W. (1908) *Introduction to Social Psychology*, Boston, Luce.

McDOUGALL, W. (1932) *The Energies of Men*, London, Methuen.

MacGINITIE, W.H. (1976) 'Difficulty with logical operations', *The Reading Teacher*, 29, pp. 371–75.

McINTYRE, D., MacLEOD, G. and GRIFFITHS, R. (Eds.) (1977) *Investigations of Microteaching*, London, Croom Helm.

McLEISH, J. (1970) *Students' Attitudes and College Environments*, Cambridge Institute of Education.

McNAIR, A. SIR (1944) *Committee to Consider the Supply, Recruitment and Training of Teachers and Youth Leaders*, London, HMSO.

McNAMARA, D. (1976) 'On returning to the chalk face: Theory not into practice', *British Journal of Teacher Education*, 2, 2, p. 155.

McNAMARA, D. and DESFORGES, C. (1978) 'The social sciences, teacher education and the objectification of craft knowledge', *British Journal of Teacher Education*, 4, 2, pp. 18–31.

McNAMARA, D. and DESFORGES, C. (1979) 'The social sciences, teacher education and the objectification of craft knowledge, in BENNETT, N. and McNAMARA, D. (Eds.) *Focus on Teaching: Readings in the Observation and Conceptualisation of Teaching*, London, Longmans.

MANDLER, G. (1975) *Mind and Emotion*, New York, Wiley.

MARDLE, G. and WALKER, M. (1980) 'Strategies and Structure: some critical notes on teacher socialisation', in WOODS, P. (Ed.) *Teacher Strategies: Explorations in the Sociology of the Classroom*, London, Croom Helm.

MARLAND, M. (1975) *The Craft of the Classroom*, London, Heinemann.

MARTON, F., HOUNSELL, D.J. and ENTWISTLE, N.J. (1984) *The Experience of Learning*, Edinburgh, Scottish Academic Press.

MARTON, F. and SALJO, R. (1976) 'On qualitative differences in learning II — Outcome as a function of the learner's conception of the task', *British Journal Educational Psychology*, 46, pp. 115–27.

MASLOW, A.H. (1954) *Motivation and Personality*, New York, Harper and Row.

MASLOW, A.H. (1968) *Toward a Psychology of Being* (2nd Edition) Princeton, N.J., Van Nostrand.

MEICHENBAUM, D. (1977) *Cognitive Behaviour Modification*, London, Plenum Press.

MEREDITH, G.P. (1948) 'The method of topic analysis', *Educational Development Association*.

MEREDITH, G.P. (1966) *Instruments of Communication*, Oxford, Pergamon.

MILLER, G., GALANTER, E. and PRIBRAM, K. (1960) *Plans and the Structure of Behaviour*, New York, Holt, Rinehart and Winston.

MORGAN, C. LLOYD (1894) *Psychology for Teachers*, London, Arnold.

MUSGRAVE, P.W. (1979) *The Sociology of Education*, London, Methuen.

NEISSER, U. (1978) 'Memory: what are the important questions?' in GRUNEBERG, M.M., MORRIS, P.E. and SYKES, R.N. (Eds.) *Practical Aspects of Memory*, London, Academic Press.

NEWBLE, D.J. and JAEGER, K. (1983) 'The effect of assessments and examinations on the learning of medical students', *Medical Education*, 17, pp. 25–31.

NEWELL, A. (1974) 'You can't play 20 questions with nature and win', in CHASE, W.G. (Ed.) *Visual Information Processing*, New York, Academic Press.

NISBET, S. (1967) 'The study of education in Scotland', in *Scottish Educational Studies*, 1, 1, pp. 8–17.

NODDINGS, N., GILBERT, K. and LEITZ, S. (1983) *What Do Individuals Gain in Small Group Mathematical problem Solving?* Paper presented to AERA: Montreal.

NORMAN, D.A. (1982) *Learning and Memory*, San Francisco, Freeman.

PASK, G. (1976a) 'Conversational techniques in the study and practice of education', *British Journal Educational Psychology*, 46, pp. 12–25.

PASK, G. (1976b) 'Styles and strategies of learning', *British Journal Educational Psychology*, 46, pp. 128–48.

PASK, G. (1976c) *Conversation Theory: Applications in Education and Epistemology*, Amsterdam, Elsevier.

PEDDIWELL, J.A. (1939) *The Saber-Tooth Curriculum*, New York, McGraw-Hill.

PEEL, E.A. (1962) *Joint Working Party on the Teaching of Educational Psychology in Teacher Training*, London, British Psychological Society and Association of Teachers in Colleges and Departments of Education.

PEEL, E.A. (1971) *The Nature of Adolesclent Judgment*, London, Staples.

PERROTT, E. (1982) *Effective Teaching*, London, Longman.

PETERS, R.S. (1977) 'Education as a specific preparation for teaching', in PETERS, R.S. *Education and the Education of Teachers*, London, Routledge.

PIAGET, J. (1971) *Science of Education and the Psychology of the Child*, London, Longmans.

PITMAN, E. (1982) 'Transactional analysis: An introduction to its theory and practice', *British Journal of Social Work*, 12, pp. 47–63.

POLLITT, A.B., HUTCHINSON, C., ENTWISTLE, N.J. and DE LUCA, C. (1984) *What Makes Exam Questions Difficult?* Edinburgh, Scottish Academic Press.

RAMSDEN, P. and ENTWISTLE, N.J. (1981) 'Effects of academic departments on students' approaches to studying', *British Journal Educational Psychology*, 51, pp. 368–83.

RESNICK, L.B. and FORD, W.W. (1981) *The Psychology of Mathematics for Instruction*, Hillsdale, N.J., Lawrence Erlbaum Associates.

ROSENTHAL, R. AND JACOBSON, L. (1968) *Pygmalion in the Classroom*, New York, Holt, Rinehart and Winston.

ROSS, A. (1984) 'An education for tomorrow's teachers', in ALEXANDER, R.J., CRAFT, M. and LYNCH, J. (Eds.) *Change in Teacher Education*, London, Holt, Rinehart and Winston.

ROSS, D. (1883) *Education as a University Subject*, Glasgow, J. Maclehose & Sons.

ROWAN, B., BOSSERT, S.T. and DWYER, D.C. (1983) 'Research on effective schools: a cautionary note', *Educational Researcher*, 12, 4, pp. 24–31.

RUTTER, M., LEBOVICI, S., EISENBERGE, L., SNEZNEVSKIJ, A.V., SADOUN, R., BROOKE, E., and LIN, T-Y (1969) 'A triaxial classification of mental disorders in childhood', *Journal of Child Psychology and Psychiatry*, 10, pp. 41–61.

SALJO, R. (1976) *Qualitative Differences in Learning as a Function of the Learner's Conception of the Task*, Gothenburg, Acta Universitatis Gothenburgensis.

SCHMIDT, R. (1982) *Motor Control and Learning*, Champaign, Ill., Human Kinesics Publishers.

SCHRODER, H.M., DRIVER, M.J. and STRENFERT, S. (1967) *Human Information Processing*, New York, Holt, Rinehart and Winston.

SELIGMAN, M.E.P. (1975) *Helplessness*, San Francisco, Freeman and Co.

SELMES, I. (1985) *Approaches to learning at secondary school: their identification and facilitation.* Unpublished Ph.D. thesis, University of Edinburgh.

SIMMONS, C. (1982) 'The use of transactional analysis', *BPS Education Section Review*, 6, 93–6.

SIROTNIK, D.A. (1983) 'What you see is what you get — consistency, persistency and mediocrity in classrooms', *Harvard Educational Review*, 53, 1, pp. 16–31.

SKINNER, B.F. (1968) *The Technology of Teaching*, Englewood Cliffs, N.J., Prentice Hall.

SLOBODA, J., O'CONNOR, N. and HERMELIN, B. (1985) 'A case of extraordinary musical memory', *Proceedings of the Experimental Psychology Society*.

SMITH, F. (1982) *Writing and the Writer*, Heinemann Educational.

SMITH, L.M. and GEOFFREY, W. (1968) *The Complexities of an Urban Classroom*, New York, Holt, Rinehart and Winston.

SMITH, R.N. and TOMLINSON, P.D. (1984) 'RAP: Radio-assisted practice. Preliminary investigations of a new technique in teacher education', *Journal of Education for Teaching*, 10, pp. 119–34.

SNYDER, B.R. (1971) *The Hidden Curriculum*, New York, Knopf.

SOLNICK, J.A., RINCOVER, A. and PETERSON, C.R. (1977) 'Determinants of the reinforcing and punishing effects of time out', *Journal of Applied Behavior Analysis*, 10, pp. 415–28.

SPENCER, H. (1855) and (1929) 'What knowledge is of most worth?' in *Education, Intellectual, Moral and Physical*, London, Watts & Co.

STAMMERS, R. and PATRICK, J. (1975) *The Psychology of Training*, London, Methuen.

STANTON, R. (1982) *Basic Skills*, London, Further Education Curriculum

Development Unit.

STENHOUSE, L. (1975) *An Introduction to Curriculum Research and Development*, London, Heinemann.

STEVENS, M. (1968) *Observing Children who are Severely Subnormal*, London, Edward Arnold.

STONES, E. (1979) *Psychopedagogy Psychology Theory and the Practice of Teaching*. London, Methuen.

STONES, E. (1984) *Supervision in Teacher Education: a counselling and pedagogical approach*, London, Methuen.

STORY, P. (1973) 'Cambridge School Classics Project'. In Schools Council, *Evaluation in Curriculum Development: Twelve Case Studies*, London, Macmillan Educ.

STOTT, D.M. (1978) *Helping Children with Learning Difficulties*, London, Ward Lock Educational.

STUBBS, M. and DELAMONT, S. (1976) *Explorations in Classroom Observation*, London, Wiley.

SULLY, J. (1886) *Handbook of Psychology for the Teacher*, London, Longmans, Green & Co.

SUTHERLAND, P.A.A. (1982) 'An expansion of Peel's describer-explainer stage theory', *Educational Review*, 34, pp. 69–76.

TAYLOR, J.K. and DALE, J.R. (1971) *A Survey of Teachers in their First Year of Service*, Bristol University Press.

TAYLOR, W. (1969) *Society and the Education of Teachers*, London, Faber and Faber.

THOMAS, L.C. (1979) 'Construct, reflect and converse: the conversational reconstruction of social realities', in STRINGER, P. and BANNISTER, D. (Eds.) *Constructs of Sociality and Individuality*, London, Academic Press.

THOMAS, L.C. and AUGSTEIN, S. (1984) 'Education and the negotiation of personal meaning', *BPS Education Section Review*, 8, pp. 7–36.

THORNDIKE, E.L. (1913) *Educational Psychology*, New York, Columbia University.

THORNDIKE, R.L. (1982) 'Educational measurement — theory and practice', in SPEARITT, D. (Ed.) *The Improvement of Measurement in Education and Psychology*, Victoria, Australia, Australian Council for Educational Research.

TIBBLE, J. (1966) *The Study of Education*, London, Routledge and Kegan Paul.

TOMLINSON, P.D. (1981) *Understanding Teaching: Interactive Educational Psychology*, London, McGraw-Hill.

TOMLINSON, P.D. (1985) 'Matching teaching and learning: The interactive approach in educational psychology', in ENTWISTLE, N.J. (Ed.) *New Directions in Educational Psychology I: Learning and Teaching*, Lewes, Falmer Press.

TORGESEN, J.K. and LICHT, B.G. (1983) 'The learning disabled child as an inactive learner: retrospect and prospects', in MCKINNEY, J.D. and FEAGANS, L. (Eds.) *Current Topics in Learning Disabilities*. Norwood, N.J., Ablex Publishing Co.

VERNON, P.E. (Ed.) (1957) *Secondary School Selection: A British Psychological Society Enquiry*, London, Methuen.

VERNON, P.E. (1980) 'Modern educational psychology as a science', in GORDON,

P. (Ed.) *The Study of Education Vol. 1*, London, Woburn Press.

WALL, W.D. (1979) *Constructive Education for Special Groups*, London, Harrap UNESCO.

WALLER, W. (1932) *The Sociology of Teaching*, New York, Wiley.

WARNOCK, M. (1978) *Special Educational Needs: Report of the Committee of Enquiry into the Education of Handicapped Children and Young People*, London, HMSO.

WASON, P. and JOHNSON-LAIRD, P. (1972) *Psychology of Reasoning*, London, Batsford.

WEBB, N.M. (1982) 'Student interaction and learning in small groups', *Review of Educational Research*, 52, 3, pp. 421–45.

WEDELL, K. (1980) 'Early identification and compensatory interaction', in KNIGHTS, R.M. and BAKKER, D.J. (Eds.) *Treatment of Hyperactive and Learning Disordered Children*, Baltimore, University Park Press.

WELFORD, A.T. (1968) *Fundamentals of Skill*, London, Methuen.

WERTHEIMER, M. (1945) *Productive Thinking*, New York, Harper.

WHELDALL, K. and MERRETT, F. (1985) 'Training teachers to be more positive: the behavioural approach', in BENNETT, N. and DESFORGES, C. (Eds.) *Recent Advances in Classroom Research*, Monograph of the British Journal of Educational Psychology.

WHITE, P. and WHITE, J. (1984) *Practical reasoning and educational theory*, an unpublished paper, University of London Institute of Education.

WHITESIDE, M.T., BERNBAUM, G. and NOBLE, G. (1969) 'Aspirations, reality shock and entry into teaching', *Sociological Review*, 17, pp. 399–414.

WILLOWER, D.J., HOY, W.K. and EIDELL, T.L. (1967) *The School and Pupil Control Ideology*, University Park Press, Monograph No. 24.

WILSON, J. (1975) *Educational Theory and the Preparation of Teachers*, Slough, NFER.

WOODS, P. (Ed.) (1980) *Teacher Strategies*, London, Croom Helm.

WOODS, P. (1985) 'Pupil strategies', in BENNETT, N. and DESFORGES, C. (Eds.) *Recent Advances in Classroom Research*, Monograph of the British Journal of Educational Psychology.

Author Index